Praise for *Going to Solace*

"When the people in our lives bring out the best in us, community functions at its optimum. Through their connection with a hospice, the characters in *Going to Solace,* each in their own way, discover resilience in themselves of which they were unaware, spurring them to take on challenges they previously thought impossible. Amanda McTigue masterfully sets us down in a small town in the Appalachian Mountains where we see in each of her characters reflections of our own capacity for caring, forgiveness, and integrity."

—*David Robert Ord, Editorial Director, Namaste Publishing; author,* Your Forgotten Self

"What *The Help* did for the Deep South, *Going to Solace* does for Appalachia. It is rare to read an author's first novel, close the book and think, 'This is a great story, maybe destined to become an enduring piece of Southern literature.' Set in the hills and dales of North Carolina's Blue Ridge Mountains, McTigue's not-soon-to-be-forgotten characters belie Southern stereotypes as they struggle with life's great ending moment. Through extraordinary storytelling—poetic and descriptive—a six-day journey unfolds resonant with universal themes of family, friendship and intersecting cultures. Readers will relish the sparse, but precise use of the dialect of the mountain people—it's delightful and literate."

—*Waights Taylor Jr., author,* Our Southern Home: Scottsboro to Montgomery to Birmingham—the Transformation of the South in the Twentieth Century

"*You are not alone.* That's the message every hospice worker brings to those facing terminal illness—and it's the take-away from this wonderful book. At last, storytelling that isn't grim! The characters became so important to me, I *had* to know what happened to them. This is writing infused not only with a sense of humor, but also a "sense of human," a quality I deeply admire in my colleagues in terminal care."

—*Karen Kenney, Hospice of the Valley, Phoenix, AZ*

"Amanda McTigue's *Going to Solace* is a romp in Appalachia like none other that you have taken. Quirky characters, intimate stories, local humor and sadness (all written in note-perfect "home-talk") capture the lilting cadences of the best of Southern writing, both its poetic and its Gothic elements. Just as you wipe away your tears of compassion, like a stand-up comedienne, McTigue has you weeping with laughter."

—Carol Benet received her Ph.D. in Comparative Literature from the University of California, Berkeley

"There's sleight-of-hand here, don't miss it. Beneath the surface, the author welcomes us (*all* of us) by playing with assumptions about race, ability and cultural heritage. Others' stories become ours, multiple stories become one, exploring what happens when we're brought together under the terrible, leveling shadow of death."

—Lynne D. Morrow, Ph.D. Professor, Music and American Culture, Sonoma State University

"*Going to Solace* is one of the most beautifully written novels I've read in quite a while. Kudos to Amanda McTigue for capturing so well the lyricism of the local dialect of these characters. I consider this book to be not just fiction, but a true work of literature."

—Frances Caballo, Owner, ACT Communications; Social Media Editor, Redwood Writers/California Writers Club

"McTigue is a master of discernment who transports us to a world in which great richness of character underlies small town ways and abiding truths arise from the eternal contest of fear versus hope. *Going to Solace* is an exhilarating work, full of notes exquisitely rendered with empathy and humor. It makes blood rush to the head and heart, just like the fresh mountain air its characters breathe."

—Robert Kertzner, M.D., Associate Clinical Professor of Psychiatry, UCSF

GOING *to* SOLACE

AMANDA McTIGUE

Harper Davis Publishers

For Tom

Going to Solace / Amanda McTigue. -- Colorado Springs, Colo. : Harper Davis Pub., c2012.

p. ; cm.

ISBN: 978-0-9819153-7-1 (cloth) ; 978-0-9854930-0-4 (pbk.)

Summary: During Thanksgiving week 1989, a handful of mismatched folks cross paths at a hospice called Solace in the Blue Ridge Mountains. Through interweaving points of view, some funny, some sad, this novel illuminates the altered states of shock and clarity that come as loved ones (and hated ones) pass into death.

1. Hospice care--Fiction. 2. Death--Fiction. 3. Mothers--Death--Fiction. 4. Blue Ridge Mountains--Fiction. I. Title.

PS3613.C75 G65 2012
813.6--dc23
2012937614
1206

Cover and page design by Tanya Quinlan.

Table of Contents

Prologue

Saturday

Sunday

Thursday

Characters

FAMILIES

The Earlys

August Early, retired trucker
Theodora Early, his wife
Catherine Early, their daughter
Sue-Sue and Serena, Catherine's daughters

The Dulls

Maggie Dull, aka Maggie Dulé, event planner
Dolores Dull, her mother
Dalton and Baylor, her brothers

The Greeveys

Cadence Greevey, on leave from the eighth grade
Verleana Pole Greevey, her mother
Bobby O. Greevey, her father

CARETAKERS

Dr. Moazzem Narduli, oncologist
Dee Dee Hipps, RN, Solace supervisor
Bear, RN, Solace supervisor
Hazel Gurley, Solace RN, helping the Earlys
Burnice Kling, Solace RN, helping the Dulls
Lana Hendren, Solace RN, helping the Greeveys
Kitty Pearl, Solace LVN, nurse in training
Cherille Meade, Solace cook
Isah Oduya, Solace aide

FRIENDS and LOVED ONES

Pam and Walker Crowe, owners, Mountain Man shop
Beau McCallum, owner, Rexall drugstore
Miss Susan Neville, next-door neighbor to the Earlys
Curtis-Michael Hipps, manager, Pay Less Pantry and Dee Dee's husband
Jonelle Hipps, mother of Curtis-Michael Hipps
Paco Esparza, Bobby's partner
Amelia Payle, Maggie's assistant
Viktor Ivanek, Maggie's friend

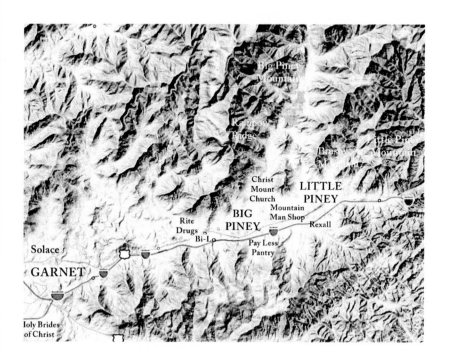

Prologue

From the Blue Ridge Mountains
In the Town of Garnet

God spare you the need, but should one of your loved ones take sick—mortal sick—and need a place from which to die, you could do worse than Solace. One hundred years ago, it was the home of a logger. In those days only tree men had the wherewithal to build big homes and this one was fine indeed—bricked, rambling, companioned by a pair of sizable tulip poplars. Over time, the land around it got sold off for cheap housing, but back in the 1970s, do-gooders saved the homestead from demolition. Turned it into what they call a hospice. Which they named Solace.

Solace.

Just the one word. Like God.

It took some getting used to. People got fussy. "We don't buy food at Grocery or do our wash at Laundry." But they came around. Pretty soon everybody was saying, "They sent him to Solace," or "She's headed to Solace" without batting an eye. Even the newspapers printed it that way.

You may remember a few years back, the warm winter, 1989. That was the year Rite Drugs moved in next to the Bi-Lo. There was snow fifty miles north, but here in Garnet County, summer overstayed by months. The balsam got too dry. Folks worried about a fire up on Brushy. Not that the heat had any bearing for some, but for others, it was a marker as was every detail of life. Part of the import of such times, in such circumstances, when it's the everything that seems to stick, that can't be shaken off.

SATURDAY

November 18, 1989

I Go To Prepare

August Early
After Breakfast

The nurse went inside to his wife. Mr. Early stayed put on the stoop.

He had seen to his breakfast, such as it was. There was no telling the difference between one cup of coffee and another, so he'd taken to fixing the powder kind with a spoon and hot water. Of no mind to do any cooking that needed cleaning, he was off eggs entirely and onto the toaster waffles with syrup. One plate, no pan.

He had all the dogs out front with him now, something his wife would never abide. Theo had a horror of losing even one to a deer. It had been her experience that once a hound got something as fleet as a deer in its nose, it would give chase up hollows and down clear across the county, never to be seen again. She'd had him work the dogs like a pack, sleeping them together in the back run off Brushy and letting only one out at a time to sweep the hillside while he kept an eye out.

But now Mr. Early couldn't be bothered. *They want out, let them out,* he thought. *They run away, let them run.* He'd run too if he could.

He'd been doing the dogs that way for a while without her knowing since she never left the house anymore or even her bed. Still, not one of them took off after nothing. Years of pack-raising made an invisible tether that kept them sniffing off this way or that, then bounding back before too long.

You might to see this, Mr. Early thought at his wife. *They know who puts food in their bowl.* He closed his eyes, but all he saw was Theo in her sick bed, so he opened them again.

Miss Hazel came out on the porch—*clomp, clomp*—two hefty tie shoes, bright white, echoing off the planking. She was a big woman the exact color of a wet potato. Judging from the lines in her face, nothing resembling a smile had appeared there in many a long time. Mr. Early crooked his neck to look, still sitting but turning up to where she stood.

HAZEL GURLEY, R.N. She always wore the clip-on badge for home visits, even though nobody would mistake her for anybody else. It was part of the uniform, he supposed. They might oblige it over at Solace, that nurses wear badges like the police, in case somebody took it upon him- or herself to question their remedies. She came to the house on her own in her own car, had been doing so for months now.

"Your wife neewwds a bell," Miss Hazel humphed.

He'd done what he could to get used to her, striding as she did into his very home, addressing him as if they were kin.

"Her breathing's getting bad. She needs something by the bed in case she wants to call you but can't."

Mr. Early nodded. That made sense, but where in God's name would he find a bell?

Even not speaking, Miss Hazel followed him. "You don't need nothing fancy. Some pennies in a cup she can make a racket with. Or a shoe she can bang on the table."

"I'll find something," he said.

Miss Hazel stepped down to where he was sitting. Her tone went from gruff to teachy. "Now, if she gets bad, you may have to bring her to the hospital. You call Curtis-Michael, he'll come right up the hill with the ambulance. I left his number by the telephone."

Mr. Early rose to shake her hand, saying, "I'll do it," all the while thinking, *Over my dead body.*

The hospital's the place you go to die. That's what his mama said. She would not set foot in one until it was time for her to go and by then she was gone so they had to carry her in. Even her babies were birthed at home.

But not Theo's. She'd gone to the Holy Brides of Christ to have their one and only, to have Catherine. Mr. Early had not been able to go with her. In those days there was no way he could turn down a shipment. Hauling paid the bills. "Maybe just as well," Theo said to him meaning, *Maybe just as well for* you, *but not for me.* She said Catherine had come a-screaming into this world just fine. Might to have gone out the same way—no one knew for sure. Found her dead in the street, the needle still in her arm. Screaming or maybe just drifting off into a cloud of the drugs, either way she'd stayed shy of a hospital to do it.

Mr. Early watched the nurse trudge out to her car. The dogs did not stir for her going. They lay plopped down, hither-thither, in the morning's first patch of sun, blinking, panting, about as interested in car-chasing as the gravel they lay on.

"You tell them she's Dr. Narduli's patient," Miss Hazel called back to him through her window as she rolled off down the mountain.

There's No Place Like

Maggie Dull
After Brunch

Maggie finally tracked down a Dr. Narduli at the Holy Brides of Christ. Talk about memory lane. She and her pals used to call it "Blessed Babes" with the sarcasm that passed for wit in her teenage years. Catholic to its gilt gills, Holy Brides hospital sat in the middle of greater downtown Garnet like a rococo spaceship perched on the less-than-hospitable landscape of Planet Protestant. Maggie ought to know. Garnet was home-*not-so-sweet*-home.

It took her a dozen calls to various clueless office clerks before she could establish that this Narduli character was indeed her mother's doctor. "Medical oncologist," a snippy, self-identified hospital coordinator informed her. As if she needed informing.

Maggie peeled off her mini-skirt, swapping it for sweats and leg-warmers. She'd work the phone, then hit the gym. With luck she'd make her new step aerobics class, but there was the small matter of checking this guy's *bona fides* before dialing him direct. She slogged through a mind-numbing rhythm of cold-calls, explanations and call-backs requiring *repeat* explanations. Happily, her research netted enough flotsam to get the story: Narduli, first name Moazzem, with medical credentials from what must have been his native India and Houston, Texas. Global village stuff. No way to tell if he was competent. Maggie wondered how Garnet was taking to him and he to Garnet.

It was Dr. Narduli who was presiding over her mother's course of chemotherapy, though in this case (per the polite, perfunctory voice on the phone) he was presiding over nothing, because her mother had apparently elected to drop the chemo maybe six months before. Maggie was hearing *that* for the first time.

"Would this be Miss Dull?" He spoke with the care of someone schooled in English better than the English-born, his words made musical by a hint of accent.

"Dulé," she corrected him. She'd changed the name the second she hit Palo Alto. What on earth had her parents been thinking? You're born Dull, you change the name. That seemed clear to Maggie by kindergarten, Day Two, with her classmates exploiting the obvious disadvantages of her surname on the playground. But her father must have had some sentimental attachment to *his* father's name. And her mother—hallucinating from the *Doris-Day-happy-ever-after* drugs they administered to all women of her generation—her mother had apparently been ecstatic to become a Dull. It was all so tribal. It had taken Maggie to undo the legacy. Maggie never had been Dull.

"How is she?"

A beat. Not even worth explaining to the doctor why she'd have to ask after her own mother's status.

"Comfortable," he said.

"How long?" she asked.

Another beat.

"People can surprise you."

"When they *don't* surprise you?"

"A month," he said.

"Thank you." She meant it. Like all her kin, most especially her mother, Maggie did not pussyfoot. It was obvious she would have to go home.

A Penny Earned

Pam Crowe
Closing Time

"I got to get home!"

Pam Crowe nearly sprayed her Coca-Cola all over the magazine rack. What was this world coming to? You drop in to the Rexall for some chit-chat and here comes the child, howling like a banshee.

"Cadence Greevey, where are your manners?"

Cadence froze in the doorway next to a display of Thanksgiving table goodies, fold-out paper turkeys and acorn-stamped napkins.

Pam looked at Walker who looked at Beau. Eyebrows rose all around. It was for Beau to say something—this being his shop, for goodness sake—but seeing as he wasn't quick enough on the draw or even *on* the draw for that matter, Pam took it upon herself to do the talking. She used her mommy voice.

"Come on in quiet now and speak to us like a normal, civilized person."

Cadence stayed put, rocking where she stood, one foot on the shop floor, the other on the sidewalk. Her backpack, piled as always with somethings-or-other and set too high on her shoulders, made it look like she'd keel over any second. Truth be told, it was way too small for her, the same Sesame Street backpack her mother'd been trying for years to wean her of—"Years!" she told Pam—but apparently Cadence fell to the floor crying if anybody tried to take it away. What with Noah's flood and all, her mother had apparently given in. But giving in did not come naturally to Pam Crowe.

"What do you mean yelping like a stuck puppy? Mr. McCallum might to have had customers in here. Now what do you say?"

"I'm sorry, Auntie Pam."

"And who else?"

"I'm sorry Uncle Walker."

"Who else?"

"I'm sorry Mr. McCallum."

"That's right. Remember what your mama says, Cadence. You're a — what? You're a—"

"I'm a big girl."

"That's right. So, if you're a big girl, and you *know* you're a big girl, why aren't you wearing your big-girl dress today?" Pam shot a look over her husband's way. "Walker, honey, tell Cadence how much you like her big-girl dress."

Pam should have known she couldn't count on the men to backstop her. Both Walker and Beau got to shrugging, checking the floor around their boots instead of addressing the child directly. Mind you, everybody was used to Cadence. "Her thinking don't keep up with her growing," that's how it was said around town. Still, the child needed guidance. She was getting into her teens. Her mama had tamed her hair down neat enough into those braids, but she looked like she'd stuffed herself into a second-hand doll's dress with its too-short hem and puffy sleeves and that silly apron overtop.

Cadence swiveled in the door, her eyes glued to the clock in the front window, the plastic one shaped like a cat with its tail counting *tick-tick-tick*.

"I got to get home!" Her voice was once again too loud. "I can't come to work, no more, Mr. McCallum. That's what I come to tell you."

Beau crossed two substantial arms over his increasingly substantial midsection. He still had on his white coat, the one he wore so that customers would believe the medicines he gave them were the right ones. His eyes popped round behind his glasses, the lashes magnified long and black even with his hair gone white. Wiggling the tips of his fingers, he waved Cadence toward him, clearly fixing to do some counseling when—

"Oh, no!"

In a flash she was running past him, past them all, shucking her backpack which fell—*Thunk!*—on the floor while the three grown-ups talked over one another saying, "Whoa! Take it easy! Where you going?" Lickety-split, she was at the wire rack filled with birthday cards.

"Somebody made a mess!" Cadence began sorting frantically. "They's envelopes in front so you can't see no pictures. How's a gram-mama gonna see the one with the butterflies? Or a daddy, how's he gonna find the one with the bat smacking the ball as a special gift for his boy? I had them perfect yesterday, Mr. McCallum, I swear I did!"

"Don't swear, Cadence. Stop that flapping." Pam reached for her as Walker fetched her backpack, but the girl would not be diverted. One, two, three, she spun the rack, putting everything back in its place and then turning to them with a big smile. "We get it right at Rexall," she said.

Beau smiled. "Yes, we do. I taught you that, didn't I?"

"Yes, sir. You said for me to straighten the candy bars and chewing gums and swipe the dust off the kitty-cat clock and then when somebody pays their money for their treats with their medicines in a paper bag and they say, 'Bye now' at the counter, that's when I say, 'We get it right at Rexall.' But I can't come no more, Mr. McCallum. I'm sorry."

Cadence ran for the door, snatching her backpack from Walker as Beau called after her, "Is it your mama, honey? Is she okay?"

Cadence whirled. "She's fine. She is fine-fine-fine. I got to go."

And out she went.

"Well."

That was Beau, speaking for the three of them.

"Well, indeed," Walker nodded. Pam sidled in beside him.

They found themselves standing in a tight circle at the center of the store as if they'd gathered for prayers. Beau pointed back toward a card table and folding chair behind the register. "That's where I let her finish her lessons in the afternoon. There wasn't that much else I needed doing."

Pam nodded. "God love you for taking her on."

Walker leaned back on his heels, hands shoved deep in his pockets. Pam felt her heart tug. He'd gained enough weight these days to where his belt sat well below what used to be his waist, barely keeping his dungarees up over his backside. Not from any sickness, those extra pounds, just from being old. A calamity the three of them shared.

The men conferred.

"You suppose her mama's taken a turn?"

"She said she's fine."

"No way to know."

"Maybe we could ask at church."

"We cannot drop by," Pam reminded them. "Verleana Greevey is not one to countenance a visitation, planned or un-."

"I wonder how I'll get her medicines to her," Beau mused.

"I wonder how you'll get anything done what with Cadence gone." Walker put on such a face of woe they all three burst out laughing.

"Come on. Let's get some eats." Beau hit the back door. "Mexican or Chinese?" He tossed his white coat over a broom handle, all the while speculating with Walker as to the weather and its impact on hoped-for holiday shoppers. But Pam was only hearing out of one ear. In fact, she was so distracted, Walker had to grab her elbow right quick to keep her from pitching clear down the steps.

"Here's what I want to know," she said. "How'd that child get herself into town? And how on earth is she getting home?"

FORD EVERY

Cadence Greevey
At Sunset

The easiest way home was Little Piney Road, Cadence knew that, but Cane Creek was faster. The creek trail cut straight up the mountain because its water cut straight down. Which made for steep going, sure enough, but you couldn't beat it for speed. There wasn't much Cadence liked about being a big girl except having the longer legs that made running quicker, and climbing more like walking as a giant with big, giant steps.

Tick-tick-tick. She kept seeing the twitching tail of the kitty-cat clock in her mind, counting off the seconds as if to say, *You're late! You're late!* But it wasn't fair. She'd planned things so carefully. Her mama slept for hours these days, so Cadence figured she could scoot down to Big Piney right as Mr. McCallum was closing, say three words to him and scoot right back before her mama knew a thing. How could she have known there'd be visitors? How could she have known Auntie Pam would want to talk-talk-talk? Now she was surely late getting home and *what-if what-if what-if* her mama woke up in her sleeping chair with nobody there?

The creek trail had slopped down to soupy mud in the hot weather. Cadence hated the way her backpack pinched as she steadied herself, arms out wide so as not to slip and dirty her dress. Her "dirndl," that's what her mama'd taught her to call it. A dress with an apron was all it was, but it was right pretty, or so Cadence thought. Her grandaddy, who was once over the ocean, had brought it back with him, first for her mama and now for her. Lord knows, it was tight, Cadence having grown all the way into herself, but it was nice, with tiny rose flowers all over and the apron with just a few stains but white.

At the flat rock—her sliding rock of a summer—Cadence left the creek trail and immediately started climbing, hightailing it straight up the mountain. Her shoes were a mess all right, but so far her dress was perfect except for some raindrops shaking off the laurel branches she used to pull herself along.

Bang! Cadence let the screen door slam, calling "Mama?" remembering too late that her mama was most likely sleeping. Remembering her shoes too late too. She ran back to the front door to toe them off on the mud mat.

"Mama?"

There was no answer.

What-if what-if what-if? Cadence ran for the bedroom door. The La-Z-Boy was empty. Always, when Cadence came in to check, that's where she'd find her mama because that's where she slept. She'd been doing that way since Cadence's daddy got himself good and gone. In fact, the very next day her mama had telephoned down to Curtis-Michael Hipps: "Come take his bed out of this house." Since then she slept sitting up in a chair. It was a scary sleep to look at, her face loose, her mouth wide open. Wide open, not a little open.

"Mama?"

Cadence ran for the kitchen and there she was. Barefoot in her nightgown. Not speaking or making any sign of knowing Cadence was there, but just one after another laying a slew of bacon, a whole entire package on a special microwave tray they'd bought at the Second Time Around store. Oh, how her mama loved bacon. *Her* mama, she said, had come up through the Depression when people ate nothing but bacon or bacon fat, Cadence couldn't remember which. So her mama's mama—that would be Granny Gaylene who was Gaylene Pole on an envelope–Granny Gaylene had learned a taste for bacon and served it all the time. She'd raised her kids on it, all ten of them including Cadence's mama—Verleana—Verleana Pole until she married Bobby O. Greevey and then she was Verleana Greevey and stayed that way, even when he was gone from the house. Cadence knew all the stories from her mama telling them over and over. She knew who was what and by what name. She knew that it was bacon that kept them alive to be talked about at all.

And now here her mama was laying out a whole pack of Jimmy Dean, setting the timer on the microwave and pushing the big button that said START. The plate went round and round, but—Cadence couldn't believe it—there was no bacon inside. It was still sitting on the counter. Then the microwave was beeping and her mama was turning to get her a paper napkin with that tray of raw bacon in her hand like she was getting ready to eat it.

Cadence had to say something right quick. "Mama! You can't eat that bacon. It's not cooked yet!" Lord, the look she got. Her mama brooked no back-talk, even in her sickness.

"Let me carry it for you, mama. Let go." It took all kinds of sweet talk for Cadence to pry the bacon away, but she did it, all the while holding her own mama by the hand like a baby, leading her back to the La-Z-Boy to square her away, tucking a blanket up and around. Everywhere Cadence's hands went, her mama's followed just a second later, as if she were trying to learn a dance.

"You still hungry, mama?"

"Heavens no! I couldn't eat another bite." Like she'd swallowed a whole pound of bacon and some pancakes beside.

Cadence knew right then. She knew it was time and she knew where to look: in her mama's special book, the one with the sparkly castle on the front and a princess riding in a coach. That's where his phone number was. Not under G. Under B for Bobby.

Never Look A Gift

Bobby O. Greevey
After Supper

As quickly as Bobby was reaching, hands dripping from the sink with the first ring, Paco beat him. It was a game they played—*Fastest guy, Last to die*—some competition having to do with reflexes and waning youth, a holdover from their courting days. Paco covered the receiver and mouthed, "Big case," then put on his prosecutor's voice.

"Rivera residence." His face dropped. "It's for you." He passed the phone over, his black eyes blacker. That's how Bobby knew. *Shit.*

"Hello?"

"Daddy?"

"Cadence? Wow. Hi. I didn't recognize your voice."

It wasn't a little girl voice any more. It was — what? Not deeper, but firmer maybe. Bobby switched places with Paco, handing over the dishtowel.

"Long time no talk. What's going on?"

"It's the bacon, daddy. It's not cooked and she's trying to eat it and she turns on the microwave and there's nothing there—"

"—Slow down—"

"—so I put it out back. I put the whole pack of Jimmy Dean in the wood box where it won't smell up inside the house, but no bear can get to it 'cause I locked it up good."

Here Cadence paused.

"Okay. Well, good girl. That was good." Bobby could not get his brain in gear. He walked himself into a corner of the breakfast nook, as far from the kitchen sink as the phone cord allowed.

"Help me out here, honey. What's this about bacon?" He knew Paco was listening.

"Mama's eating bacon 'cause I went down to Mr. McCallum to tell him I can't work no more and I wasn't gone long, but maybe too long 'cause Auntie Pam was there and the birthday cards was a mess and I could see the kitty-cat clock, but Auntie Pam was talking and mama says be good and listen to your elders so that's what I did, so I was late coming home…"

"Cadence!" Bobby had to raise his voice. He heard her hold up on the other end, her breathing noisy in the phone like a child's, like a baby really. *Damn.* She was worse than he remembered.

"Where's your mother right now?"

"I'm not supposed to say."

"You can tell daddy," he said, thinking right away, *Verleana's gone and left the child.* Instinctively, Bobby turned to Paco who was leaning, almost sitting on the sink, smoothing his wine glass up against his cheek. It was hard to tell what was going on in that head of his.

"Mama says I'm not supposed to tell, but then she also says, 'Tell the truth.' So which is it, daddy?"

"That's a good question, honey. Let's see…" Bobby came back to the counter, pouring himself another glass of merlot. "The first rule is: tell the truth. All the other rules aren't as important as that one, okay? So tell me where your mother is."

"She's here."

"Is that the truth?"

"Yes, sir." It'd been a while since Bobby'd heard "Sir." No one said "Sir" or "Ma'am" in Cincinnati or anywhere north of the Nowheresville he'd once called home except in court and that was Paco's territory.

"Okay, put Mama on the phone."

"I can't. She's sleeping."

"That's okay. You can wake her up."

"No. It's sick-sleep."

"What's sick-sleep?"

"That's when you can't wake her up."

Bobby caught Paco staring. He'd traded his wineglass for a pair of bright yellow plastic gloves.

"Listen to me now, honey, is your mother okay?"

"She's sick."

"She's sick…" Well, at least the woman wasn't dead or run off with some loser. Bobby was absolutely sure that "sick" meant drugs.

"Do you mean drugs, honey? Is Mommy taking drugs?"

"Yes, sir." A pause. Then, brightly, "I help her."

Bobby wilted onto the bar stool, his glass clattering to the counter. Paco stayed focused on his dishwashing, the faucet up full blast.

"Daddy?"

"Give daddy a minute to think."

If this didn't beat all. Apparently Verleana was now a drug addict. After pounding the Good Book night and day about how he, Bobby, had gone the way of the Devil, here she was sending her kid—*their* kid—their simpleton-at-best kid—out on the streets to procure for her. Maybe even shoot her up. Bobby was steaming.

Cadence's voice, so polite, so respectful, piped up again. "I help mommy, daddy. The nurse taught me."

"What nurse?"

"The nurse showed me how to write down the medicines and did she take them or not."

"Your mother has a nurse?" Bobby watched Paco carefully *not* look up.

"She comes every day," Cadence said.

Whoo-ee. Bobby stood and spun the bar stool on one of its legs. He'd have pulled a Fred Astaire and danced with the damn thing if the phone wasn't in his hand. "Okay, honey, I've got the picture now. Let's work with daddy and find that nurse's phone number. What's her name?"

"Miss Lana."

"Miss Lana what?"

"Miss Lana."

"Okay, Miss Lana. Did she leave a phone number? Let's find it together." Bobby smiled in Paco's direction. It would be all right now. He wanted Paco to know it would be all right, but Paco stayed hunched over the sink, scrubbing the broiler pan. Steam billowed around his giant plastic hands.

"How about right there by the phone, Cadence? Do you see a number written down?"

"Yes, sir."

"What does it say?"

"Solace."

"Oh, Solace? Good girl. Give daddy the number."

Coming For To Carry Me

Maggie Dull
After Aerobics

"It may be time for Solace." That's what Narduli had said. Apparently Maggie's mother was a candidate for in-house hospice care. Maggie hoped so because bi-coastal supervision was not an option.

She got busy packing the trimmest of bags. Countdown to Holiday Hell, and here she was flying to the boonies. Not what you'd call a career booster, but then again, who was she kidding? Career? Hers was a job. Euphemized in the trade as "event planning," it was in fact merely party-throwing for the rich and incorporated. Indeed, years of professional festivity had eroded Maggie's sense of mission to sheer rent-paying.

Thank God for her Access miles, considering the airline wouldn't see fit to stake her to a flight *before* her mother died when she could actually do some good. At best, booking at the last minute on Thanksgiving week, she'd have wound up paying a small fortune to ride at the back of the bus. But with her Access status, Maggie popped into first class, no questions asked.

She tight-rolled some pantyhose, then combed the walk-in. Nothing like a modern condo for primo closet space. What should she take? Beach wear? Arctic gear? Maggie decided on layers: pile for chill, peel for heat. Always comfortable, always put together.

Then she walked every room in her ritual pre-lockdown inspection, un-plugging appliances, consolidating trash. She owned the place lock, stock and barrel. Plus, there was a modest chunk of cash in the bank. And neither was divorce booty, thank you very much. Maggie had always made more than her ex-. In fact, he had taken *her* to the cleaners with the settlement. Spilled milk. Besides, there was an upside to Splitsville: reducing one's dependents to a big fat zero made running off to the hinterlands that much easier.

Off came her leotard and cross-trainers, on went a teddy and robe. Maggie slid into the kitchen alcove her realtor had pitched as a "breakfast nook." To Maggie, it was cocktail central. She knocked back what would surely be the first of several Fuzzy Navels, ticking down her checklist: two corporate year-end wrap-ups, five private holiday parties ("holiday" meaning festive, but not identifiably Christian), three of them for first-timers. Maggie made more than half her yearly income in this last quarter, not to mention building her client base. Great holiday bashes begat more of the same. Failure, on the other hand—and failure meant any occasion even marginally less than "Spectacular!" "One in a Million!"—and her business would dry up in a heartbeat. The field was too damn competitive. Every bored Palo Alto wife thought that because she could throw a dinner party, she could do what Maggie did.

Checklist complete, Maggie dialed Amelia on the mobile.

"Dulé Associates." Amelia picked up anytime, anywhere, even on a Saturday night. That was their deal. Without the wherewithal to afford a mobile phone of her own, Amelia was delighted to have Maggie underwrite the latest in telecommunications in exchange for on-call status.

"It's Mags. Listen, my mother's sick." (She wondered, did Amelia even know she had a mother? Going on three-plus years working together, but Maggie was pretty sure she'd never mentioned her folksy folks back in the Pineys.) "I have to fly home for a couple of days. That means you hold down the fort."

This was new territory. To date, no one had done any fort-holding at Dulé Associates except Maggie herself.

There was silence on the other end of the phone. *Good,* Maggie thought, *I have her attention.* When she dropped the bomb, Amelia actually screamed, real screaming, horror movie stuff. Apparently that was the kind of thing mentioning a 5K bonus could do.

"If you ace this gig," Maggie told her, "You will pull down one big, fat wad of cash."

"Really?" Amelia squealed.

"Really."

"So what do I have to do?"

That tickled Maggie no end. It was gratifying to know the girl had been listening all these years. Rule number one at Dulé: nail down your terms. So Maggie did some nailing: "It means raves across the board. It means every client re-books. And it means you snag at least three new customer referrals."

"Done."

Wow, I should have tried this sooner, Maggie thought. Clearly, the co-pilot was ready to pilot.

Arranging for a lift to the airport—that all went down like butter. No doubt, Amelia's attention was elsewhere, dreaming of ways to blow her 5K windfall with that good-for-not-much boyfriend who mooched off her. Maggie heard *beaucoup* "thanks a lot's" as the only associate in Dulé Associates signed off.

Phew. Maggie drained the last of her last Navel. Maybe her business would survive. Maybe she'd be able to sneak out of town and sneak back again with no one noticing. Maybe the whole entire course of history would not take a catastrophic turn before she got back.

She took another look at the note, flattening it on the banquette, its familiar, hyper-neat printing a testament to the penmanship of yore:

DO NOT DROP BY. DO NOT VISIT. I WILL NOT
ACCEPT PHONE CALLS. I WILL NOT ACCEPT
MAIL. I DO NOT WANT TO SEE MY CHILDREN.
LOVE YOUR MOTHER.

"Love your mother?" thought Maggie or, *"Love,"*— with a comma—*"your mother?"* Imperative or salutation? And what was this about children? There were no children. There was only child, one child. Only Maggie. Yes, there were other living progeny. Two sons, two once-upon-a-time brothers. But Dalton had long since disappeared. For all anybody knew he was lying in a ditch or holed up in some mansion, a millionaire with a new name. And Baylor had cut their mother off altogether since the Christmas when she told one of his daughters she was fat to her face.

Nevertheless, the second Maggie got the note, she'd called Baylor.

"Mags," he said, "have you imagined all these years that when I say 'she's dead to me' I'm talking figuratively? As far as I'm concerned, she's already in the ground. You let her ghost your life, it's on you."

It's on me, indeed, Maggie thought. *Someone has to deal with it.*

She stared down at the note. Attached with a paper clip was a piece of scratch paper, torn from what looked like a grocery bag, scribbled on in pencil. Maggie did not recognize the hand:

YOUR MOTHER REQUESTED ME TO SEND
THIS TO YOU. I AM SORRY. BURNICE.

"Requested me?" Maggie abhorred grammatical sloth, not to mention that tone of pity: "I am sorry..." Sorry for what? And who, in God's name, was this Burnice?

We Gather Together

Burnice Kling
After Hours

Burnice Kling wagged both index fingers: "Don't even think about sending me back to Miz Dull!" Announcing it straight to Dee Dee's face. Dee Dee Hipps, Queen of Solace and in all ways Burnice's boss. Normally, Burnice did not make a habit of puffing up to a supervisor, but things had gotten out of hand. In all her years of nursing, Burnice had never quite seen the like.

"There's something wrong in her house." By "her," she meant Miz Dull. "Y'all'll think I'm some kinda crazy woman, I start talking about it."

"We already do." Dee Dee winked at Bear. Which, of course, made him laugh.

What a pair they were, like orphan salt and pepper at a picnic. Bear managed all Solace nurses in-house while Dee Dee looked after the home-visit staff. Burnice knew to watch her step. These two might be mismatched, but God help the nurse who tried to work the one against the other.

Bear planted his feet, lifting his belly off his belt. Tall as he was, he looked like a telephone pole, rough hewn of a dark wood, gouged from the weather, his tattoos, at least the ones you could see, fading off him like peeling paint. "What's the deal, Burnice? You fixing to fire your patient?"

She tried her sweetest, kindly-nurse voice; "Miz Dull is throwing things."

"So? You've seen that before."

"Yes, sir, I have."

"Then what gives?"

"This is different."

"Different how?"

Bear wasn't smiling. Burnice wasn't either. She met him stare to stare while Saint Dee Dee coo'ed, "Now, now, you two."

Honestly, the woman could be irritating, patting down a head full of blond curls that had come into this world neither blond nor curly. Dee Dee peered over her glasses, tapping her clipboard with one pink fingernail. "Give me a minute. I thought I saw a new note here on Miz Dull."

Bear leaned over her shoulder. "What's the story?"

"Colon," she said.

It's not the cancer, Burnice thought, *it's Satan himself.* She looked around for somewhere to sit, but nothing looked safe. Space was so tight at Solace they'd had to improvise an office in an outsized pantry at the back of the old farmhouse, an unofficial bone yard for furniture too frail to leave in patients' rooms. The place was filled with worn-out chairs, tables, lamps. And, of course, flowers. Scattered around, balanced on every collywopple surface, was an ever-changing assortment of the get-well-soon bouquets that were always left behind when loved ones passed. No one at Solace had the heart to waste even one flower, so they got scooped up and plonked down in the "office" until they died. Volunteers came by once a month from the Holy Brides Gift Shop to collect the vases.

Certainly, Bear knew better than to try sitting, given his bulk. Instead, he hovered over Dee Dee, leaning in, then raring back.

"It's the holidays for Christ's sake—" he checked himself "—I mean, for *crikey's* sake. Sorry, Dee Dee." She nodded, but he was off to the races: "Holy Brides is full. Every Solace bed is taken. We've got field nurses driving all over creation to accommodate the patient load. And now you come in here wanting to take a client off your list?"

"Bear, Bear, Bear, Bear—" Dee Dee did her usual, unriling the man, setting him down off his high horse. "Here it is. Look. We've got a note says Miz Dull's daughter's coming in from California. That should help." She turned to Burnice, "There's nobody with Miz Dull now, is there?"

"Not a soul," Burnice said thinking, *Can you blame them? Who would wait on a body with the Devil taking up residence right there next to the bed?*

Dee Dee chattered on. "Usually family shows up and everybody straightens out."

Burnice knew any possible straightening could only come from Jesus resurrecting himself direct to the Dull house, but those were thoughts best left unsaid. She sent her eyes to the ceiling: *Lord, keep my tongue in my head where it belongs.*

Dee Dee resumed her curl patting. "We've got Miz Greevey coming in-house; Lana says she's taking a turn. And Hazel's got her hands full with Miz Early. There's just no way we can reassign you, Burnie."

"No way, no how. It's hump time." Bear'd learned to talk like that at the V.A. counseling shell-shocked vets.

"Bring it up at staff meeting and maybe someone will have an idea for you," Dee Dee purred. She'd learned to talk like *that* at supervisor training. As if taking on the Devil might be an occasion for helpful hints.

Burnice took herself on over to the door. "I'll handle it."

Dee Dee kept up her purr. "We can talk about it tomorrow."

I've done my talking, Burnice thought, swinging her purse off a side sofa. She used a different tone to make herself clear: "I will handle. Miz Dull. Myself."

"Atta girl." Bear threw Burnice his best buck-up-the-platoon smile. "Welcome to Hell Week!"

"Bear!" Dee Dee protested. "You know I don't like that rough talk."

"I mean *swell* week," he said, laughing at his own joke. He picked up a vase of dried baby's breath, one wilting, silver balloon stuck in among them. GET WELL SOON! it said. He tossed it into the trash, then swung the lot, wastebasket and all, up off the floor, smacking it clanging with his clipboard, hoisting it overhead as if to ward off something coming from the sky.

"You know what we say in the Corps…"

Burnice and Dee Dee had heard it a million times. They said it along with him now, matching the boom, the bellow of his voice: "I-i-i-in-coming!"

SUNDAY

November 19, 1989

THERE'S A FIRST TIME

August Early
After Church

Mr. Early had never set foot in an elevator before. Not to mention a hospital. He'd seen them plenty of times on the television though, so he was able to walk right from the parking lot through those first big glass doors that—*Bang!*—split out from each other without anybody touching anything—HOLY torn from BRIDES—and then those second glass doors that split out identical just a step away for him to go in.

He was scared all right. On television, hospitals were nothing but hallways and they looked real narrow, and people—doctors, he divined with respect to the white coats—would tear down those hallways pushing tables that must have been on wheels with, of course, the patient lying slab-flat on top, so you couldn't hardly see him. And there'd be a bunch of doctors too, each one carrying something high up in the air and yelling, so that if you'd found yourself in one of those television hospitals, you'd hear them barreling around the corner. Still he was afraid he would not hear in time and they'd crash right into him there in the entryway and he'd be hurt, but it would be his fault just the same.

It wasn't like that though. It was a vestibule there at the hospital just like where you came in over to the Christ Mount. That's what the preacher called it, a vestibule. The plain space, big and quiet, where you first took your hat off before walking into church.

Mr. Early was grateful to stand for a minute and get his bearings. He could feel his heart in his wrists jumping up against his shirt cuffs which were buttoned. He could feel just the starting-to sweat coming on his upper lip. He told himself it was natural.

There was a square polished block in front of him looked to be of limestone. Behind it, a row of orange chairs, all locked together. But there was nobody around. In this hospital it was quiet.

He stood a while because he could not figure which way to go. Finally some folks came around to his left. They stood staring at a wall. He saw two round knobs with arrows there. *That must be the elevator,* he thought. *Like on television.* He figured these people most probably knew how to operate an elevator and so they'd be good for him to ride with.

He eased in behind holding his hat.

They were a family, that's what he made out of them. There was a man and a woman and a little boy who liked hanging onto the overalls around his daddy's knees and swinging and pulling on them until his daddy said, "Quit."

It occurred to Mr. Early they were in the hospital too and so likely they too were visiting the sick. Or even the dying. *Of course, somebody might have had a baby.* He could hear his wife's voice saying that. She said he always looked for the bad in things.

Ping. There was a bell sound. The wall split open from the middle just like the entry doors had done. He let the family step in first as he had planned. Then it was his turn.

Mr. Early had grown up on a farm like most of the folks whose people had come from the Piedmont, and he knew just how a horse might feel stepping into that elevator, because they used to take the livestock up the road to Mr. Kinnel's big Avenel Farm to weigh them and that meant shooing them into a tight one-animal pen whose floor was really just a scale bottom suspended on big 2,000-pound springs. He'd be the first to tell you that animals don't like to be stepping out on any ground that's spongy or loose or in this case spring-bouncy, and Lord, you should have seen those animals spook. They'd come straight back at you, all fours in the air to throw themselves right down on their backs if they could—he'd seen one do it—before they'd commit any weight to that floor, because they could feel it, just setting that one hoof or sometimes at the most two, the front two, in. They could feel it when the footing was not to be trusted.

Mr. Early was sorry he'd thought of the horse up in the air now because that was where he wanted to be, walking onto the elevator floor and feeling it bob like the big scale. Lord, the heebie-jeebies it gave him up his heels. Why'd he have to go remembering that?

"Four, please," said the father.

Mr. Early looked over at him and smiled. The boy was still ratcheting back and forth off his father's knee.

"It'll un-nerve you," Mr. Early said to the boy, thinking to let him know it was all right to be scared. But the boy only seemed to be interested in what it looked like to look at Mr. Early with his head hanging upside down while still standing but leaning off his Daddy.

"Quit," said the father. He stepped toward Mr. Early dragging the boy. "Quit," he said louder and the boy quit, standing up.

The father lurched in so close that Mr. Early had to turn with him and then could see—*Oh, the buttons.* Buttons with numbers. That's what "Four" had meant.

The father pushed 4 and stepped back, handing the boy to his mother. She was a squared-off woman, loose-skinned, her face in folds like a bloodhound. Mr. Early thought maybe it was her kin they were coming to see. Maybe her old mother was dying of a feeble heart and them coming to pay their respects. Maybe all the while they were waiting in the elevator, her mama was passing from this world to the next, cursing a God that would let her die alone. He could hear Theo getting after him in his head again: *Always looking for the bad in things.*

The doors banged into each other so hard they shook the floor. *Kerblam!* Something took hold of them. *Kachung!* Now they were going up. Even with no windows Mr. Early could tell they were moving. Something in his stomach told him so.

The fourth floor, which he could see with the doors opening, looked to be some kind of baby birthing place. He got that impression by the balloons and the lots of children like at a picnic. The family spilled out mother first, head down, dragging her kinfolk behind. *That woman don't look baby-happy,* Mr. Early thought. More like she was bothered because her *sister* had the baby and she wanted another one but couldn't no more.

A couple on the outside of the elevator stood looking in. Then looking some more.

"Afternoon," Mr. Early said.

The gentleman, an older man of the color of a good bay horse, met Mr. Early's eyes and nodded. He stepped sideways so that he and his Mrs. could come in together since she had his arm tight. She was dressed up in a round pink hat like a tin of snuff set on her head and a veil crimped off it and her good high shoes so that she was walking carefully and needed his support. They were a fine pair the two of them, just as proud and walking proud as a pair of old hounds, stiff but with dignity, still dressed from church.

Mr. Early had not been able to attend this morning. It was going on three o'clock but here this gentleman had on his shining blue suit with a striping tie and she a dress pearlescent. Must have been they'd kept their clothes on to come to the hospital. Might to have gone home from the service first and sat real careful so as to stay church-perfect. Maybe the Mrs. had brought him an aspic from the icebox, but neither of them hungry much or talking until it was time to start the car.

The couple found their place to the right of Mr. Early. The gentleman, being knowledgeable, knew to push his button right away, which was 8.

"JESUS JOSEPH H. MARY MOTHER OF GOD WAI-AI-AI-AIT!" A long-limbed boy, all laces and elbows, ran full bore, throwing his body, mucky sneakers and patched jeans into the closing elevator doors—*Whomp!*—as they thumped into him and jerked back open.

Right behind came a passel, enough of them jamming in to where Mr. Early had to move to make room. *They had ought to be a family,* he thought, *but no daddy.* Five, maybe six of them, every last one antsy-pantsy, shuffling and fidgeting to make the floor bounce. One hopped over in front of the older couple, pushed the 7 button and hopped back.

The elevator didn't give any one of them much room so everybody hushed up standing that close.

Mr. Early saw the woman was got up in an old pair of sweatpants cinched high on the ankle with a tie rope hanging at her belly and some tippy slip-on shoes Theo would have worn inside with a bathrobe, not out for company. The woman's long hair lay flat down on her neck like a wet horsetail lies off the tailbone, her skin the color of tired biscuit gravy. She had on a plain T-shirt with a stain up on the left side and sure by the hang of it, she didn't seem to be wearing no bra. Mr. Early couldn't help knowing. Didn't take but a glance to see a horse's lines, how it'd been eating, was it foundered or favoring or just how the animal'd been worked, in traces or for saddle. He could size this woman in a minute.

Her family got eased down finally and wasn't bouncing the floor no more when, damn, if the mama didn't pipe up out of the blue, loud like you'd hear at the Garnet County Trotters Auction saying, "I FORGOT TO TELL YOU. THEY HAD TO TIE FRANKLIN TO THE BED. HE'S STILL COMING OFF THE DRINK." Just as loud as you please.

Mr. Early did not make a sound, did not move a muscle, not one muscle of the mouth or blinking or nothing that would show that he had heard this, and even all the while thinking, *My word.* The couple to his right was quiet too.

Ping. 7. The big family went scrappling off.

7 must be where you come to dry out, Mr. Early thought. *And maybe the drugs too.* The place where Catherine might have gone if she had not gone instead to that needle in her arm, leaving behind her mama and her daddy and her own precious babies, twins girls, the sweetest little darlings you ever did see, who had never done a thing to deserve her leaving them that way.

The elevator rose. It was just the three of them now. Mr. Early did not engage with the older gentleman or his wife in her Sunday hat. Her eyes had not left the floor since their stepping in. For his part, the husband fixed his gaze firmly upon the light behind the row of numbers above them with his eyes hard and black and his chinline set, seeming to say, *We must not speak!* as if he was looking at the American flag coming out into a wind.

They should make a coin of him, Mr. Early thought.

At 8, the gentleman walked out with his Mrs. right close on his elbow. There wasn't a nod or even a glance in Mr. Early's direction, so intent were they on that place they were going to. *Which is how it should be,* Mr. Early thought. *They must to have their minds on someone who needs them, a grandmother with the sugar shakes or some fool of a nephew who's rolled the tractor over his leg.*

The elevator doors closed. Mr. Early was alone. There was a jerk, a howl, metal-on-metal, booming down and back up the dark pitshaft that was surely just to the other side of his feet.

Lord, he thought, *Where is she? Where is Theo?*

When the doors finally came open at 9, which was the highest number, there was a little man standing in the widening gap, a short man with coal-black hair wearing lots of clothes—a white doctor coat unbuttoned and then a blue jacket stuck on top.

The man caught sight of Mr. Early. "Can I help you?"

"I. I." Mr. Early kept saying "I." He was having a hard time saying anything at all. "Early?" he asked.

"Oh," said the man. "She's here. You're in the right place." Now the doors were bucking. The elevator wanted to go. The man raised his voice, "Cordelia! Mrs. Early has a visitor!" swinging himself in and jabbing toward the buttons as Mr. Early stepped out.

An enormous woman leaned into view from the hallway. "Come on, honey. Shake a stick." She had on all white, pants and a tuck-in blouse. Her blue name tag said CORDELIA. She waved him down to her.

Mr. Early passed between two low counters with lots of people in white behind them, mostly women but some men, standing among a jumble of metal poles and tubes and those bags hanging off them he'd seen on TV. Light came down from up high onto the people there, so that everybody seemed to be glowing in a special glowing place. Not one of them cast their eyes up as he passed.

The nurse got her arm all the way resting on his shoulder which was easy since he wasn't a tall man but she was a right large woman, pushing him along next to her. "You must be Mr. Early."

"Yes, ma'am."

"Your wife's been looking for you."

They walked by doors and doors, some closed but mostly open with inside every one of them an old person on a bed.

"Here we are." Miss Cordelia coaxed him forward like they used to do the horses up to the big scale.

The first thing he saw was blackness, dead blackness in front of his eyes, even though he didn't feel a faintness, and thank God because that would have been an embarrassment.

And then he could see.

Theo.

She was there in the bed just like on the soaps, wearing a plastic mask that was a pretty color of green like a Coca-Cola bottle and some kind of faded print dress covering her body.

She could talk in the mask. "Did you see the people about the insurance?"

He immediately turned, starting into the hallway, but Miss Cordelia was there to catch him. "You don't have to worry, Mr. Early. We checked her in when she got here. You can go down on your way out and show them the Blue Cross. Have you got it?"

He nodded.

Even hours ago not being able to breathe and mad as a hornet, Theo had gasped out for him to bring the Blue Cross card when he came. That was after Curtis-Michael and the boys had come up the hill with the ambulance and got her on the stretcher.

Miss Cordelia swung him back around. "We've got a nice recliner chair, Mr. Early, see? So you can sit with your wife and be comfortable and you can even sleep here if you like. There's juice and coffee down with us at the station. You feel free to come on by if there's anything you need."

She positioned him to sit in the chair which he did, just on the edge of it, with his hat in his hand. And then she left.

"Theo..." He couldn't help the tears coming though they stayed in his eyes.

"Don't you cry on me, August Early. Don't you cry on me. I'm the one should be crying." Her voice was better than this morning, but her breathing was as odd as could be. "They're giving me this oxygen." She pointed up past her head to something that looked like an oversized Ball jar wall-mounted. There were numbers on it. "I'm on 5," she said. "I couldn't get but 2 at home."

At home Miss Hazel had called and gotten them a machine that you plugged in the wall. The man who brought it said it pulled oxygen out of the air or it made oxygen, Mr. Early wasn't sure, but that it was oxygen in the house, and so nobody could smoke no more. He said that oxygen could set your house on fire. Mr. Early hadn't had a cigarette since nor his wife neither and she'd been smoking even with the sickness.

Theo's eyelids closed even with her looking straight at him so he wondered whether she was still watching him through the skin. She did not move. After a time, it appeared she was sleeping.

Thoughts kept chasing around-around-around in Mr. Early's mind. When he was a boy in second grade, his cousin had got his eye whacked out with a hoe. That's when his mother said, "Sometimes God is a mischievous mean old cuss." Mr. Early was of a mind to agree with her.

It wasn't but two minutes he'd been in the shower that morning. He'd put off bathing for days just because of the plumb bare chance this kind of thing could happen, but finally he'd gotten in, just to rinse he thought, and it being morning was usually a good time for Theo. So he hadn't heard at first. She must have been calling for him a minute or more. Calling for him as best she could without being able to breathe. A mean old cuss to play tricks like that when, only the day before, Miss Hazel said she should have a bell and Lord save them, if they hadn't found a bell that very night, or Theo had, a real silver one she kept with her mother's things in a trunk filled with the nice china and cloth pieces they never, ever used. Things she was saving for Catherine, Theo said. Now she was saving them for the twins.

So Mr. Early was poking a towel in his ear and that was why it'd taken longer than it should for him to hear the high, frantic tinkling of that silver bell which was her only way of calling him to come into the room and find her waving and ringing and gasping, "I can't breathe. I can't breathe."

A mean old cuss.

Looking over at his wife, Mr. Early wondered what he should be doing. *Just sit with,* he supposed. That's what Theo said when one of her women-friends was sick: "I'll be over to sit with."

Out of the blue, Theo turned her head to him. "I'm going to sleep some," she said, her eyelids still closed.

Mr. Early waited. She did not speak again. He squared his hat on his lap. He told himself the twins would be all right. Miss Susan Neville would look after them just fine. He told himself he could sit quiet now. Theo needed for nothing. He told himself he could do nothing until he knew what to do next, until his wife's eyes opened and she was with him again.

Where There's Smoke

Maggie Dull
After Take-Off

They were well more than halfway across the country, Maggie on her third vodka tonic. That's when she caught a whiff of something truly terrible—a piercing, acrid odor. Right away, she knew. She looked around to see if anybody else had caught it.

Why did she bother? Surrounded by the Fraternity of the Great Unaware there at thirty thousand feet, their faces slack to airport thrillers and binders full of spreadsheets, Maggie was once again way ahead of the pack. The pear-shaped fellow next to her did not so much as lift his gaze.

The smell intensified. Maggie stretched the synthetic substitute the airlines called a blanket across her nose to serve as an improvised gas mask.

Ten seconds. Mr. Pearbelly next door shuffled some pages. Twenty seconds. Mr. Pearbelly stuck a paper clip between his teeth. Thirty seconds. Still no sign of recognition. Thirty seconds is a very long time when you know that your plane is on fire.

Maggie was tired of being first. As in, first to know. You can bet that during the all-important registration phase of Pre-Birth, Maggie had muscled her way into the *Make-Me-a-Smart-Kid* line. Probably even made a stink about it when it was her turn to order up a life. That's when the proverbial Powers-That-Be should have kicked her ass right back to the *Think-It-Over* line. But no-o-o-o. Like every other dummy, Maggie must have asked for smarts. She must have asked to know things before other people did.

It was one thing to get her hand up first in social studies class. It was quite another to take on the whole clairvoyant drama. Back when Maggie was a kid, it was called ESP. She used to wake up in the middle of the night knowing that something was about to happen. Knowing the way you look at something red and know it's red. The way you can't *not* know it's red.

Like the big one. The night she woke up thinking, *Uh-Oh,* and straightaway hearing what sounded like snakes climbing up the back wall of the house. Not that she had any idea what snakes crawling up a house might sound like, but that's what came to mind. Snakes. *Slither-slither-slither.*

All it took was sitting up in bed to see—*Oh.* The sound wasn't snakes, it was fire, shooting up from the roof of the Eargles' trailer in the lot out back. The *slither-slither-slither* was actually *crackle-crackle-crackle.* The snakes were flames.

She'd run down to her parents' room to knock on the door they always kept tight shut. Knocking until she heard her daddy's voice—"What?"—his roar dissolving into the wet cough that erupted any time he took a deep breath.

"The Eargles' trailer is burnin'," she yelled, coming in.

"That's just dreaming. Go on back to sleep."

"All right. But the Eargles is going to be one sorry family in the morning, no thanks to you."

That shot her daddy out of bed. He hated when she sassed. Heaving himself over to the back window, a big man in big underwear, he drew the curtain back. It was quite a sight by then, the whole trailer up in flames.

"Good God, Dolores," he bellowed. "Call the fire station."

Sure enough the entire Big Piney brigade had to come up the hill, one fire truck and a bunch of guys in flatbeds. By then, the trailer was a goner, but nobody got hurt. At least that's what her mother said.

Not that anybody ever thanked Maggie. That wasn't the point. The real drawback of the first-to-know program was that she was never first enough. If she were, the Eargles would still be in their trailer. And a gal whose mother was dying of cancer would not only *not* get on Flight 252 on that particular Sunday, she'd also warn everybody else to stay off an airborne fireball-waiting-to-happen.

Maggie wondered when it would be time to get up and knock on the pilot's door herself since, predictably, not one of the service attendants was in sight. *Hiding in the galley, no doubt.* You wouldn't think there'd be enough room for them all in those tiny service zones between sections, but apparently there was. Maybe a few were in the lavatories hoping it would "blow over," pun intended.

Forty seconds. At long last heads started to come up around the cabin. One. Then another. People began looking around. A few hands went up to noses. Eyes met. A murmured voice or two.

Meanwhile, the smell worsened. *Sharp enough to choke a small farm animal,* Maggie thought. *That's what it takes to get people's attention.*

Mr. Pearbelly finally looked up from his inventories. He glanced at her with the blanket over her nose. And *smiled.*

Stuck on Charon's boat dock with the Pillsbury Dough People and we're going down, Maggie thought. *The story of my life.*

Bing. A call bell sounded. In a flash, here came the flight crew, racing up and down the aisles with large plastic bags, sweeping everything off passengers' tray-tables—napkins, bottles, half-filled glasses. If you weren't quick, your cheap paperback would be gone too.

Is this the pre-conflagration routine? Maggie wondered, *We neaten up before we blow up?*

One of their brave sky hostesses got on the horn, managing an impersonal voice-over that tinkled with faux cheer, inviting them to bring their seatbacks and tray-tables to their full upright and locked positions.

Cabin clear, once again the crew disappeared.

Silence. Blankets and pillows held over faces now. Tears down one woman's cheek. Meanwhile, Mr. Pearbelly had gone back to reading his charts. Perhaps the guy was slow, perhaps the cognitively-challenged cousin of some mogul, flown around on sham business trips, pretending to read inventory-to-shipping ratios in order to look busy.

Enter the gods: *deus ex machina* in the form of the pilot's voice descending from overhead speakers. Firm, very male. A lovely Southern drawl. Sexy, really, and calm. Calm to beat all calms. The man might as well have been instructing them to look out the left side of the plane for a terrific view of the Grand Canyon.

"Ladies and Gentlemen," he said. "We got us a funny smell on board."

A funny smell!

"We're right over Little Rock, so we're gonna take ourselves down there for a minute, just to make sure everything's okay. They've cleared us for landing. Why don't you go ahead and buckle those seatbelts nice and tight..."

That's when they rang five bells.

Bing. Bing. Bing. Bing. Bing.

'It tolls for thee,' Maggie thought. *Three bells, you're landing. Five bells, you're going down.*

Sure enough, immediately—more than immediately—the plane dropped. It did not descend. It did not swoop. It dropped, angling steeply to the left. If her seatbelt hadn't been fastened, Maggie's face would have found itself plastered somewhere up by the overhead call buttons.

Free fall lasted ten to fifteen seconds. Time got wonky. The acrid smell stung throats and eyes around the cabin. Clouds tore by, giving way to ground, ground rushing up, a crazy quilt of farmland rotating as the plane's left turn spiraled into a skein of landing strips, plummet narrowing to close-up.

Then Maggie was back in real time. *Bang!* Tiny wheels, giant jet slamming down, shooting past a phalanx of fire trucks that were already speeding alongside, trying to keep up as the plane sped by. Brakes shrieked. Maggie's seatbelt raked unyielding across her lap.

A bubble of hope rose inside her, as if careening on land in a giant can of exploding Sterno were any more promising than flying that way.

They taxied to a swift stop in the farthest corner of the farthest landing strip. Maggie could see the terminal in the distance. LITTLE ROCK, a sign said. It was little all right. No other planes in sight. They probably didn't want folks landing for an Ozark vacation right next to the funeral pyre of a burning 737.

Fire trucks formed a line on both sides of the jet from the nose all the way back to the tail. Teams of men converged, push-running mobile staircases—the kind that people used before jetways were invented—toward each of the airplane's exits. One of the stewards wrenched open the forward door from inside.

A spaceman entered the plane. Swaddled in silver, his feet encased in puffy boots, his hands stuffed into gauntlets, he maneuvered awkwardly, tipping from side to side just to get his suit through the door. A spherical helmet, screwed neckless to the torso, hid the person inside. He was moving in slow-motion. So was Maggie's brain. *A spaceman?*

As he turned to scan the scene, his mirrored faceplate reflected a cabin full of astonished people staring dumbstruck back at him. His right arm rose. A single mylar finger performed the universal pantomime: *Come this way.*

Maggie's brain began to catch up. Maybe this was fire gear. Maybe fire-*ball* gear. Maybe they would all be blown to heaven and only the spaceman would survive, thrown clear of the burning wreckage, saved by his heat-shielding bubble wrap.

A stewardess asked for calm over the intercom, but there was no need. The Dough People made not a peep. Minds not yet comprehending, they rose as one, their bodies shuffling into line—*So polite,* marveled Maggie—shock reducing them to habit, summoning the rote memory of manners that is the glory of civilization itself.

We'd never see this in the made-for-TV movie, Maggie thought. On TV, people would be screaming and pushing past each other, trampling babies, restraint being anathema to Nielsen ratings.

They deplaned briskly row by row. Maggie moved into the aisle when it was her turn and not before, Mr. Pearbelly shuffling just ahead. Breaching the doorway, she caught a glimpse of orange to her right, the leaves of a lone sugar maple waving at her from the far end of the runway. Her first lungful of air was a surprise, moist and clean. And then she was running down the mobile steps. Down to personnel who grabbed her two elbows, steadying her and directing—frankly shoving—her into the already receding line of passengers walk-running toward the terminal. "Go!" they yelled. "Go!"

Risking their lives to ensure that none of us trips while fleeing a burning airplane, thought Maggie. *God bless America.*

There was eerie quiet out on the strip. She listened for a big bang behind her, but none came. When she reached the terminal door, an aide frantically waved her inside. Instead, like Lot's wife, she turned around.

As she did, a crew of spacemen on a crane rose toward the plane, bumping its midsection. Then a curved, metal door dropped down, swinging below the belly of the jet. Instantly, a dense ball of matte-black smoke poured out and up, momentarily engulfing the barreled sides of the wide body.

The spacemen recoiled. The crane retracted. There were no flames. There was no noise. Just a death balloon rotating as it ascended from the plane, evil oil-black stuff, dissipating very gradually into the air.

That was it. That was all Maggie needed to see. She had been first. She had been right. On fire at thirty thousand feet.

Entering the terminal, her mind was racing. Where was that pilot? He'd been the embodiment of courage under fire. Or over fire, literally. She should write the airline. It should go in his file. What was his name? Maybe she could meet him for a drink. *Just to thank him,* she thought. *Really thank him.*

Maggie pictured herself tearing off the pilot's jacket, the shirt and tie, the boxers, and giving her hero the time of his life right there in the middle of the Little Rock waiting area. She'd never had sex with a pilot before, but the man had said, "We got us a funny smell." He was John Wayne *redux.* He could have looked like an Ewok for all Maggie cared. She was ready to make his day.

By now she was several light-years over the moon, imagining them married, she and her pilot at a cocktail party with her telling the story of the burning plane to admiring gasps and him doing his *Aw Shucks* routine.

Someone tapped her shoulder from behind. "You wanna move up, Lady?"

Maggie saw she was in a line. A line stretching across the length of the terminal to a desk in the far distance whose placard said INFORMATION. She counted well over fifty people in front of her. Clearly, Little Rock was not prepared for a planeful of get-me-outta-here's.

That's when Maggie remembered her Access miles. First Class might not help in a fireball, but it sure as hell could make a difference on the ground. The line was just as long for the payphones. Maggie God-blessed Motorola as she pulled out her mobile and got on the horn to the central office. They rebooked her in a heartbeat. "I was on Flight 252." That was all she had to say.

Turn The Other

Burnice Kling / Lana Hendren
Afternoon

Burnice hadn't had time so much as to set down her purse and here they were, nurses—professionals all—having to half-sit on whatever stickly, broken up chair or table they could find. Honestly. Couldn't somebody at Solace come up with the resources for a proper office?

Dee Dee Hipps still had on her Sunday shoes. "Ladies, you are lifesavers," she said.

"Lifesavers." Bear echoed. "But sometimes savers need saving. We want to know how you're holding up, what with the heavy patient load. Especially you, Burnice."

Right this minute, Burnice thought, *if they are so all-fired sure they want to put their noses in my business, I'll tell them I feel like a criminal under the bright lights in the police lineup, thank you very much.* But before she could think what to say other than nothing, Dee Dee opened her big mouth. "Burnice says she wants to fire Miz Dull."

"What?!" That set the nurses in an uproar.

"We do as we're told!" Hazel piped up from over on the one-armed sofa, her thick legs splayed out in front of her, her wide feet wide. "Dee Dee assigns us—Dee Dee or Bear—and we go. That's all it is!"

"That's all it is!" Here came Kitty Pearl to join her, the two of them raising their palms as if in church. Would wonders never cease? Kitty Pearl, with her white-pink ponytail, perched next to Hazel, the grump, like a chickadee next to a buzzard. The jury was out on little Kitty. She was still in training. Everybody sensed a hurt under her meekness and wondered whether she had the strength for Solace work. And yet here she was, opening her sole mouth, her dolly-button-eyes aimed straight over at Bear.

Hazel got to tugging that same sweater she had on every day, not-quite-white wool over her not-quite-white uniform. Clearly, she was about to do some preaching: "We are called to help the needy. It don't say nothing 'bout the needy *nice*. Sometimes needy's as mean as a gander's got the run of the barnyard."

Burnice rolled her eyes. "Hazel, you and me've been in this barnyard for some time now. Don't be talking to me about goose this and gander that."

Then Lana Hendren threw in her two cents nobody had asked for, smiling like God's own anointed just because she was senior member of the home-visit staff. "Are we not Solace? Is that not our name? We are called to bring comfort."

Burnice bit her tongue. She did not want to get into it with *Miss* Lana, as she had her clients call her. *Miss* Lana in her fancy lady suit she wore even during the summer with one of those might-as-well-be-underwear blouses, and her ankle—the one dangling in the air not the one planted on the floor—her ankle zigzagging like a copperhead getting ready to strike.

Truth be told, Burnice was jealous. Lana had ways of keeping her complexion up. Her skin was the walnut color of Burnice's leather-bound family Bible and fingered down to the same butter smoothness. She looked polished the way Burnice imagined an Egyptian princess would back in Moses's time, bathed by servants twice a day in precious balms and unguents. Not like Burnice's tired skin, ashy, pale as a chickweed moth.

Lana held up a plastic plate of leaf-shaped sugar cookies with orange sprinkles. "Could be, we all need some comfort," she said. "I bought 'em special at the Bi-Lo. Y'all dive in."

She passed the plate around. Everybody took one except Bear who took two. He pointed them at Burnice. "Talk to us, Burnie. I mean *talk*-talk." He popped the cookies in his mouth, chomping them whole as he spoke. "It's rough out there, people. We gotta watch the burn-out." Bear with his war talk, speaking to them as if they were the men he'd seen through the jungle, some coming home safe, others in a box.

What exactly, Burnice wondered, *should I "talk-talk" about?* No matter how well she hewed to her Bible, she was pretty sure if she opened her mouth, she'd be branded a voodoo-er by her colleagues.

Why was it the Devil could be cited as a real-true thing in scripture, but seeing the infernal in this life was considered suspect? Among her people, it was commonplace. Aunt Mayto, Auntie Grace and even Great Uncle Otis had seen him. Folks of their generation were accustomed to such things. Certainly Burnice always kept her eyes peeled for signs of malevolence, but until Miz Dull, she hadn't had trouble with demons at work. Which was amazing considering she made her living helping folks cross over.

"It's a feeling," she said, all the while thinking, *It's a sure-as-trueness.*

"It's hateful," she said, all the while thinking, *It's the Evil One himself.*

"In Miz Dull's house, you mean?" asked Kitty, big-eyed.

"Hush," Hazel elbowed her.

Burnice could see Hazel was one of those who'd take things wrong. Rumor had it she wouldn't support saying prayers in school. Not that she wasn't Christian. Just she wasn't about to let anybody tell her what to do. That was something she and Burnice had in common.

Burnice waved them all quiet. "Here it is," she said. "Come yesterday, Miz Dull was fevery, middlin' fevery after breakfast. I could tell by touching. I was taking her temperature when damn if the thermometer didn't go crazy on me. Hot-cold, hot-cold right there in her mouth."

"Thermometers break." *Oooo,* it froze the blood, that tone of superiority in Lana's voice, as if she were correcting a child late for Sunday School.

Burnice sucked in her cheeks as she spoke. "A brand new thermometer, not one day old from the Rexall. I pull it out of her mouth and it's jumping 90 to 110 and back. I figure to try it again, so I'm swabbing, coming around the corner from the bathroom and there she is, Miz Dull, who has not had the strength so much as to turn in her sleep for going on a week now, there she is standing straight up high in the middle of the bed, her eyes bugging, pointing at me and saying, 'I reject you!'"

Burnice paused for effect.

"'I reject you!' She nigh-on spit it."

"She spit at you?"

Hazel poked at Kitty, hissing, "That's a manner of speaking."

"Next thing I know, she's grabbing anything—a bag of Attends, the tissue box, her C&D ointment—and she's throwing it straight at me. Hard. Like she's the rifle and I'm one of them cutout ducks at the county fair."

"That's assault." Dee Dee reached for her paperwork. "Why didn't you call us?"

"Another two hours and I'd be sitting where I am now telling you face-to-face."

That seemed to satisfy Dee Dee but not Hazel. Now *she* started in, eyes dark as sludge, arms pretzeled down tight to her ample bosom: "When I was a child, I used to ride the ponies down to Miz Early's place. Not my patient Miz Early. I'm talking about her husband—Mr. Early—his mama. She kept ponies to ride for lessons. Which was fine, except every time I went, she gave me a stubborn one who wouldn't go or an ornery one would get to buckin'. So one day I said to her, I said, 'Miz Early, how come I can't ride Princess or Blue Boy?' which was the nice ponies with the manners. 'How come you always put me on the bad ones?' And she said to me—I'll never forget it—she said, 'Hazel, I put you on the bad ones 'cause you're *that good*. I can't put the fainty-minded on them, I gotta put you. You are their match.' Now you can see as how that would help me. I was the one good enough to do it."

Hazel turned to Burnice: "Why can't it be the same for you and Miz Dull?"

"Seein's how I never had no pony ride or rode nothing my whole life except a wheelbarrow down to the end of the driveway, might be that *you* oughta take on Miz Dull," said Burnice, looking not at Hazel but at the place where the far wall met the floor.

"Oh, now," clucked Dee Dee and Lana both.

"I don't need to hear from Miss Holier-Than-Thou," huffed Burnice.

"Ask me for help again!" Hazel huffed right back.

"When I ask, you may speak!" Burnice roared, intent on shutting the woman's mouth for good.

Bear clapped to calm things, palming his clipboard with his hand. No one paid him any mind.

"I'll take her!" That was Kitty Pearl.

Hazel turned on her. "You can't take Miz Dull! She will eat you alive."

"How am I going to learn if I don't? I'll take your home visits, Burnice. You come on in-house."

From the corner came a voice that could stop a spooked deer in its tracks: "She is not herself..."

Everybody started. Was that Cherille Meade? Lord have mercy. Cherille who, come meeting time, squidged into the farthest, darkest, quietest corner of the room until the chitter-chatter stopped and she could get herself back to "her" kitchen. The only place at Solace, she liked to say, where God's real work could be done. Little tiny Cherille with her feet up off the floor for her shortness and her hair round like a mixing bowl turned upside down on her head.

Her eyes fixed directly to Burnice. "Miz Dull is not herself. You know that, Burnie."

At any other but meeting time, Burnice was Burnie to Cherille. The two had been known to enjoy a visit, commiserating in the Solace kitchen over some small inconvenience of their workdays. But in all their years together, neither had mentioned to the other the mysteries they entertained about things beyond.

"You got the name right," Cherille said, "but not the nature."

A ringing commenced in Burnice's ears.

"There's nothing wrong in that house. There's something wrong in her."

A tingling ran up and down both Burnice's legs and a clanging started in her head.

"She's afraid to cross, that's all it is. That's all *It* is. That's all *He* is." Cherille slowed way up. "She is not herself, Burnie, nor you neither, walking around like your hands is tied when you know what needs doing. She's like a deer with the dogs on her, backed against a tree and no way to jump 'em or kick her way loose or nothing. It's you standing between her and a dying she thinks will be all teeth and claws and howling blood."

"That's it," said Burnice. Now *she* was talking like the church choir.

"Oh, death ain't dogs," grumped Hazel.

"It's not death that's doggin' her." Cherille's eyes flashed from far-away to close, holding on Hazel and then dropping to the nothing that was in her lap.

Bear coughed, pointing to Dee Dee's papers. "We got us a note here,

Ladies. Apparently Miz Dull's daughter is coming in. Narduli spoke with her this morning."

"*Doctor* Narduli," Dee Dee reminded him pleasantly, nodding toward Kitty. "Ladies, we've already had a good chat with Burnice. She is aware, busy as we are, that we cannot reassign her."

Burnice rose to her feet, looking not at her supervisors, but at Cherille: "Fear not, I am restored; my way is clear."

"That's the spirit." Dee Dee stood too, opening her arms wide as Bear stepped in next to her. "I want to thank you, Burnice, for sharing your feelings today. You ladies of Solace are true saints, all of you. I know you don't get much thanks, or respect, or, Lord knows, remuneration of the monetary kind..." Here everybody laughed as they always laughed. "But you have our admiration and support. Right, Bear?"

"You got it," he said. Bear pointed at each of them in turn, coming last to Burnice: "You. Got. It."

Lana stood, buttoning her jacket as her fellow nurses donned coats and scarves, setting chairs back against the wall. Cherille left with Burnice, the rest close behind. All but Hazel. Lana lingered with her thinking to draw the woman out, but Hazel made a show of staying seated, intent, it seemed, upon reorganizing whatever was in her purse. So Lana made a show too, gathering up the leftover cookies, rearranging them one-by-one on their platter.

"Ever had a thermometer go bad on you like that?"

"Never." Hazel did not look up from her purse stirring.

"Me either. Probably made in some far away factory where nobody cares to do things right."

"Nobody cares about anything anymore," Hazel snapped her purse shut with a pinch.

Lana tried her brightest smile. "I'm of a mind to see what Cherille's got going in the kitchen. You want to join me?"

Hazel hesitated, stiff from her previous altercation. "I could do."

"Come on, then." Lana stepped into the hall, skirt swinging. She scooped Hazel's elbow up into hers, "I did not know you knew Miz Early."

"Only as a child."

Lana tried again, "I did not know she had horses."

"Ponies. A pony is not a horse."

This is a bitter woman, thought Lana. She flourished her Bi-Lo platter, pulling Hazel in close. "I got to get up the road to Miz Greevey, but first, let's see, can we find us a home for these cookies."

Beside Us To Guide Us

Cadence Greevey
Late Afternoon

Cadence put her nose up to the crack between the wall and the front door just the way Hershey did when he was alive. She sniffed at the air that poured through like a teeny-tiny wind.

Nothing.

Hershey would have smelled someone coming. He would have known it was somebody in the driveway long before anybody else and barked his fool head off 'til everybody knew that too. But Cadence couldn't smell a thing except that little bit of air that smelled like nothing.

Hershey was a dumb name for a dog. Cadence knew that now. She'd called him Hershey's Kiss because that's what color he was as a puppy and because she didn't have brothers to tell her not to. After all, no boy would ever name a boy-dog Kiss. When she got older, Cadence realized that and once she caught on, she just called him Hershey.

Hershey was dead in the ground behind the forsythia. The only way *he* could bark now would be to howl like a ghost dog, howl for her to come out to his grave, his black coat turned inside out as a spirit coat, ghost white even in the light, baying 'til she stepped closer-closer so that his buddies, the cat murderers and squirrel mongerers he'd met underground, could jump out and grab her.

Cadence backed away from the door. *Stop thinking about it,* she thought, thinking about it all the while.

She decided to wrap herself in the curtain by the big front window, pulling its bottom tight around her head like she'd seen people do in the pageants to play Mary the Mother of Jesus, so that only her face showed through. The curtain was a tan color, but Cadence pretended it was blue like Jesus's mama's would be.

Jesus's mama.

Cadence slipped the curtain over her face.

Stop thinking about it.

But Cadence could not until—*Ding Dong!*—the doorbell—and there was Miss Lana in the matching jacket and skirt.

Miss Lana was the prettiest lady Cadence had ever seen in walking true-life. She had come to the house most days since July, always in her fancy clothes even though nobody dressed in Little Piney except for church.

Cadence twirled herself around once, twice and then once more to show off her dirndl. She told Miss Lana she'd put it on special just for her, though, truth be told, she wore it most days now.

"Hey there, pretty girl." Miss Lana stopped her twirling, smiling at her but looking like she had other things on her mind. "I need to come inside and see to your mama."

Which was what she did, going straight to the living room chair, checking her mama's left hand like she always did which didn't even wake her this time, moving fast, opening doors and windows—"We need some air in here!"—putting on her plastic gloves, snatching up and rinsing things, setting some in the trash and some out on the back porch. Then she got to rooting in the closet for another blanket to tuck her mama in nice and tight. *Just like Mother Mary might do the Baby Jesus,* Cadence thought.

Once when she was visiting, Miss Lana told her she'd lived all the way up in Washington, DC and so Cadence figured she was a nurse to lots of important people before her mama, maybe even to the President. Cadence thought the President would be lucky to have her.

"You want to show me your book?" Miss Lana sat down to look at the spiral notebook she'd taught Cadence to write in, putting check marks under DATE and TIME and PILLS. She asked if Cadence had written everything down and Cadence said, "Yes, ma'am," which was true. She was always extra careful about the pills. Still, half her mama's hair had gone bright white on top, like Hershey would be as a ghost of himself. And then she'd gone crazy.

Cadence was pretty sure it was her fault. That's what she told Miss Lana.

"Oh, no. That's the sickness, honey." Cadence loved it when she said "honey." Miss Lana patted on the sofa for Cadence to sit next to her. "I think it might be time for your mother to come on in to Solace. Do you know what 'solace' means?"

Cadence shook her head.

"It means comfort. So it's a place where we can give your mother comfort and make her comfortable."

Cadence liked the sound of that.

"I asked Curtis-Michael, could he come up the hill and help us. He should be here any minute."

"Is he coming with the ambulance?"

"I believe he is."

Cadence loved the ambulance. She couldn't believe she might get to see it at her very own house.

"So what happened last night, sweetheart? Can you tell me about it?"

Cadence did not want to say because she knew she had to tell the truth and the truth was she'd stayed up past her bedtime watching TV which she knew she wasn't supposed to do, but her mama wasn't saying nothing, so she did.

Cadence figured she could skip that part of the story. "The pails and the washcloths."

"What about them?"

"The pail next to mama's chair always has the blue washcloth on top. The one by the toilet has the green one. Mama said I wasn't to touch them."

"Mmmm-hmmmm."

"She said never-ever-never to go near the laundry 'cause she did the wash every day the second she woke up."

"Well, yes," Miss Lana said, "because, you see, your mother is taking medicine for her cancer, and sometimes that medicine can make you sick." By "sick," Cadence knew she meant throw-up sick. "So what happened last night?"

"I looked to see how mama was doing. She's always sleeping and that's when I go to bed. But last night, she was wide awake in her chair, holding the blue washcloth and tilting for that pail. She said, 'Cadence, I'm sick,' and then she started pulling at her nightgown and there was throw-up in the bucket and some blood too. She wanted that nightgown off bad, so I helped her get it off right quick and oh, wasn't there a mess there worse than any baby's. Her chair seat was covered and bad-stinky."

"Oh, dear."

"She wanted to go in to the bathroom. She was all naked, but she wanted to go just like that, and her face is smooth, Miss Lana, but the middle part of her is sagging and the skin is really hanging down so I knew she was bad sick."

"What a good helper you are."

"No ma'am. She didn't like me to help her. She was mad. You don't cross my mama when she's mad. She sat herself down on the floor right up next to the toilet and took hold of that green washcloth so she could throw up. Then she spit. Then wiped her mouth. Then she did it again a bunch of times. Then the washcloth went in the pail. I said, 'We got to clean you up.' I did my best to rub her good with a towel all over, even between her legs with her shaking the whole time like Hershey after a bath."

"Who's Hershey?"

"My dog. Only he's a ghost dog now."

"I see," Miss Lana said, looking around as if she might could see Hershey hiding in the corner.

"He's under the forsythia."

"Oh," Miss Lana said again, this time patting Cadence's hand.

"I told Mama, I said, 'Your chair's dirty. You can't sleep there no more.' "

"You did a good job, Cadence."

"No, I didn't 'cause she went crazy and it's my fault 'cause I stayed too long at the Rexall which I told her, but she stopped me wiping with the towel. She held on so tight it was hurting me. She said, 'Put Hershey out.' Real loud like that. 'Put Hershey out.' She said she can't stand having him around the house 'cause he smells bad, but he can't smell bad 'cause he's already in his grave."

"That's the sickness talking, honey. It makes people make things up. That's why it's time to move your mama to Solace. She'll do better there. But what about you? Is there a relative who can come be with you?"

"There's my daddy."

"That's good."

"He lives in Cincinnati."

"Well, that's pretty far away."

"With Paco."

"Do you think he can come be with you?"

"He's already coming."

Cadence told her about finding him under B and calling and him saying he'd drive down right away—Right away!—to be with his girl. Which wasn't exactly what he said. He said he'd see about coming. But Cadence liked the sound of "Right away!" It's what a daddy might say on TV if maybe the wagon train was broken down and him coming to rescue his family on a horse.

"When will he get here?" Miss Lana asked.

"Now."

"Tonight?"

"Yes, ma'am." Which wasn't the hundred percent truth, but maybe close enough to be all right to say.

Then Miss Lana asked about friends and Cadence said she didn't have the kinds of friends at school to go to sleep-overs with, but Miss Lana said she meant grown-ups, so Cadence told her about Uncle Walker and Auntie Pam who weren't a real uncle or aunt, just pretend. "I'm supposed to call them Uncle Walker and Auntie Pam because they took Mama on as a helper at the Mountain Man. You know their store in Big Piney? Mama was their helper to put food on the table, that's what she said. Plus I was a helper too over with Mr. McCallum at the Rexall after school which Mama said was a blessing and never to bother him, but just to be of help. You can call Mr. McCallum," she said, "Only not 'til tomorrow because Sunday is the day of rest."

Miss Lana wrote his phone number on her clipboard. She promised she wouldn't call until morning.

They heard the ambulance coming up the hill. Not that Curtis-Michael used the siren, but it had a noisy motor, winding up the switchbacks.

It impressed Cadence no end to see a real ambulance parked in her very own driveway. Like the ones she'd seen in Garnet parked outside a house or even a school one time with her wondering what on earth could be wrong in there. Now it was *her* house with the ambulance and somebody else would be wondering why.

Curtis-Michael came inside with a couple of the boys from Big Piney. He told Cadence several times that he couldn't let a little girl ride along with them, even though she wanted to so bad.

He carried a fold-up chair with wheels into the living room and widened it. Fiddling with the blanket around her mama's knees, he wrapped her good, straightening things just enough to get her eyes open and her one arm over his neck before lifting. She looked like a plucked-up ragdoll in his arms as he swung her from the home chair to the wheeled one.

"Look, Mama, they're going to carry you!" Cadence used her big-girl voice. She leaned down, trying to catch her mama's gaze beneath the hair that had fallen around her face. "They're gonna ride you, Mama, like a pasha on a hellephant."

Even as late as last year, her mama had read to her from a color-book about the pashas because it was Cadence's favorite story where princes rode elephants like horses, only when she was little, Cadence could not say "elephant"—she said "hellephant"—so they'd made it their special way of saying it ever since.

And didn't that right there bring her mama's face straight up to hers with a pure, untroubled smile, her teeth darkened, her gums blue-gray, but beaming at Cadence like that very same pasha. "On a hellephant," she gasped.

Curtis-Michael did indeed ride her. He wheeled her out to the porch. From there, he and three of the biggest boys from high school hoisted her up to where the ambulance was parked, chair and all.

They did not use the siren driving away. Cadence watched them wind down the hill through the no-leaf trees, going not much faster than her mama would heading to the Pay Less for cigarettes back when she could do such things.

Cadence could hear the ambulance long after she could see it, the sound of the motor following Cane Creek out to Big Piney, heading toward the highway.

Only boys get to ride in the ambulance, she thought, *but maybe someday they'll let a girl be of help, put me in the back where I can fold up the chair with wheels and watch out for a sick lady—maybe a sick lady with a little girl just like me taking the ride of her life, maybe even with the siren going—and I could be there to say, "It's all right. It will be all right."*

Miss Lana came out to her on the porch.

"Can I go to the hospital?" Cadence asked.

"It's a hospice, honey. Like a hospital but more home-y."

"Oh."

"You can come and visit your mama whenever you want and even stay overnight. How about we talk about it when your daddy gets here?"

"Yes, ma'am."

"I want you to lock the door 'til he comes."

"Yes, ma'am."

Cadence wished Miss Lana would stay with her, but she was sure that, as a grown-up lady, she must have her own family—a husband and some children to go home to, maybe even a daughter—so Cadence was a good girl, a very good girl and said nothing. She only waved goodbye.

Lightning Doesn't Strike

Maggie Dull
Evening

Two and a half hours after touchdown in Little Rock and Maggie was already boarding airline number two scheduled to route her through Charlotte to Garnet. Several ex-252'ers were boarding with her, some weepy, some jitter-chatty.

"Lightning doesn't strike twice," she told them just as her mother used to tell her. But Maggie knew better. She'd read about conventions of lightning strike survivors who gathered to compare notes. They'd be the last people to say that lightning wouldn't find its way back to a preferred host since some of them had been hit more than once. Apparently such people generated a kind of victim-electro-magnetism that continually attracted corrective energy from the universe. But not her, by God. Not Maggie Dulé. Boarding her second jet of the day, weakened perhaps by a brush with the Big Bye-Bye, Maggie found herself lapsing into the very bromides she repudiated.

As a result, she didn't see it coming. For the first time in her life, Maggie wasn't first.

They were accelerating, then climbing steeply, barely off the ground, when the airplane—the *second* air transport of the day, mind you, the one that was supposed to have been immunized from catastrophe by previous near-catastrophe—made a rapid, 90-degree dip. The plane literally turned on its side.

And then, just as rapidly, righted itself.

This time, there was screaming plane-wide. Particularly right in front of Maggie from a row of Flight 252 veterans.

She wanted to scream with them. Where was their pilot with some reassuring captain-talk? Not a word from the intercom, as if nearly turning over in the air were an everyday event.

The cabin was still buzzing as two of their sky hostesses strode up the aisle toward the front of the plane. "He always does that," one was saying to the other. "He forgets to check the flaps."

Forgets? To check? The flaps?

Maggie unbuckled. She rose, half-turning in her seat. "Am I going to have to fly this plane myself?"

She might as well have been Moses with the tablets. Everybody hushed up and stared.

"For your information, I just got off a plane not three hours ago that caught fire in midair." Maggie's voice rose for the benefit of her captive audience: "That's right. Fire. Mid-air. Now, it has never been my pleasure to fly this particular airline before—clearly I had not planned on it this afternoon—but since I'm here, in your care, I want to know: Are we in safe hands or not? Please don't insult my intelligence by telling me that it was nothing. I have a pilot's license."

Where did she dream these things up? She barely had a driver's license.

"I know that we do *not* want to be rotating ninety degrees during take off. That puts us milliseconds from loss of lift. Stall. Boom. Crash. Everybody incinerated to a crisp. You don't believe me? Why don't we check?"

Maggie turned to the back of the cabin. "Do we have any off-duty pilots on board with us today? Because I'd like to get your take on what just happened."

Two male stewards approached from opposite ends of the plane.

"Fine! Would you gentlemen have a chat with the cowboy we seem to have at the throttle up there. Shake him out of his hangover or midlife crisis or whatever the hell his problem is and get us back on the ground in one piece. Because I'm on my way to visit my dying mother and the plan is for me to bury her, not her bury me."

You'd think this would be Maggie out of control, Maggie over the edge. Not even close. She was having the time of her life, watching the blood drain from a sky hostess's face, watching the entire service crew up and down the aisles freeze.

They're wondering, she thought, *whether I'll need restraints.*

One of the stewards spoke. A slim guy, shirt tucked in tight, Miami Beach tan. "Madam, we will get you to your mother safe and sound." Clearly he was enjoying her diva turn. Probably a bit of a diva himself. He flashed a mouthful of teeth rendered even whiter by the melanomic tone of his skin. "Now, can I get you something to drink?"

Good for him, Maggie thought, *The first person on this God-forsaken, lightning-twice-cursed excursion who seems to have half a brain.*

Two Smirnoff's later—on the house, as she expected—and Maggie was in better spirits, pun absolutely intended. She knew she was home free. Two strikes, maybe. Three strikes, no way. The plane flew. The plane landed. Little Rock to Charlotte. Charlotte to Garnet. Passing from the brink of death to baggage claim in the span of a few cocktails.

And then—

Where was that motel shuttle?

Glass doors split open to reveal a swanky new welcome sign suspended over the arrivals deck: GARNET INTERNATIONAL AIRPORT. *International?* Maggie thought. *Perhaps. If Nebraska is declared a foreign country.*

Through the jumble of useless wayfinding, she spotted a tiny sign—SHUTTLES—with an arrow pointing out to an island. She dragged her luggage across the pick-up zone. HOSPITALITY INN. There it was over the dashboard of a minivan. Maggie could just make out the driver inside. He was wearing a cowboy hat.

Or she was. Stepping down from the van, the cowboy hat came off to release masses of real-by-the-look-of-it, orange-red hair tangling and curling down over the driver's shoulders.

She was enormously tall. Well over six feet. Rangy in jeans and boots. And grinning, this woman. Grinning as if she and Maggie went way back. Did they? Was she some long-lost kindergarten mate?

"Hey! How're you doin'?" Grinning and striding forward. "Let me take those bags."

A woman taking bags from a woman the way a man would, lifting them with no apparent effort up into the back of the van.

"Go on and find yourself a seat. I'll be there momentarily."

Ah. *Momentarily.* Maggie knew she was home now. You wouldn't hear a word like that in Palo Alto. That was mountain-talk, home-talk.

Find yourself a seat? There was no one there but Maggie. She had a vanful to choose from.

The driver stomped on board, straddling her seat backwards like a saddle.

"New York?" she asked.

"Palo Alto."

"Where's that?"

"California."

"Oh, right," said the driver. "I lived in Reno for a while. Hated that. You want a drink before we take off?" She opened the lid of an oversized cooler beside her. "Wish I could offer you a beer. They don't let us drive with that."

A big smile aimed directly at Maggie. Crooked teeth, a little pointy.

"But I've got the next best thing. Ginger beer. I've got every kind of formula-one, tickle-you-up-and-tickle-you-down soda known to man. Knock Back, Cory's, even Emperor Lo's—that'll take the roof of your mouth out through your brain. It's cold. Let me pour you one."

She pulled a no-nonsense tumbler from a strap on the lid of the cooler, filled it with crushed ice from a bag next to the sodas, then pried open an old-fashioned pop bottle and carefully poured its golden liquid into the glass. "Always pour it sideways," she said. "Preserves the carbonation. Here."

Another big smile. Offering her the drink.

Maggie felt a sting in her throat. What was this? Tears?

"You're tired," said the driver looking straight at her. "Drink up."

The ginger beer was fizzy, fizz initially obscuring the taste. Then, there it was: raw pepper over honey.

"Good, hunh?" The driver leaned forward, her breasts tight-snapped in a lasso-print cowgirl shirt. "It tastes different when it's made with real sugar instead of corn syrup."

Her hair glowed redder with oncoming headlights behind it.

Maggie found a way to speak. "I need to get to the motel."

"I know you do," said the driver. With real tenderness. Not turning away from her. And then turning away, back toward the windshield. "Let's get you home."

You Can't Go Home

Cadence Greevey
Evening

Cadence did a twirl or two, practicing. She would twirl for her daddy the minute he set foot in the house just like she twirled for Miss Lana. He'd missed seven whole birthdays since she last laid eyes on him, but now he was coming home.

"You'd think he's the King of Sheba, the way he's taking his sweet time," Cadence said to the granddaddy clock *tick-tick-tick-ing* by the door.

She knew how long it would take her daddy to drive because one summer he drove her to his house up north. "Joe Slow needs eleven hours," he said. "I can make it in nine."

Cadence had only gone the one summer. It was nice of him to invite her, but maybe not so much fun, for her anyway. It wasn't his fault. Both he and Paco had to work, which left her to sit around at the public pool and listen to kids talking who already knew each other. She didn't know a soul in Cincinnati.

Her daddy was Bobby O. when he left Little Piney. Been Bobby O. Greevey all his life since he was born there. But up in Cincinnati, he told her he was Bob and to call him that and not to call him Bobby O. ever.

Paco called him Bob. Paco was nice. He brought home hot dinners from the Italian restaurant after work. But they were grown-ups. They didn't know how to talk to a little girl.

Cadence stopped twirling. Her daddy should be home by now. Maybe he'd got caught in a speed trap trying to make it in nine hours instead of eleven.

She ran to her mama's bedroom door. It was still pretty stinky in there.

She wanted to see, was the police scanner still on. After her daddy left, her mama kept one by the chair where she slept. Mostly it gave out a hissing sound, but every now and then a voice would come through. Her mama said she didn't want nothing to creep up on them in the night, particularly a fire, because she said a fire could move fast in the mountains. She told a story once of the Eargles' trailer catching with a nighttime blaze and how most of the family'd gotten out, but old Mrs. Eargle, Don Eargles' mother who had come to live with them, she could not move fast enough and so had burned up with all their belongings.

Hiss-shshsh. That's all the police scanner would say. There was no talk of catching a speeder named Greevey on the way home to see his little girl. Cadence thought about turning it off, but that meant two things. One, she wouldn't know if a fire was creeping up on the house in the night. And two, she would have to go all the way into her mama's bedroom to do it. She did not want to go in there anymore. Maybe she could get her daddy to turn it off when he came home.

He should call! That was a rule Cadence knew from her mama, "If you're going to be late, you call."

In a flash, Cadence ran to the telephone in the hall. She lifted the receiver. There it was, the dial tone, thank goodness. She thought the phone might have broken without making any noise to tell her so, and there her daddy would be trying to call her and not being able to get through. She stared at it thinking, *Ring! Ring! Ring!* until it came to her: *Daddy can't call because he's in the car.*

Cadence ran to the television set and turned on the news. They didn't get but two stations with a picture. Here came Chester Lopez, Channel 5—"This is Chester Lopez reporting from Charlotte"—talking to a man in a fire hat, then to a lady crying with her baby. Cadence watched a bunch of commercials go by: "Drive the new Silverado today!" and the one they played over and over again of a little boy drinking cough syrup with a big smile—"Tastes like cherries!"

At long last, she saw what she'd been waiting for: Miss April Turner, the Weather Girl, a beautiful-beautiful, dark-skinned, darker-than-Cadence girl in a jacket and skirt, both of the same color just like Miss Lana. She pointed one nail-polished finger at a thick blue line running down the TV screen with spikes off it and said, "Blizzard. Hail up north."

"Hail" sounded like "hell," and that sounded bad. Maybe it was hail holding up her daddy. Maybe he was in a traffic accident. Cadence thought when the weather got bad, folks would have fewer accidents because they'd pay more care. But she knew that was when you got the big pileups on the news and pictures of cars cut open by what they called the Jaws of Death with a mess of glass and car seat but never a picture of the people who'd been in the car because they surely looked pretty bad.

He could be in a pileup, Cadence thought, with the front of the car in his lap and the whole entire headlights back where the tail lights were.

"Ah, ah, ah."

Cadence started a rhythmic sound she'd been making ever since she figured there was nobody around to hear her anymore.

"Ah, ah, ah." Like a song with no tune.

She turned off the TV and walked around the edge of the rug several times, toe-heel, toe-heel, to calm down.

What about the bed?

She ran to her room. Because hers was the only bed left in the house, she figured her daddy would sleep there. She wondered, should she change the sheets? Instead, she smoothed the ones already there, pulling the blanket tight. Then, as a special present, she set Rabbit on top of the pillow.

Rabbit was her pelt of thick, gray fur. The Christmas when Cadence was eight, her mama had surprised her with him, brought him home from the Mountain Man, which the best tourist shop in Big Piney, everybody said so, with heaps of things Cadence loved like stuffed foxes on mounds as hard as the ground itself and baskets that the Cherokee made weaving wood like yarn. Most especially, she loved the display of perfect gray rabbit pelts that her mama kept having to tell her not to touch, because they were for city folks to buy.

Cadence was surely no city girl, nor never would be, and yet here her mama had gone and got Rabbit, tissued him in Christmas paper and tucked him up under the tree. Cadence had taken good care of him ever since. She patted him only one way, the way the hair fell, and always softly, never pulling, so that Rabbit was still as full and soft as he had been that Christmas when she'd unwrapped him.

She was sure her daddy would like him.

Her daddy.

What about the Premiums?

Cadence ran for the kitchen now, opening the icebox for maybe the hundredth time. They were still there. Cadence liked Zestas better, but she remembered how her daddy put great store by Premium Saltines. She'd put the box in the refrigerator to keep the ants out, sat it next to two Budweisers she found in the back pantry.

What drew her up short, she heard a motor coming from way on the other side of the valley. She could hear like that in the Pineys—anybody could—one side of the mountain catching the barest twig snapping on the other.

Bang, she was out the front door in the chill.

She listened hard. Evening settled in, the dark firs getting darker, the tangle of rhododendron and laurel that surrounded the house beginning to disappear. Cadence tracked the sound. It was a car, or a truck maybe, rounding Rainbow Ridge, rounding *around-around-around,* then heading straight toward her. Straight toward her!

And then turning away.

Cadence heard whoever it was turn to follow Cane Creek down off the slope. Some lucky family, most like, driving in to Big Piney for Mexican or maybe Chinese. But not her daddy.

Not her daddy.

A Good Man Is Hard

Bobby O. Greevey
Evening

Bobby was on the home stretch, about two thirds of the way from Cincinnati, climbing Windy Gap when the snow hit. It was a hell of a storm. Like that, he went from flying to inching. He could no longer tell what was pavement and what was ditch.

He followed the swath in front of him, tracks left by a truck apparently since they were double-wide. Or had been. Almost immediately they were filling with slush-hail, blurring but passable. When the tracks went a little to the left, Bobby steered left. When they curved right, he dogged them, careful to stay inside those parallel channels since outside, he knew, his tires would have no purchase.

That worked just fine until he caught up with the truck. True, he could see his way better guided by the tail lights, but he couldn't abide it, the crawl. The way things were going, he'd never make the Pineys. There was nothing to look at but the same pitch air and slew of confetti, bright snow bouncing before him, each flake, rough-edged like frozen lint, suspended in the red cones of the tail lights.

Jesus, he was going to die of boredom. No decent radio. Bobby tried the dial again, spinning it up-down, up-down. Nothing. Finally, a fiddle cut through the static. *Oooo,* it was Clint. Clint Black crooning about killing time, how killing time can kill you, how sitting in a bar drinking yourself blind moping about killing time can kill you dead. Lord, yes. Just what Bobby needed. He cranked that sucker, singing along, banging the dashboard in time to the kick drum.

Bobby loved him some country music, especially when he was driving. Loved to hear his own voice booming off the windshield like when he was a boy in his daddy's truck, his daddy singing along too. Of course, Paco couldn't stand the stuff. Wouldn't listen to it in the house. He called the man Squint.

Here came the pedal steel now, a snaky descending line thick with reverb when—*phwish*—Clint's voice dissolved into static.

Shit. Nothing but hiss. Disgusted, Bobby turned the radio off, literally turning it, rotating a nice, chrome-appointed dial, not punching some cheesy plastic button.

God love you, Krystal.

He felt her slipping a bit.

Come on, baby.

He eased up on the gas. Krystal was game all right. Lord knows, she was totally prepared, flashing four new Eagle Ultra-Grips custom-mounted down below. But she'd never been a heavy vehicle. She sat light enough on her tires that Bobby knew he couldn't rush her in any kind of weather. Sure enough, the minute he backed off the gas, Krystal calmed right down, steadying into the truck tracks ahead of her.

Bobby smoothed his hand around her polished steering wheel, its proportions surely modeled on some sea-captain's notion of what an automobile might need: shoulder-width in diameter, thin, hard and perfectly round.

"The kind of thing you don't see anymore," Paco had said. One of the many things they'd both admired when they met her the summer they bought her.

Krystal was a 1957 Plymouth Belvedere. Two-toned, with the lower half a shade he and Paco laughingly referred to as "dirty quartz," a description that covered more than her exterior paint job. It was Paco, God love him, who gave her her name. "Born in Detroit," he'd said, "but baptized right here in Cincinnati." Baptized indeed.

Paco called it, "A match made in heaven." Or "marriage." Maybe he'd said "marriage." He'd been talking about the car. Bobby wished he'd been talking about him. Because he still wondered on bad days: *Why me?* Here's Paco, the keeper of all things antique and rare, the rich child of a rich family raised among the hoi-polloi down in Mexico City. It was obvious from that first beer at the Hardwood, Bobby knew slim-to-nothing of the refinements that

Paco could recite in his sleep. So what had Paco seen in him?

Maybe a guy who knows how to fix stuff. Bobby was smiling now. *Maybe a guy who can make a Krystal hum.*

He sure knew how to make Paco hum.

Snap out of it! Bobby smacked the steering wheel with the heel of his hand. Enough with the snail's pace. It was past ten. He had to get around that damn truck.

He let Krystal drop back maybe fifteen feet so that he could swing her out in an easy angle to minimize any fishtailing.

Come on, baby.

He rotated the wheel slow and steady. The tires bit into an encrusted snow ridge to his left, then skidded over it, slipping like a water-skier down the outer slope of a wave. He managed to hold her with firm steering and a little more gas. She hobbled over the peaks of slush into fresh, smooth powder.

Pulling alongside the truck, Bobby had to concentrate. He missed his chance to see the face of the only other guy dumb enough to be out on that road, but he had to focus on what was ahead. Accelerating gradually, he went from a crawl to enough of a clip that he left the truck's headlights behind him until they dimmed to vanishing.

That's when Bobby realized that passing might not have been such a good idea. All he could see now was white. There was no way to tell what was road, what wasn't. There were no exits, or none he could see. Pulling over was out. Some other idiot driver—maybe the trucker behind—might plow into him thinking he was someone to follow. Besides, if he stopped, he was pretty sure Krystal wouldn't start again. The snow would build an icy glue around her tires. He'd be found inside her, frozen dead by morning.

So he kept pressing on through the wall of flakes. After a while, the wipers couldn't keep up. Snow scooped down close to Krystal's hood and then up again at the last second straight into the windshield. It made his eyes jump. He tried the hi-beam. He tried the low. He slowed way up. Then slowed some more. But no one came along. All he could hear was his own tire crunch.

He didn't need any fancy college degree to realize that his "rescue fantasy," as Paco called it, was doomed. They'd both watched the weather report that morning standing as they always did, addressing the TV with their coffee mugs like strangers in an airport, determined to catch the latest. They both heard cute Miss Jo Wong, premier news-anchor-hopeful in her pressed-tress coif, saying, "Fluke storm. Snow to the south." Saying, "Slow going through Windy Gap." But did Paco say anything? All Bobby wanted to hear was one little, "Don't go." That was all. One little, "I'll worry about you..."

Bobby asked Krystal for more speed. He'd show Paco. He'd make the Pineys, do the whole round trip, but, by God, he wouldn't call. He wouldn't talk to Paco until he got home. Maybe storm footage and a little overnight silence would melt the ice on Mount Tough Guy. Maybe they could bypass Paco's usual "What's the big deal?" and go right for a prodigal reception. Bobby saw himself in their front door, Paco tearful, kissing him on the neck and cheek, berating him for being so foolish as to brave the Great Blizzard of '89, Bobby puffing his chest out to say, "What? I grew up in the mountains. It's nothing to me."

Then he was thinking, *Where's my steering?*

The car started to pitch.

Thinking, *This is not road.*

The weight of the car where he was sitting was no longer there. No weight. Weightless. The right wheelbase buckled. *No, wait,* he thought as he ascended, *I'm flying.*

I'm flying.

Snowflakes moving horizontally now. Silent flight, off the ground for sure. He was seeing the inside of an ice cream cone wrapper, white, conical, tapering, zooming in as its seam spiraled out around and past him. He was rushing toward the widening hole at its end, its dark point suddenly becoming his whole view.

Things accelerated beyond him. There was a curious absence of sound. And sensation.

Then he felt a snap across his left shoulder.

He heard a voice.

"Daddy."

He saw ice cream all around him, vanilla, shattered sugar cone strewing the ground.

"Daddy."

He saw the fuzz of Krystal's visor angled directly at his eyes, the lattice of a perfect spider web suspended in fine lines against a white background.

From the spider web came a face. "Are you with us?"

Bobby waited for the face to speak again.

"Cadence?" he asked the face.

Now he heard Cadence's voice on the phone: "Daddy? Mama went off crazy."

He could see that the face above him was not Cadence. It was a man he did not know. It appeared that the man was speaking to him, framed by the web.

"What's your name?" asked the face.

"Bobby O. Greevey," he said, trying to take it back as he heard himself say it because Paco had never once heard either the *Bobby* or the *O*. "I mean Bob."

The spider web got moved out of the way. The face leaned in, then turned. Fur tickled Bobby's forehead.

The face righted itself, eyes to his eyes. "Bob!" for some reason yelling at him. "Bob, I'm Travix."

Bobby could feel he was lying down. The sky above him didn't look much different from the mix of dark and snow all around it, but something was pressing into his back. That told him he was flat. Someone was holding his hand. It was not Paco.

"Okay."

Had he said it or heard it?

He could see Cadence's face now the way he remembered it when she was little. But her voice sounded different. "Mama went off crazy. She don't know Hershey's dead."

Bobby closed his eyes. What did she mean? Hershey the dog? Cadence kept on chattering. He had a headache and she would not stop talking.

"Are you all right, sir?" A face loomed. "What day is it?"

God, his head hurt. Cadence wouldn't stop, "Last night, Daddy, I got one of the pillows off the bed and I gave it to her in the wheelchair because she might to wake up with a neck ache and be mad at me, so I poked her with the pillow, Daddy, and that woke her up some and she took it like she wanted it, but she didn't put it under her head. She holded onto it like it was her pet. Like Rabbit."

Rabbit?

"Cadence, stop!"

"She hugged it with her eyes closed, so I told her, I said, 'Mama, you can pretend like this is your baby, like I do Rabbit' and then she said, 'I never had one,' and I said, 'You never had a baby?' and she said, 'No! I never had a stuffed animal!' Real mad."

Now Bobby saw flakes coming into his eyes and things going by. He was on his back sliding on a sled, moving, being moved. There was a lurch. He was lifted. A big noise. Then no more snow. He was inside a can, metal, lights in his eyes. Overhead were silver bars with hooks and a bag, a clock to his left.

It was an ambulance.

The man's face leaned over him, over his arm. "You're all right."

"Cadence?"

Still she was jabbering. She sounded upset. "Did Mama never have no stuffed animal when she was little?"

"Stop!" Bobby couldn't take the talk-talk-talk.

The man's face, busy overhead, looked down at his hand and pulled the ring off. Paco's ring.

"Stop!"

"Can we call Cadence for you?" The man's eyes met his. "How can we get in touch with her?"

"Paco!"

All the while Cadence kept talking. Bobby could tell by her voice she was crying. He didn't want any crying. He was sharp with her: "Cadence, nobody had stuffed animals back then."

"Oh," she said.

On the phone, yes. She'd said "Oh" on the phone. *When was that?* "Do you want me to come?" He remembered now he'd asked her that. She had not answered.

The man's face overhead came in close. "Who's Cadence?"

Then Cadence was speaking, not answering him but saying so quiet, "I didn't know there was no stuffed animals."

Ah. It all snapped together in his head. This morning. He'd been on the phone with Cadence. He'd turned to Paco to say, "I'd better go." He'd said into the phone, "I'll see about coming." Then to Paco: "I'd better go."

But nobody said, "Don't." Nobody said, "I'll worry about you."

"Calm down, Bob."

He heard his name. Then somebody squeezed the fleshy part of his hand. It was not Paco.

Bobby must have asked, because the man's face above him that was not Paco and not Cadence smiled and said, "No."

Now he could hear himself asking it again: "Am I dead?"

"No, you're right here," said the face.

"Oh."

He heard Cadence say "Rabbit" as his eyes closed.

Make Me Like One

Maggie Dull
After Supper

Maggie sat on the insufficient slab of foam rubber that the Airport Hospitality Inn referred to as a mattress. The phone rang in her ear. Too many times.

DO NOT CALL.

My God, Maggie thought. *What if mother is dead? What if I came all this way…?*

Then she heard, "Hello?"

The voice was weak, but it was her.

"Mother, it's Maggie."

"Maggie?"

"How are you doing?"

"Oh…" the voice high and wandering, "A good day. We're having a good day here."

We? Maggie thought. She was aware of music in the background. Loud music. Who was that? Dolly Parton?

"I know it's been a while, but I happen to be in Charlotte for a conference." Lying to her mother was like breathing. "I've got an extra day. I thought I might swing by to see you. If that sounds all right."

DO NOT DROP BY.

A pause. Too long a pause. Then——

"When are you coming?"

"Well, it's a long drive." Maggie was spinning the yarn, even though she was maybe twenty minutes away. "How 'bout if I come for lunch tomorrow? Would that be all right?"

"That'd be all right."

"Good. I'll see you then."

Phew. She was in. It had been a gamble, the time off, the flight—flights!—but it had worked. The old bird sounded too weak to quibble.

I DO NOT WANT TO SEE MY CHILDREN.

The note lay next to the suitcase on the bed. Maggie tore it up. Both notes. The one from her mother and the one from Burnice, whoever the hell she was. Tore them into pieces small enough that no motel maid, no matter how curious, could ever put them back together. Flutter-flutter-flutter they went into the dreadful, plastic wastebasket that was standard motel issue. Then she snapped down the locks on her American Tourister and went looking for a drink.

She was standing at the elevator next to a Coke machine when she heard her mother's voice again: *The first shall be lost.* Ha! The woman never got those sayings right. No, in this case, the first was last. Maggie, the first born, had been last to flee the homestead. It had taken forever to shake off a semblance of filial duty that had become quite hollow in order to decamp to the other coast.

Home is where the harm is. Another of her mother's favorites, this one totally on the money.

Where was the elevator? Maggie needed a drink. The call light was dark, the motor silent. She punched at the buttons, both UP and DOWN, as if the problem might be directional. Nothing happened. Clearly the damn thing was broken. She decided to walk down.

Who was it who said, "You can't go home again?"

Apparently you can, she thought, *last or lost. Mother Dull, here I come.*

Her laughter echoed in the cigarette stink of the motel stairwell.

The Devil May Cite

Burnice Kling
Night

Burnice knew those parted from their right minds could manifest a sur-
passing sharpness from time to time, a gift of vision that pierced the veil.
Miz Dull had called it straight: devils was in her house. That she'd confused
Burnice with the Enemy was a case of mistaken identity only, a transgression
to be expected given the addling of sickness and medicines and the hours
and hours and hours alone.

But Burnice had no such excuse. She'd been compounding delusion with
foolishness, looking outside for devils, when all the while she could have
gleaned their nature from her Bible. Were they not called spirits? Evil to be
sure, but shadow enough to dwell on the inside of a body, squirreled up tight
in the heart and lungs, crowding heaven from the mind.

And now here came Cherille, a cook for mercy's sake and nothing more,
speaking with the wisdom of the prophets, saying to Burnice, "You got the
name right but not the nature." Saying how, for some folks, devils were
but mortal terror in all its shapes and life, hiding behind the eyes, puppet-
pointing fingers to distract all priests and healers, crying "Over there! Over
there!" while taking tighter hold within.

"Un-loose those hands," Cherille had said, and, Lord, just hearing the
words, was Burnice not instantly unbound? Did she not feel the company
of her people long departed gathering around her, whispering, "Yes indeed,"
with Aunt Mayto's voice the loudest, asking how on earth she had lost her
good sense. The good sense to know how to do. Which was the province of
every Kling, a legacy going back generations.

For Klings knew the world never learned by teaching. The world learned
by its own doing. The busier the better. Those that saw devils turned out to

be the lucky ones. How much easier to chase a fiend without than banish thoughts within. Drive off phantoms, even *phantom* phantoms, and the fear would run off too.

It was time to get busy, Burnice knew it now. Because at any minute, the real thing, the Powers or Dominions or Whosoever might come down among the living, the Holy Anointed of Heaven would come knocking, fixing to take Miz Dull up to the Promised Glories beyond and—she might resist! Convinced that hell was calling, Miz Dull might put up a fight. What would the angels to do in such a circumstance? What could they do? Drag her howling up toward the Pearly Gates, maybe not even getting that far, maybe not sanctified to force a body, or a soul in this case, into salvation? What a terrible discordance that would be. Looking for devils, Miz Dull might miss her Maker altogether.

Burnice wished that for no one, not even a cantankerous, ungrateful, past-fit-for-eating cauliflower of an old woman.

She began by gathering what she could lay her hands on in her own house. Which was paltry. But didn't Jesus say that the last shall be first? *No shame in the paltry,* Burnice told herself, *only glory.* And glory it would have to be to turn Miz Dull's eyes from devils to angels. Burnice knew what she needed was raiment, as Matthew said, raiment "white as the light."

Now, white had never been a color Burnice was drawn to. Partly because she wore it most of her waking life. Partly because pale never did anything to offset the washed-out pallor God had given her. In her own life, she gravitated to the purples, the royal blues. Hues of majesty.

So she began with her work whites. On went a wash-and-wear dress, exactly the color of no-color chalk. Younger nurses said she was old-fashioned not to wear slacks, but the fact was, no pants had ever been made to narrow and widen as did her waist, her hips, her thighs.

From her shoes, she had to choose between work tie-ons or Easter sandals, white with thin straps and a tiny peep-through flower of pink leather on the toe. In the end, much as she would have liked to step out in her better shoes, she knew it would be a night of work. She chose the tie-ons.

Gazing in her closet mirror, Burnice was disappointed. White she was becoming. Transfigured, she was not. Angels flew, after all. In paintings their apparel always fluttered as if in a wind.

Being a sturdy woman of a certain age and a great conviction about the dignity that befit her, Burnice never appeared in garments that could be described as fluttering in the least degree, but she did have a full-length slip. It was nylon and shiny, not only white as the light, but *light* as the light.

Burnice pulled it out. *I'll look some kind of crazy,* she thought. On the other hand, who would see her? Only Miz Dull and perhaps those from the Great Beyond looking down from the clouds. Why not try it? What harm could it do?

So there, in the privacy of her bedroom, Burnice shimmied the slip on over her uniform. No doubt it was odd worn on the outside of things, lumpy with the tucks and darts of the stiff polyester below. But it added a shimmer around her legs, an overskirt that moved a little when she turned.

She remembered a fringe shawl that had been her mother's, stuffed in a bag at the top of the closet. She tied it around her shoulders, pushing the tassels this way and that until they hid the awkwardness of the slip straps over her uniform.

Now she was beginning to flutter.

She felt a brightening around her. Ideas sparkled up as she went. She remembered mice helping Cinderella in the cartoon movie as a child. *This is the Holy Spirit!* she thought. *The angels have come to help!*

What about jewelry? She had a strand of pearls. Not the good kind, cheap ones from the Rexall back when it spanned two-stores-wide and stocked most anything that Piney folks might need. Her mother had worn them to church and to socials. After she passed, they had come down to Burnice. "Like mother, like daughter," Ezekiel said.

For earrings, she wanted something to catch the light there to either side of her eyes. She tried the glitteriest diamond-glass she had.

All that remained was her hair. There were two church hats in the closet, but both were bright with color. Instead, she took her good table cloth, white linen, and wound it the way she might a towel after a shower, covering her whole head.

Pearls. Diamonds. A crown of cloth. No one would know her. Which was the whole idea.

She finished herself with a dusting of talcum on her arms, hands, neck and face. Just enough to render her countenance like dust, her general appearance other-worldly.

Walking out the door, both arms strung with bags of necessities, Burnice tiptoed. There was no sense in alarming the neighbors should any one of them throw off the covers and step to the window on a too-warm midnight to spy her sneaking angelified out of her own house.

Burnice pulled in on the gravel drive. She figured any folks upslope were set back far enough off road that stands of balsam between them and Miz Dull would cotton the sound. If not, they'd surely know her car. There had been evenings—none quite so late as this, of course—when Burnice had come up at the end of her shift, fumbling in the early darkness of winter for the key under the mat. No one had taken any notice back then and she was extra quiet now.

With Miz Dull snoring away as loud as any man, Burnice had the run of the place. She kept the lights low, moving the upright halogen from the living room to just outside the bedroom door. It was a bright light, she knew and high. It would be perfect for her visitation.

That and the tinsel. Lord save us, as Burnice was leaving her house hadn't some angel whispered in her ear: "Tinsel." Of course! With Christmas coming, she'd have to get it down from the attic anyway. She'd brought along the whole box, combing the strands as flat as possible and arranging them to lie with ends to ends.

Oh, but with all of her preparations, she had forgotten music! How had she gone out the door without considering timbrels and dances?

A portable radio sat in the Dull kitchen, the kind that played cassettes. Burnice picked through a drawer full of tapes. Not much in the way of the sacred there. No gospel. Finally she chose Dolly Parton, thinking the cheer in the woman's voice, even when she sang of sad things, might transmit the proper spirit.

But in the end, it was the tinsel that did it. She set the radio player next to the halogen, so that all she needed to do was punch one and switch on the other. Then, with everything in place, she took the entire box of tinsel, held it high over her head and shook it, sprinkling every last strand out, then tossing the box aside, then punching and switching, so that the light and the music exploded together and she was standing there in the doorway of the bedroom shouting over Dolly, "Miz Dull, I am come."

Burnice expected the poor woman to startle, but damn if she didn't actually plane up from the pillow. It was amazing the strength she summoned, one minute tongue sucked back in snore, the next pushing herself upright while reaching right away for the tissue box there on the side table and rearing it back to let fly, only to freeze, tissue box in hand. Burnice could *see* her seeing her, the shock. She could see her take in the shimmer, the flutter and white, the tinsel twisting sharp spirals of light off the halogen.

The tissue box flew by Burnice's head. *Bang!*

"You Daughter of the Beast!" Roaring and grabbing now for a tube of ointment. "You may deceive Eve but you shall not deceive Dolores. I cast you out!"

Bang! The tube of ointment skidded past Burnice's feet. "Begone you deaf and dumb!"

"Not dumb!" Burnice sang it out, stopping her in mid-hurl. "Miz Dull," she said, "I am Burnice." After all, she had no intention to mislead the woman, just shift her sense of what was what.

"It's me, Miz Dull. It's Burnice."

Whereupon, there began a transformation. Miz Dull's mouth went from rageful, bared-baying teeth, to a simple, silent O, wide and round and quiet, as her eyes stared.

"Bur-nice?"

"Yes, ma'am." Burnice never left the doorway. "I have come to you because God called me to," bringing the woman along now. "I have come to tell you that you are right. That you have been right all along. They's devils in your house. All manner of the unwanted up around you, plaguing, fixing to take you where you surely don't belong and have not earned to go."

What a cry came up from Miz Dull at that moment. Tears got her, boiling up from inside, springing from her eyes to flood her cheeks. Her nose ran like a child's.

"Hunh," came out of her and then, "It's true, it's true."

This was relief. Burnice could see it.

"They come to torment me," she said. "I have sinned. My children. My boys. I have been hateful…"

Burnice reached down for the tube of ointment, shedding tinsel. "That's all right now," she said. "You know your Bible: 'In my father's house are many mansions.' Many mansions with many rooms, and one of them just for you, Miz Dull. Wouldn't be nobody in heaven if they turned out us sinners, would they?"

Miz Dull snuffled, shaking her head *No*.

"No, ma'am. But do you think for one minute that Heaven is for the lazy?"

Miz Dull looked to Burnice's face, surprised by the teacherly tone.

"There's no room in Heaven for the lazy, Miz Dull. So we got to get busy. We got to set you up so the angels can find you and the devils shy away."

"That's it," said Miz Dull, quieted now, amazed.

"You and me, we got to prepare a place for them. Offer manna for the Blessed. Lay out devil-warders for the Enemy. And you, Miz D? We cannot have you slopping around in no rig-rag with Jesus on the way. You want you your finery on for Him."

Miz Dull snuffled again. "You are an angel."

"No, ma'am, I am not. But the angels sent me to you sure as I'm standing here. So let's you and me, let's make them welcome."

Truth to tell, it was the most gratifying evening Burnice had known on the job or off. She'd heard "Love your enemies" all her life, but never come into the living of the verses that followed: "Pray for them which despitefully use you and persecute you."

She did a whole lot more than praying that night.

First she got Miz Dull sitting straight up in the bed, pillow boosted, so the woman could boss to her heart's content. It was like the sickness was gone, such a flush rose in her cheeks.

"How shall we adorn you?" Burnice asked.

"Gold!" was the answer. Miz Dull wanted gold, not white, for her Jesus' coming. But there was no gold in her closet, only yellow.

"Yellow is the poor man's gold," Burnice assured her, rolling the woman this way, then that in the bed, trussing her up in a brand-clean nightie of a strong butter color.

That was a start. Next, scrounging, Burnice found a scarf of sunflowers and a shawl in a sun-ray pattern. On they went. Followed by jewelry. Not real gold, of course. Miz Dull took a moment to fret about it, but Burnice was one step ahead of her: "Jesus will see the real in it." They put on plentiful bangles, loose ones that wouldn't trouble her circulation. Miz Dull would not be talked out of her daisy earrings, big ones like the wheels of a chariot. Burnice worried they might poke her in her sleep.

Next, Burnice tied the woman's sweat-flat hair into knots, tucking them up neat and tidy over each ear, so that she could lie back on her pillow with ease.

Finally—this Burnice had brought—a souvenir from a fancy lunch her own mama had made when Burnice finished nursing school, all the family coming from every corner of the far-flung South. It was a crown. Paper, to be sure, but a crown nonetheless. Burnice had kept it folded neatly over the years so that it rounded up again to sit straight on top of Miz Dull's head between the two knots of hair.

Together they festooned the bedroom, Miz Dull pointing, Burnice doing. They used scarves as bunting, draping from lamp to chair, from chair to doorknob, looping swags of color. It was a revel, a pageantry, ornamenting everything to say, "Come on in, angels. It's a party."

They had a time, all the while Dolly singing in the background. Burnice fixed cocoa along with two Saltines slabbed with butter the way Miz Dull liked them. Smiling, chewing, she said to Burnice, "I want you to write me a sign."

"To say what?"

"NO VACANCY FOR THE EVIL ONES. TRY ON DOWN THE ROAD."

They laughed and laughed.

Miz Dull turned serious. "Do me one in gold to say ALL GODLY ARE WELCOME."

Burnice wrote them. The gold one being in dark yellow crayon and bigger than the devil one.

"Now you put them on my door."

"I will," Burnice promised. "I will."

Miz Dull's eyelids were closing. "Will you come again?"

"As long as you need me. The Angel Me, not the Devil Me. Do you know how to tell the difference?" Miz Dull managed to rock her head side to side.

"You shall know me by my pearls," Burnice said. She held them off her neck. "If I'm wearing them, I am Angel Me. If I'm not, you will know you are looking at an apparition, a shade sent from the dark places to impersonate me and don't you believe for a second what I may say then. Trust in the pearls, Miz Dull."

The poor thing could no longer keep her eyelids open. Most nights she slipped off into an angry sleeping that was fitful. This was different. Her face was peaceful, even dropped over with the crown slipping down.

Burnice carefully removed each chariot-wheel earring.

Out in the dark living room, putting on her raincoat, Burnice felt, for all her righteousness, something like a criminal. Was this how Jesus felt, the Son of God in the guise of man?

Whoo-ee. She knew she'd best shake off such jabbering, even silent in her mind. She could hear her mother's voice: *Don't see no halo up around that head of yours, Miss Something. Just two feet on this earth where they belong.*

On her way out, Burnice planted the devil-warders: charms and poisons meant to announce, most especially to Miz Dull, how she was safe from all but the most holy. A half box of rock salt went down along a highway of white fabric running from the front door to the bedroom. Anyone with any devil sense knew those salts would burn into the thorniest of cloven hooves. A hand mirror hung in the hallway was set to repel the repellent. And a full bottle of rose water was poured into an open dish to choke any lingering fiends. Burnice even set her old baby rattle on the sideboard as a weapon to brandish in the face of apparitions.

Lastly, pulling the front door quietly to, Burnice scotch-taped her signs, NO VACANCY and ALL GODLY, beside and below the knocker. Perhaps in the light of day, she told herself, Miz Dull might find herself sufficiently restored to get up out of bed and walk with her, leaning on her arm. To wonder at all that had been accomplished on her behalf. To see posted on her own door the welcome and the repudiation, fair warning to all who considered entering there.

Abide With Me

August Early
After Hours

It had taken some time for Mr. Early to sit himself back in his hospital chair. He was afraid he'd wake Theo, so he stayed right on the edge as long as he could until his back and shoulders went achy. Then he lowered himself very slowly. The leather seat, rubbing on itself, crunched and something metal-sounding popped inside. He paused between chair noises to see if her eyelids moved, but they didn't.

A purpling light came in through one skinny window that could not be opened.

There was no clock.

Theo's hands lay outside the little slip of blanket they'd given her. Mr. Early thought maybe they were cold. Maybe she'd like them better under the cover. But they looked as beautiful as ever there. Beautiful hands, everybody said about Theo, and she kept after them with cream and a red file she used on the nails.

There came a time, with him sitting, that the little man from the elevator, the one with the coal-black hair, came walking in, his jacket still stuck on top of his doctor coat. He was messy-looking in a nice way, like a bird dog coming up wet out of a lake, a duck hanging wings akimbo from its mouth.

Theo opened her eyes, drooping her head sideways to look at him. He circled the bed and took her hand.

"What are you doing here?" he said looking straight down into Theo's eyes and smiling.

"I come to see you," Theo managed from inside her Coca Cola mask.

Mr. Early saw right away that she was flirting with the man, bald-faced flirting, and damn if the tears didn't come again. He had to stand to see if he could shake them from spilling.

The little man looked up. "You must be Mr. Early."

"Yes sir." He feared the man could see a touch of the water there in his eyeballs, but if he did, he did not seem troubled by it.

"I am Dr. Narduli."

"Yes sir. I'm pleased to meet you."

Mr. Early had not met him before. Theo would not let her husband come to the appointments. He was to drive her, she said, and wait in the truck. And he'd done it, because when she said she needed him to do it that way, it was like something bad would happen if he said, "No." Like Miss Hazel told him once on the porch after a visit, "Your wife knows just how she wants to do it, don't she?"

The doctor asked Theo questions about what had happened and how she felt. She answered him through the mask. He held onto her wrist, all the while looking up at the wall, not telling anyone what was in his mind.

Mr. Early heard words his wife had used before, numbers and names of medicines. But Theo surprised him. After a while of talking, she said to the doctor in a louder voice, "I don't want to go home. Please don't send me home."

Now, Theo was not the kind of woman to ask anything of anyone. She'd never had any toleration of being beholden, but this was her asking, Mr. Early could see it. She was asking straight to the doctor's face, so that he had to think, *Maybe they can send you away from a place like this even if you don't want to go,* and thinking at the same time, *Why don't you want to come home?*

Dr. Narduli's eyes came back to her. "We talked about taking advantage of the hospice setting at Solace. Is that what you want?"

Hospice sounded like hospital to Mr. Early.

"Yes, sir," Theo said, all the while squeezing the doctor's hand with her two.

Mr. Early turned his face to the hallway. *Why don't she want to come home?*

The doctor walked around the bed to speak to him. He said that his wife was breathing better now. He said Mrs. Early was one of a kind and to call him any time.

"Yes sir." Mr. Early shook his hand. He had trouble meeting his eyes.

Then the doctor was gone.

Partly to make conversation and partly because he felt it, Mr. Early allowed as how it was mighty thoughty of the doctor to be there of a Sunday. Theo was in no mood to talk. "That's his job," she said.

When the dinner tray came, Theo did not stir much. She looked at the food and closed her eyes. The nurse told Mr. Early that it would be all right for him to eat it, but he didn't want to, even though his stomach was hungry.

As the light from the outside failed, the lights in the room set to low level kept Theo from disappearing altogether. From time to time, her brow twitched and she would mumble something into her mask that he could not understand. Or her hands would start moving as if she were doing something he could almost make out, tossing coleslaw maybe or hand-washing her underwear in the bathroom sink.

Mr. Early put his mind on the twins. He wondered, had they had their dinner and if so what Miss Susan Neville had fixed for them. He wondered, would she feed the dogs or leave them to scrounge in the woods 'til he got back. He wondered when exactly he would get back.

After a time, a woman who had walked by the room twice before, walking slowly as if testing her legs, stopped the third time and came in the door. She asked if his wife's name was Theodora. He said it was, wondering how she knew. She asked the question in a normal tone of voice, not quiet, and so woke his wife. But Theo didn't seem to mind.

The lady said that her name was Theodora too and then she began talking about it. Her father had wanted a boy, she said, but never had one and so, believing her to be his last child, had named her for himself, and was it the same for his wife?

Theo said, Yes, her father too had wanted a boy. She took the mask down off her face to continue. The joke had been on him though, she said. He had gone on to have three more children after her and two of them were boys.

"Did he name any of them Theodore?" asked the lady and his wife said, "Yes." That would be her brother Teddy, who had got himself dragged under a train when he was thirteen and died.

"It must have been confusing," said the lady.

She was elderly, tiny-waisted, with a girl's body. She wore pants and a silvered blouse that shone in the light. Over that she had a vest of thick red material like the velvet on the seat cushions at the Christ Mount and gold threads on top of that making a pattern. Her hair was wound, a puffy white.

She looked nice standing in the doorway. Mr. Early wasn't sure whether to ask her in. There wasn't but one chair. He didn't know what Theo would want.

"Family must surely be a strange thing," the lady said smiling at his wife. "It was wrong of my daddy to do me that way because children can be so very cruel you know. They used to tease me in the classroom and call me Theodore. Once, in fifth grade, the teacher read the roster wrong and everybody laughed. I was mortified, you can believe me. In my day, of course, a girl wore only dresses, but my schoolmates would call after me and tell me to put on trousers like the other boys. Was it the same for you?"

"Yes," his wife whispered. Her breathing was more labored without the mask.

"Daddy was determined that I grow up to marry a doctor and I was determined I would not," said the lady. "And now look at me."

She laughed. His wife laughed too.

"Well, it's good to meet myself, Theodora."

She said it. Then she looked at Mr. Early.

"Goodnight."

She left the doorway.

Theo closed her eyes and set about putting her mask back on. Her hands were shaking. She had a hard time getting the elastic into place, what with her long hair coming loose from its clasp.

Mr. Early put his hat down to help. His hands on her back told her to sit forward. She held the mask to her face while he pulled her hair into a makeshift ponytail, opening and closing the clasp around it as best he could. That made it easy to set the elastic up around her ears. He placed his hand on the rounded bone at the front of her shoulder as a sign and she lowered herself back to the pillow.

He returned to his chair.

"You'll have to bring me some of my things," she said. She was speaking slowly, pacing herself. He looked for something to write with. "My cosmetic case is all fixed. It's by the bathroom door. And there's an overnight bag there too."

She had already packed.

"Yes."

"And my pillow. They put something rubber on this one. It don't feel right."

"Yes."

She took a moment to breathe.

"I believe she was one of the Brides," she said.

It took him a moment to follow her.

"One of the Holy Brides of Christ. They still run the hospital."

"Why would you think that?" he asked.

"Nuns. They all wear pants like that."

She took a moment to work on her breathing. Every time she closed her eyes he could not tell whether she would open them or whether she had gone to sleep.

She spoke again. "I do believe that she is the last of the Holy Brides."

She breathed.

"I believe I read that the others died."

She breathed again.

"That means she lives up on the hill in the church all by herself."

Her eyes stayed closed. She said nothing more.

It occurred to Mr. Early that his wife had been making up a story, that maybe she had been making up stories right along, maybe lots of them, maybe all her life. And just not telling him.

No News Is Good

Cadence Greevey
Way Past Bedtime

Cadence nearly fell off her chair. *Ring, Ring, Ring!* Finally, the phone was ringing. Surely it was him.

She'd made a promise to herself that come morning, if her daddy had not showed up in real-true life, she would find a way to call him. Or ask Mr. Mc-Callum to do so. Or Uncle Walker or Auntie Pam. She promised herself that come a decent hour, which she allowed to be ten o'clock in the morning, she would go ahead and dial until somebody answered.

With nighttime surrounding the house, thick and dark, she'd stationed herself on her little rocker, the one made for a child with its worn red velvet seat. She was way too big for it now, but she didn't care. She'd pulled it up next to the phone table, rocking with Rabbit in her lap until—*Ring, Ring, Ring!*

"Daddy?" she asked.

"Cadence?" It was a voice she did not know. "This is Paco, Bob's friend."

"Paco."

"Yes. Do you remember me? Remember visiting us in Cincinnati?"

"Yes. Thank you for inviting me."

A pause.

"Honey, I have some bad news, but it's not too bad. Your father's been in a car accident."

Cadence sat back down with a bump on the little rocker. She could see what she called the Jaws of Death pulling her daddy out of a pile of metal.

"Cadence?"

"Yes."

"Bob is all right. At least that's what they told me. He's in a hospital."

"So is Mama."

"No, this is a different one. In Virginia. I talked to his doctor."

"Dr. Narduli?"

"No, his name was Stack. This is a different place, honey. Your father is in Virginia. This is not your mother. We'll see tomorrow whether he should come home or maybe come down to you. We don't know that yet. Will you be all right?"

"Was it the snow?"

"What?"

"Was it hail?"

"There was a storm and your dad got in an accident."

"Is he dead?"

"No, honey, like I said, he's in the hospital. Is anybody there with you?"

Cadence looked at herself looking at herself in the night-mirror of the window. She looked down at her lap.

"Rabbit."

She waited for him to say something, which he did, but it took a minute.

"What's the name of the hospital where your mother is?"

"Comfort."

He repeated the name a bunch of times and then stopped. He asked where. She told him Garnet.

"Who has been helping you, Cadence?"

"Miss Lana. Mr. McCallum. Uncle Walker and Auntie Pam."

"Can you call your aunt and tell her what happened?"

"She's not really my aunt. She's pretend. I can't call until ten o'clock in the morning. If I call early, Mama says it's rude."

"That's fine. Call her in the morning and tell her what happened. Or if you want, I could call her."

"No, I know how to do it," said Cadence.

"Will you be all right there tonight?"

"Fine-fine-fine." Her gaze drifted to the corners of the dark window as if she could see the yard beyond, out where ghost dogs might congregate, where Hershey-turned-white might make his appearance at any moment, drooling the way he did on a car ride, but maybe the drool now would be blood.

Cadence turned herself back into the room, rocking very quickly.

"Here's what I'm going to do," Paco said. "I'm going to call you tomorrow to tell you how things are, okay?"

She thought, *Well, I'll be down to Comfort,* but she didn't say it because she could tell he didn't understand how things were.

"Do you have an answering machine?"

"Okay!" She wanted to get off the phone now.

"I'll keep you posted."

"Okay-Okay!" sing-songing, like the refrain of a lullaby.

"All right. Goodnight, Cadence. Do you have our number?"

"Okay-Okay!"

She waited, rocking. Eventually he hung up. She could hear the dial tone. That's when she knew it was safe for her to hang up too.

She was tired.

The grandaddy clock *tsk-tsk'ed,* scolding, *So far past your bedtime, young lady!* It was the first since the sickness that Cadence missed her mama, the old mama. She missed being tucked in, being read to.

Cadence slid into her bed, snaking under the blanket, barely disturbing it and not getting under the sheets at all. She didn't even take her clothes off. Because they were already warm. Because it was wrong to do. Because she could go to sleep in her whole clothes and there was nobody to say nothing about it. She could even lie on top of the sheets instead of underneath so the bed didn't need much making in the morning and wouldn't nobody say a thing about it.

She lay sideways, placing Rabbit carefully over her right hand, skin side down to be sure the fur was open to the night air and not to be disturbed. The other hand she squinched between her knees, the way she liked. Her eyes fixed on the one window, on a vague dark wiggling beyond that must have been branches stirring in a night wind. She went to sleep.

MONDAY

November 20, 1989

That's One Small

August Early
Morning

It was a nurse who told Mr. Early he could not drive Theo to Solace in his truck, a desk nurse, one of many standing behind the high counter under the bright lights at Holy Brides. While most of them wore white, this one wore blue, pants and a shirt covered with sailboats in tired colors. None of which helped Mr. Early reckon who he was talking to since this nurse was a man, but his nametag did not say DOCTOR, it said NED.

So he must to be a nurse, Mr. Early thought.

It was hours before Theo would be going anywhere. Still, as soon as she caught wind of the ambulance ride she pitched a fit. She said she hated the idea worse than anything that had happened in the one day she'd been in the hospital. She could not abide people making a fuss.

"But you came here in an ambulance," Mr. Early reminded her.

Theo's face reddened up from the neck like a flower opening real fast. "That was Curtis-Michael driving," she said. "Curtis-Michael Hipps. He's got some sense. He might to be my own child, coming up in every one of my Sunday schools since he was five." The red in her cheeks splotched gray. "I know them ambulance boys, August. Give them half a chance and it's 'Look at me! I'm a big shot!' screaming around town like some fancy-pants with them lights flashing and the sirens going and everybody staring, and me there in the back not able to do nothing about it."

Her talking set Theo to coughing. Mr. Early stood through it, smoothing the bedclothes. He knew not to touch her directly when she was worked up.

That's when Theo sent him out to the counter to tell whoever was there she didn't want no ambulance carrying her nowhere. She said to tell them she wasn't wearing the oxygen mask, so she was plenty able to ride in a truck like a normal person.

The nurse called Ned did not smile or not-smile as Mr. Early said this. He barely looked up. "Hospital policy," he said. "There's nothing I can do."

Mr. Early stood for a moment considering. He wondered whether, if he took Theo out of the hospital right then and there, if he put her in the truck and drove her to Solace himself, whether they would put him in jail for it. But what if she took sicker by the sheer effort of walking and riding, so that by the time they got there she was a whole lot worse off because of his foolishness? It seemed there was nothing to be done.

It took Dr. Narduli to quiet her, coming in cheery and fast around the bed saying, "Looks like you're breathing better," until he saw that her breathing might be better, but her mood was surely not.

It took the doctor letting Theo talk, nodding *Yes* as he did so, listening as she reviled the very notion of an ambulance carrying her anywhere, anyhow, anyway. It took him asking her finally eye-to-eye, "Mrs. Early, in all our time together, have I steered you wrong?"

That stopped Theo cold. "No sir, not never." She smiled her crimp-lipped, girl-smile. Mr. Early had to look away.

The doctor's voice soothed. "*You* know you don't need an ambulance. And *I* know you don't need an ambulance. But guess who does? The people who have to take care of you. It makes them nervous if they don't have their special equipment with them."

Mr. Early did not know where the doctor came from, but he spoke like the actors on television who played kings and royal folk.

"What if something were to happen? Here I entrust you to them and something goes wrong and they don't have what they need to fix it. We have to consider their feelings. Will you help me with that?"

If Theo answered him, it was not with words.

Through the long narrow window by the bed, Mr. Early could see a strip of concrete wall, stained and pebbly like wet sand. Above it, a lilac sky was yellowing to gold.

Then Dr. Narduli was asking him, could they speak.

Stepping into the hallway, Mr. Early realized that he had not taken off his parka. Theo said he'd sleep in it if he could. But the doctor wasn't doing much better. He had the buttons of his white coat to where one side was hanging down longer than the other. He spread his feet out and planted them, standing strong, short as he was, crossing his arms and casting a solemn look from left to right like a county fair judge eyeing the stock. His words came clipped and proper. "Mr. Early, we've got a nice room for your wife at Solace. It's more like home than this place. I think she will feel better there." His eyes shifted upward. "The staff is so good, I don't have to make rounds. That means you won't see as much of me as you do here. But they will keep me posted as to how she's doing. And they'll contact me if she needs anything."

Mr. Early nodded, keeping his eyes on the badge that said DR. NARDULI.

"Do you have any questions?"

The first of his words sounded to Mr. Early like him clearing his throat, but he got them out: "What I want to know is, can I come there anytime?"

"Any time." Dr. Narduli re-planted each foot as a preacher might. "They're prepared to have you sleep there if you wish to."

Mr. Early nodded.

"They have a kitchen. They will make all of her meals. You'll see. They provide excellent care."

Mr. Early nodded again. He wasn't sure he could ask his question. He raised his eyes up past the doctor's shoulder to the sign on the wall that said MEDICAL PERSONNEL ONLY.

"I - I'm thinking on why."

"Why what?"

Mr. Early could not reply.

"Why Solace?" the doctor asked.

Mr. Early felt himself looked at. He could not look back.

"Are you wondering why she might want go there?" The doctor waited for Mr. Early to nod *Yes*. "It's somewhat unusual, but then your wife is an unusual woman." He said it respectfully. "It's my experience that sometimes a person is too fond of home to be sick there."

Mr. Early knew the doctor was trying to tell him something. It was in the sound of things.

"Or it could be that home feels like a place that needs cleaning all the time. Maybe it calls to her when what she needs is rest."

Mr. Early hadn't thought of it that way. Or either way. What he had thought was that he hadn't taken good enough care of his wife, hard as he might have tried, and that the doctor would say so, having been asked straight to his face and honor-bound to tell the truth in such circumstances. Mr. Early thought about asking had he done right, but he could not. Instead he put his hand out, mute. The doctor clasped it like a seasoned rider patting at a horse's neck to say, *Good job.*

"Take care." The doctor was off down the hallway. No doubt seeing to others that Mr. Early knew must be waiting for him.

"Don't forget my pillow, August."

He was in the bathroom packing things up. He told her he wouldn't, even as he worried that he might, since the pillow was behind her head so he could not put it with her bag to remember.

"And don't forget the shampoo."

"Theo!" he said, right sudden. Right sharp, truth be told. Sharp enough to hold her up a minute. "There ain't nothin' in here but is yours. How am I going to forget something?"

Theo did not answer him. She would not for some time. He could hear her breath rasping in and out like a cough in slow motion. They'd kept the mask off her to make sure she could breathe enough to be moved, but as the morning wore on, it had gotten harder for her.

Mr. Early finished up. Anything that could spill he closed tight and stood upright, pushing things close together in the bag so they'd hold each other straight. He'd learned a lot watching how Theo did things.

He got as far as the bathroom doorway. "Why don't you want to come home?"

Lord save us, he knew the look of fed-up-ness that came over his wife's face. "August Early, honest to Pete, you try a body."

He set her bag at the door. She could look at him any way she damn well pleased, he was having none of it anymore. It was for her to speak.

Which took a minute. Theo ducked her chin, picking at the strings on her nightgown. When she finally commenced talking, her face looked washed through like the blankness of sky between a rain and the sun.

"August." She took turns breathing and talking. "This is my last. I do not want to be home—like this—and you not able to do nothing about it. I want to be where they's people can help me."

That sounded right. That sounded like Theo.

She took another breath.

"Bring me my bag."

She poked around inside, disturbing his careful arrangement of things, pulling out, finally, one of the little packets with a washcloth inside. The smell was like medicine when she tore it open. She set to cleaning her fingertips, then touching the corners of her mouth.

"Do I have nothing on here?" she asked, turning her face for him to view full on.

"No, you're clean."

She held up the torn packet. "I want you to promise me something."

He fetched the wastebasket.

"Promise me."

He nodded, staring deep into the basket like it was a pitshaft long abandoned by miners, filled with a swill of cold, black rain water and the lone body of a little girl who'd fallen in and drowned. Theo stared with him.

"I don't want to know," she said. "I do not want to know."

Breathing.

"I do not want to feel what I felt yesterday."

Mr. Early looked up from the hole and the body and the black water he'd been seeing.

"There's things they can do if I get bad. You're going to have to tell them like I'm telling you now: when things get bad I do not want to know. You understand me, August?"

He nodded.

She said it again like a schoolteacher, "You tell them what?"

"That you don't want to know," Mr. Early said. He had a picture in his mind of her not being able to breathe.

"That's right. Will you do that?"

"Yes'm," he said.

Mr. Early was years-on her husband, papa to their one dead child and now having to bring up two grandbabies besides. Even so, from time to time he caught himself speaking to Theo like she was his mama. It was how he'd been raised to do.

"You won't forget," she said. Saying it, not asking.

"I don't forget nothing, Theo!" He was irritable now. How'd she get on that jag of his forgetting? He'd never forgotten nothing in his life. A stick of butter maybe once at the Bi-Lo, but he was always to work on time, to church on Sunday and to where he was supposed to when he was supposed to. Didn't that count for nothing?

Theo kittened down. "That's all right, then," she said.

Mr. Early snatched the bag off her lap and set it next to a paper sack filled with things the nurse said they could keep: a hospital toothbrush, mouthwash, a comb and a few of the medicine cloths in packets. He ran over in his mind one more time the bathroom picked clean, the empty hangers in the closet, the nothing left on the bedside tray.

There wasn't a thing for him to do now but sit and wait for the ambulance. Theo's head drooped. Mr. Early lifted the recliner clear off the floor, big and heavy as it was, in order to shift it closer to the bed. He wanted things so that, while he was keeping an eye on Theo, he would always be seeing the pillow there under her head. That way, he knew, he would not forget it.

Freedom's Just Another

Maggie Dull
Mid-Morning

The blue-gray of the ridge top, a feathered line of balsam, molting sour-woods and poplars, led Maggie from Garnet east to Big Piney by way of 51. Turning off the highway onto Main, she had to hit the brakes big time. Folks in town were moving at half speed, shambling along sidewalks or easing vehicles into ample, head-on parking slots as if docking enormous spaceships.

Thank God I dressed, Maggie thought. How could any population miss the fashion boat so entirely? Surely they watched television. Everyone in America did. Where was the fake Chanel, the upscale polo, the fit-for-office fitness-wear that even your average middle-aged *Hausfrau* on the West Coast could pick up for a song? Here even the youngest women sported dowdy stuff.

Making her wardrobe selection that morning, Maggie'd reached for the shortest skirt in her suitcase, the lime green, *Tennis-anyone?*-inspired number that telegraphed her post-divorce aerobicization. Yes, she'd joined the Jane Fonda revolution. Her marriage may have failed, but, by God, she'd make sure her abs didn't.

You can *go home again,* she thought, pulling into the Pay Less. *You can go home and pretend to be the fantasy of success you swore you'd become.*

Her plan had been to breeze through town, a blur in the rearview mirror, noticed, then gone before anyone had time to wonder, *Could that be Margaret Dull?* But the breeze-through scenario tanked immediately. Maggie had but to climb out of her rented Tracer—powder-blue, no less—when she right away saw three people she knew at the gas pump.

First came the Crowes, Pam and Walker. Age had not done them any favors, but then again they'd always looked old. They were carrying their morning coffees, crossing to a beat-up minivan, no doubt on their way to open the Mountain Man. Amazing how a gift shack like that, a literal ma-and-pa, could survive the tsunami of corporate retail sweeping the country. *The advantage,* Maggie thought, *of doing business where not much business is done.*

The second they saw her, they waved, as if it were the most natural thing in the world, Margaret Dull popping in out of the blue after so many years.

Maggie waved back. Did they not remember who she was? She thought it more likely they remembered every detail of her formative years skulking around the store, one of a pack of shifty teenagers haunting the Mountain Man, killing time on hot summer afternoons just to eye the boys going by on their bikes. Oh, they knew her all right. They were just doing the mountain thing. Obeying the Blue Ridge code of unflappability where nothing calls for commotion except maybe a bear in your bedroom or a rattler in your sink. And even then, a rifle or a clean shovel strike was all it took to take care of the situation.

At least Walker raised his coffee cup. Pam barely glanced over she was so busy extracting a donut from the bag he was carrying.

Meanwhile, over by the second pump, Maggie saw her mother's buddy, Beau McCallum, filling his pickup. Lord, he looked tired. So did the truck, a battered Chevy, well past fifteen years old and two-toned, the upper half being white enamel, the lower sheathed in mud with a familiar WE GET IT RIGHT AT REXALL on the bumper.

Damn, if the man didn't recognize her instantly. "Long time, no see, stranger," he called out, one quick glance up from the pump handle and then back to top things off.

"Hey, there." Maggie waved, her mountain twang locking back in.

Hail the prodigal daughter, Maggie thought. Surely her mother had not spoken well of her since she'd run off to the far coast and married and divorced and never come home. Surely Mama Dull had honed a spell-binding tale of abandonment, never mentioning that it was *she* who had driven her children off. Never mentioning DO NOT VISIT. Not a peep about DO NOT DROP BY. That would not be part of the Dull saga she'd be likely to share with others.

Maggie got busy gassing. Apparently Pay Less had not gotten the memo about that miracle of modern transaction, the credit card swipe. Here Maggie was free to fill her tank before ever having to prove her ability, not to mention willingness, to pay for it. Such a thing was unheard of in Palo Alto where too many folks were ready to gas and go.

Maggie headed inside with her wallet.

Wow. She might as well have been fifteen again. Not a thing had changed at the Pay Less. The identical, ancient shelf units. Maybe a few more bags of chips, some compound Coke stains on the floor, but otherwise things looked the same only dirtier. Like a moldy postcard of a technicolor locale.

Maggie cased the refrigerator section. She started to reach for the usual bottled water when it occurred to her, *What a waste of anonymity. Why not dive into the universe of guilty pleasures?*

So she pulled out an icy bottle of cream soda. Then she worked her way around the snack aisles looking for—there she was!—Little Debbie. Racks stacked with the cutest little face you ever did see. Her pink straw hat still set back on her head so as not to interfere with the red curls. A smile so bland it communicated the essence of what lay within: cream. Cream sandwiched between mushy patties of pure sugar masquerading as oatmeal. Maggie picked up two. *Whoo-ee. Home at last.*

She was plunking down a few bucks at the counter when she heard her name.

"Maggie Dull?"

She'd know that voice on her deathbed. Addled, on the brink of the Beyond, she'd hear that deep baritone saying her name and know who it was.

Sure enough, she looked up to see, standing behind the cashier, Curtis-Michael Hipps himself. Every bit the linebacker's body she remembered from that scratchy, worsted sofa out on the Hipps' screen porch junior year. And the Hipps' basement senior year. And the wooded slope behind the Dairy Queen that last summer. There was nothing like a cul-de-sac when the trains hurtled by.

Thank God she'd chosen the lime skirt. An industrial green unknown to the Pineys either in nature or personal adornment, it clung. She knew she looked great.

Curtis looked the same only bigger. Jowls, for sure. Saggy muscle at the shoulder but not in a way that made much difference. Maggie liked the weight.

"Curtis-Michael," she said, the way his mother used to chide when he came in late, Maggie tucked under his arm. "Curtis-Michael Hipps." She shot him a gaze right past the dumbstruck cashier.

"I like your hair," he said, without batting an eye.

She dished it right back. "Shucks, you saw through my disguise. I was hoping no one would recognize me."

"It would take more than a hairdo," he said.

Hairdo. That was so Curtis.

He'd been sure they were going steady. Not that he'd formalized anything. But when he found out they weren't—that she'd been just as happy to see a little of Monroe Bickle on the side—he'd broken up with her right then. Right before she left for college. Made a big to-do of it. Although she'd tried to appear devastated, the fact was, Maggie knew she'd be moving on. Curtis had been great for starter sex. He'd been willing to try until he pleased her, letting her show him things like, as big as he was, to roll over once he'd gone where he was going, because it was hard to breathe under a guy with that much body.

Maggie noticed the ring as he came around the counter. He, on the other hand, wasn't looking anywhere near her ring finger. But his eyes did catch the real estate below her skirt line. Maggie couldn't stop a smile coming. *Damn,* she thought. *What's it been? Maybe six or seven minutes in town and I'm ready to jump some high school memory?*

"What's shaking?" she asked, affecting the caricature of a smooth hipster that would never play on the West Coast.

That got him running through his catalogue of pride. He'd apparently ended up marrying Dee Dee Watkins from Flat Rock High. After Maggie'd left, of course, directly after. Maggie didn't know the name, much less the face. Probably a pretty girl. Curtis had always been a sensible guy. His mother had done a good job beating into his head the horror of unplanned pregnancy. Maggie hoped he'd married for what he would have called love.

On and on he went. *Blabbity-blab.* Letting her know that he was happy, prosperous. He'd started out with Ray over at the Jeep repair place and moved on to manage the Pay Less Pantry. He volunteered with the fire department and the EMS guys. There were some kids apparently. Maggie found her mind wandering.

No way Curtis would have ended up following her. College was never on the horizon for him. No doubt that was part of his appeal now. Simple men and Little Debbie's. *You can go home again.*

He came up for air long enough to ask what brought her to town.

"My mother."

He didn't react. It was a tribute to her mother's all-fired misanthropy that she'd managed to keep even her dying off the local radar. Maggie was glad. She hadn't come all this way for pity parties.

She swept her arm around the Pay Less. "So all this is yours."

"Only if something's wrong. I just work here."

"You always on?"

"Way too much." He laughed.

Maggie pushed her bills his way. She could see that he wanted to say something, but maybe wasn't going to. So she went on ahead and said it for him. "I know it sounds crazy, but maybe one of these nights we could grab a bite to eat."

She told herself she might need to unwind over a few beers with a friend. Even if he was married.

"You bet. Big Piney's got Mexican now, even Chinese." No suggestion about bringing the wife along. Maggie was watching him pretty closely. He still had not checked her left hand.

It was good she'd opted for the short skirt, because turning around and banging through the screen door that had lost its spring with PAY LESS peeling off its backside, Maggie knew he could get a look at legs that hadn't changed too awfully much since the last time he'd laid eyes—and other anatomical members—on them.

Happy ways are here again, Maggie thought. Another motherism. Everybody talked about the disconnects, the devolutions involved in coming back to one's hometown, but what about the fun?

Suddenly it was good to be out of Palo Alto. For all its West Coast, free-love liberalism, Maggie had never enjoyed being trashy there. Flirting with a married man who probably had a very nice wife and a great set of kids—that happened all the time. But not for fun, for keeps. Out there it was serious, home-wrecking stuff. *Yawn, yawn.* Maggie being her own a case in point. She'd been seeing Viktor maybe—what?—thirteen, fourteen months now. On the side. For him, on the side. He had a perfectly adequate wife. And even though he complained of the clandestine meetings, the *Sturm und Drang,* the fact was, he loved, absolutely *loved* the guilt. Suffering over the damage he was doing—*that* was the turn-on for him. For Maggie, it was just the sex. Good sex, mind you, but it seemed overwrought now. She'd known it was ending months ago. One of these days she would call the whole thing to a halt. And, if Maggie had anything to say about it, the wife would never know. No muss, no fuss.

"Hey, woman!" Curtis was trotting out behind her. "Making so much money you don't need your change?" He was waving a ten and some singles. "So what are you doing tonight?"

Maggie cocked a hip to one side. "I only just got here, Curtis. Figure I ought to spend some time with my mother."

"How 'bout tomorrow?"

Maggie looked down. Somehow in the talking, the walking, she'd torn open one of the cream pies. Little Debbie's head had sheared right off. Maggie took a whomping bite, smiling over at Curtis. *Bang.* The sugar hit. A Debbie rush sharp enough to shatter teeth, the cream, fluffy sweet. Maggie felt a trace of it on her lipstick. She leaned over to keep any crumbles from sticking to her blouse.

She kept on chewing as she spoke. "You free every night of the week, fella? What about that family of yours?"

"Old friends don't come through every day. Dee Dee can take them."

Mmmm-hmmm, Maggie thought. *And who will take you?* Laughing his way. Him laughing right back. Her standing by the powder-blue Tracer, tossing the empty wrapper into the trashcan, a clean three-point shot sweeping straight in. Him standing square, one foot in an oil puddle, one foot on a potato chip bag, all take-it-or-leave-it cool. You couldn't beat Curtis-Michael for that air of disinterested interest.

"Let's see how things go. You want to call me up at the house tomorrow? Same number."

"I'll do it. You give my best to your mama."

He turned, purposeful, striding back into the Pay Less. He looked great in jeans.

Once again, Maggie was one with the Tracer, fully gassed. She pulled onto Main Street, rolling her window down. What with winter-turned-summer, the air was balm.

She thought she'd take a back road from Big to Little Piney. Balancing her cream soda, left hand on the wheel, she caught the light wrong at the Rexall and had to wait.

And wait some more.

She punched around the only four radio stations that came through in the Blue Ridge. Country. Bible. More Bible. And then, out of nowhere, the Fine Young Cannibals. Singing their heads off about how some woman was driving them crazy, how they couldn't help themselves. Maggie's fingers tapped out the guitar riff on the steering wheel. What a great tune to work out to. She wondered if there might be a half-decent aerobics studio within driving distance of home.

Still no green light.

Across the street a young woman was sitting at a bus stop. A teenager given her general body size, but wearing ankle socks. Maggie caught what looked like a cotton summer dress under the girl's open coat. And a smock. Or an apron. Some kind of Christian cult? That would be nothing new in this neck of the woods, fundamentalism boiling down to whatever "fundamentals" each local preacher chose to insist upon.

But you had to love Big Piney for maintaining its bus benches, all tarted up with home-spun advertising. One side of this one said MOUNT, the other said MAN with the odd girl sitting in between on what appeared to be the painted portrait of a bushy-bearded rube.

That's a prize-winning photo, Maggie thought.

The light finally changed. Maggie cruised up Peach Street. There was good old Walker Crowe standing out front of his shop arranging a jumble of washtubs and watering cans painted with daisies. Tourist bait even in November. Surely at this time of year only the locals dropped by to chat, not to buy anything. How did the Crowes survive?

Maggie punched up a country station. She caught Dolly in full bawl, wailing about yellow roses. Her mother had always sworn by Dolly Parton. She'd sing along in the car, high and out of tune, while Maggie played with an actual dolly in the backseat. Maggie couldn't remember ever hearing anybody sing quite as badly as her mother before or since. Clearly, people who did, did so in utter solitude. Which was what having her daughter in the backseat must have meant to her mother.

Maggie got halfway up the mountain when she checked her watch. *Damn.* It was still too early.

With no one on the road, she swung the Tracer 180 and headed back. How about dropping in at the Mountain Man? Maybe they'd have a knick-knack she could take to her mother. Maybe something for Viktor. A coon-skin cap or some de-Toqueville-gone-kitsch slice of Americana. It would be her break-up offering to him, a parting gift from the Hollywood Squares.

Hers was the only vehicle in the parking lot except for the Crowes' mini-van. Walker was nowhere to be seen. Maggie pulled down the visor mirror: hair, makeup—flawless. One deep breath and she was out, tottering along the cracked sidewalk in her heels, weaving through an obstacle course of ye-olde-souvenir stick brooms and smiley-face wind chimes toward the OPEN sign on the door.

Never Did Run Smooth

Pam and Walker Crowe
Shop Hours

Because the bus stop was around the corner, neither Walker nor Pam noticed a girl there. Besides, Walker had his hands full. His wife was having one of her China Doll days as she called them. "You break me, you take me." That was how she warned Walker to steer clear of her. On China Doll days he spent every waking moment distracting her from the bouts of tears that blew through like summer downpours coming up over the mountains, drenching things and then rolling on.

Which drove Pam crazy. After all, she wasn't the only one with moods. He got testy too. On mornings like these, she would just as soon leave him behind. "Stay home," she'd say. "I'll mind the store."

But Walker was not one for spending even two minutes by himself. Never had been. Whither she *went-est,* he would go.

It was a disappointment for both of them—having to come back into the shop full-time after years of building the business to where they could afford someone else to mind the register. And on this morning of all mornings: the Monday before Thanksgiving, slowest of God's own slow days. No question, business over at the Bi-Lo would be hopping, turkeys flying out the door along with bag stuffing and stacks of canned onion rings for green bean casseroles. But the Mountain Man wouldn't pick up until Friday after everyone had downed their feasts, watched the Macy's Santa glide by in his float-sleigh on TV and then snoozed from nap time right on through 'til morning. That's when foot traffic would pick up in town. The Crowes always did a decent business in Christmas goo-gaws: corncob angels, hand carved crèches and the like.

Walker had offered to drive down to the store with a sign saying "Closed Until Friday," but Pam would have none of it. She told him it was a message from God. How else could one explain losing their one-and-only-ever-in-life employee? Verleana Greevey, one minute able-bodied, the next un-abled, just like that. What could it be but a lesson? At whom might the Lord be pointing His ever-loving finger if not at them, indulging in premature retirement as they were, frippering any number of perfectly good days here on earth in the kind of indolence meant for beyond the grave?

All fine and dandy, Walker thought, *but could the woman heed her Lord with a glad heart?* What with her Mighty Sighs of the Martyr, he'd had just about enough of Pam's woe talk, trundling down Rainbow Ridge in the Nissan with nobody and nothing on the road except Jonelle Hipps' Pekinese relieving itself on a mailbox.

It was his idea to go by the Pay Less first. Pam could make coffee just as good at home, but he knew she was partial to those bags of little powdered donuts they kept by the check-out. The kind their doctor had told them was clean off the list seeing as how they both could lose at least fifty pounds and only then start looking at the big sizes in regular department stores.

"Life is too short," Walker told her pulling in at the gas pump. "We get no donuts on the *regular* diet, but nobody said nothing about the *treat* diet." The treat diet. That made Pam laugh. Which made him laugh. She repeated every word to Curtis there behind the register, which made *him* laugh too.

For the first time in days, they were sweet with each other, toting up their Jumbo Javas, plopping down a king-size bag of donuts—"Get the big one!" Walker told her. They'd busted it open before they were hardly out the door, coffee tilting just this side of spillage, fighting each other to reach in for a first bite and laughing, thank merciful heavens, laughing.

"That was Margaret Dull," Pam said, mouth half sugar-glued, as they got in the car.

"Mmmm-hmmm."

"Dolores' daughter."

"Mmmm-hmmm." Walker was chewing too much to say more.

"She looks out of a magazine."

He swallowed. "She lives in Hollywood," he said, reaching in for yet another donut, even as he racked the steering wheel around one-handed to get them onto Main.

"She looks like a movie star."

"I believe it's the television shows." Talking and eating made him spit some sugar onto the dash. "She writes one or makes money on one. Something like that."

"She looks good."

"She does look good."

That's what they were saying—Walker could swear on it—when they turned off Main to Peach. That was why he had no recollection of any girl at the bus stop. Because Pam was busy saying, "No wedding ring on her finger."

"Is that the first thing you women notice?" he asked as they pulled into the parking lot. They juggled coffees to get the shop door unlocked. "I believe I heard that she's a divorcée." Walker used the fancy word with a wink back to his wife.

"I wonder if they's children."

"Mmm-mmm-mmm," he mumbled meaning, "I don't know."

Somehow between donuts and the pleasure of shared censure, they felt their moods lifting. Perhaps it wouldn't be so bad, a day of nothing-much in town instead of sitting at home.

Walker set up the sidewalk display: watering cans, wind chimes, the old stick brooms. He was in good enough spirits, coming back inside, to say he wasn't sure, but that it might be his turn to dust. As if either of them ever forgot whose turn it might be. And didn't they both hate doing it? They each held to the principle that tidying daily meant never tidying much. Even so, after all these years, the wisdom of Solomon could not offset a dread over chores that made the one keep vigilant track of how hard the other was working.

He was poking a long-pole duster into the ears of a wall-mounted stag when in sashayed Miss Margaret Dull herself as if summoned by their speaking.

Pam right away noted her hair. More than two colors of brown and blond. Mounded up and rounded round with curls swooping every which way including one loop dead between her eyes. That meant money. And the tightness of that sweater coming off the one shoulder. Pam saw a grown woman dolled up like a soap star on a morning talk show looking for some-body to ask, "How do you do it?" so she could say, "Drinking from the Fountain of Youth."

"If it isn't Margaret Dull!" Pam managed.

"Good morning, Miz Crowe. I saw y'all over at the Pay Less."

"Don't you look fine these days."

"Oh, you are too kind." Margaret did a swivel half-circle there to take in the shop. "I'm so glad ya'll are still here."

Pam wondered how much "ya'll" Margaret was using in Hollywood.

"Thought you'd be sitting out on your porch by now. Let the business go."

"Don't get me started," Pam said.

Here came Walker, propping up his dusting rod and swiping his hand across a cleaner patch of his work pants to stick it straight out to Maggie.

What on earth is he thinking? Pam wondered. Men shook hands with men, all kinds of men, strangers and buddies alike, but not with ladies.

Walker looked surprised too, even though it was his own hand waving out there in the breeze like that. "Good to see you, Margaret."

She bypassed the handshake, leaning in to peck him on the cheek. "Call me Maggie. Somebody says 'Margaret' and all I hear is my mother calling me out."

Pam shook the bag of powdered donuts her way. "You visiting your mama? We haven't seen her in a while, have we, Walker?"

"I was in Charlotte for a meeting. Thought I'd swing by."

Of course Maggie didn't take a donut. *Probably one of those that won't touch sugar,* Pam thought, *or anything else that might put on the pounds.*

Maggie was already nosing around the store. Walker nodded at Pam. They'd worked out a shorthand: folks who walked in off the street were ei-ther lookers or grabbers. You could tell two steps in who was who. Lookers dawdled, wasted your time and left no money. Grabbers, on the other hand, got in and got out.

Grabber, Walker mouthed to his wife.

"Mother used to speak of the redbirds y'all had. Do you carry them anymore? I want to bring her a little something. She's partial to redbirds."

Walker pointed to the back. "That's Edsel Mudd carves them. He's still up on Rainbow. There's a flock setting there on the window."

"A flock," said Maggie. "That's cute, Mr. Crowe."

"Call me Walker." He escorted Maggie down the aisle between the hunting knives and the pelts, re-buttoning his sweater vest and pants-wiping his hands one more time.

Pam watched the tug of Maggie's skirt from leg to leg. *Here's a woman who likes a man,* she thought, noticing at the same time how her husband, so many years past courting, was setting his one clean hand almost, but not quite touching the small of Maggie's back.

"Oh, look at what you've done." Maggie spied the carvings on a ledge, arranged as if they were real birds congregating after a long flight.

"That's Verleana did that," Pam called after them, so that Maggie had to turn around. "You recall Verleana Greevey? Husband ran off and she had to go back to work, praise God. She's been with us for years. Enough to where we could leave her with most everything in the shop. But she's took sick now. We're not sure when she'll be back."

"Or if," said Walker.

"Or if."

Walker was pulling redbirds off the window shelf, handing them to Maggie who palmed each one in turn, lifting them up and down as if their flyweight held any importance.

"We hear you're out in Hollywood."

Maggie laughed. "Hollywood, no. I'm in what they call Silicon Valley."

"That's California?"

"The other California." Maggie frowned as she considered the birds, looking down to her hand and back to the shelf the way a bird itself might do.

Pam stayed put behind her counter. "We hear you're doing television."

Maggie laughed again. "Only the way everybody else does—by turning it on. No, no, I'm an event planner."

"What's that?" Pam and Walker spoke together.

"I put on parties for people."

"Sounds like fun." That was all Pam could think to say.

"Fun for the clients." Maggie brought her chosen redbird straight to the cash register, Walker trailing.

Pam said later, that must have been when Maggie asked about the girl at the bus stop, in the time it took for them to imprint her credit card and call in the number. Neither could remember what they'd said back to her. Probably too busy on the phone with the bank or wrapping the bird to pay much attention.

But Pam did remember Maggie saying "strange:" "Who is that *strange* girl?" Pam remembered, because it crossed her mind, not in an entirely charitable way, that surely anything in the Pineys would strike Maggie as strange coming from a world where parties needed planners who were not you, the party giver, but some gussied-up gal from the mountains looking like TV fixing to make you and your life look like TV too.

Off Maggie went—"I'd best be heading up the mountain." She blew an air-kiss at Walker's cheek, squeezing his shoulder, Pam noticed, with a ringless left hand, the redbird satchel peeking out from her purse.

Reclothe Us

Maggie Dull
Noon

The driveway looked good. Had someone graded the gravel of late? Of course it took Maggie a minute to see anything else because, as was true for all mountain properties, the road came in above the house at roof level. From there she had to climb down the old stairs fashioned of cut railroad ties. They had gotten rickety, flaking splintered wood, edged by overgrown grass whose every blade, even with the warmth, was brown.

There's no fooling grass, she thought. Grass wouldn't trust a spell of false summer. Regardless of the heat, it went on ahead and did its dying, knowing it was time. Must have been the position of the sun told it that.

In the back of her mind Maggie was running a tab: *Mow the grass, check. Stair repair, check.* She assumed it would all come out of her pocket. No way the brothers (or brother, the reachable brother) would offer a red penny of thanks-for-bringing-me-into-this-world tithing. *How sharper than a serpent's tooth,* indeed. She wondered how much it was all going to cost.

The Motorola screamed. A blue jay jumped into the air with the sound. Maggie fished for it in her purse wondering what time it was in California. It was Viktor.

"What's up?" Maggie asked, mid-stair. Pea vines had crept from the tree line to choke what was left of a scraggled vegetable patch below her, its withered tomatoes and unpicked squash deflating toward greenless ground.

Wonder of wonders, Viktor, who never called to chat, was calling to chat.

"Is this a bad time?"

"Uncanny."

Who could she get to pull back those pea vines?

"I miss your legs."

"Viktor—"

"Around mine."

"I am at my mother's door, Viktor."

"I like missing you."

Maggie snorted, "You wouldn't have it any other way." She lifted her voice into a girlie octave. "Oh, here's mother! Mmmmm-moi…" miming a home-coming kiss at nothing into the phone so that it sounded like truth 3,000 miles away. She slid into an impersonation of tearfulness, "Mama, I'm so glad to see you!" Then, "Viktor, let me call you back," and she was off, killing the phone and stowing it. She didn't feel bad. He liked the tough love thing. It was why he chose her to begin with.

Rounding the stairs now, she made a mental note to source a yard man. Maybe Pam or Walker Crowe would know whom to call.

She was at the front door before she registered what she was walking on: a black rubber mat strewn with—what? Granules. Sparkling white. Mica? No, rock salt. A box of it sat beside the door. In 70-degree weather?

The door itself was loosely framed with a single line of Christmas lights, still blinking in the daylight. *Good Lord.* Were they left over from last year? Maggie noted an extension cord running to the porch outlet. Was that rated for the outdoors? How apt an ending to the family saga, her mother wittingly or un-, burning down the puny legacy that was the house of Dull.

A ladder running to the roof was propped up by the front door. On the doorknob, affixed by a rubber band, hung a schedule for bus routes out of town with, scribbled over top, BON VOYAGE.

And then there were the signs. Two of them on letter-sized paper, scotch-taped below the doorknob. NO VACANCY FOR THE EVIL ONES on the first and ALL GOODLY ARE WELCOME on the second, only one of the O's had been crossed out to read GODLY.

A cuss cursed, Maggie thought. The lamentable if predictable disintegration of a death-rattled woman living by herself. She heard hillbilly music playing inside. Was that Dolly?

Maggie knocked.

Nothing.

She tried looking in through the window, but the curtains were drawn. Hanging off the rod was a haphazard line of—what was that? Tinsel, hanging like reverse gravity on a faraway planet where the grass was silver and grew upside down from the sky.

Get a grip, Maggie thought, grabbing the doorknob. It turned smooth as butter.

She was straddling the mat to avoid tracking salt into the house, calling "Mother?" even as the damn mobile rang, so that she had to fumble with her purse before her eyes found the vision of a creaky banshee turning in the middle of the living room, arms wide open, swathed in God-only-knows what, sleeves and scarves swinging this way and that, a swirl of garish yellows, sing-songing up toward the ceiling, "I go to prepare a place for you!"

"Hello?" Maggie said into the phone and "Mother?" right after.

The banshee's eyes came down to her. Then a scream just as Amelia's voice chirped in Maggie's ear. Of course it was Amelia. She was calling at the appointed hour for her appointed update.

"I'll call you back!" Maggie said loud and firm with her mother's screaming no doubt audible in the background, turning off the phone and dropping her purse as her mother backed away crying, "Get thee behind me oh ye of little faith!" pawing her two hands in front of her, sleeves and scarves swishing back and forth.

"What in God's name is going on?"

"In God's name!" her mother roared, snatching up and brandishing the twig broom that lived beside the fireplace. "No room at the inn!" She swung the broom side to side.

"Mother, it's me." A more unhelpful phrase Maggie could not have come up with, but it was the best she could do.

Her mother, already exhausted, hunched over for breath, the broom between them, punching at Maggie with each word, "Where—are—the—pearls?" A paper crown tilted over some Princess Leia -do of hair knotted above each of the woman's ears.

Time to call for the straight jacket, thought Maggie.

The place was a hurricane wreck. Clothing lay everywhere, stuff wound from lamp to lamp. And what was she standing on? White fabric, cheap, rolled out through the living room. A plate piled high with pink sugar wafers sat on the hearth, a jelly jar of something bright orange beside it. My God, was it bacterial? How long had it been there? Glitter covered every surface. Maggie wondered what kind of industrial rig it would take to vacuum all that up.

It was the music that snapped her out of it, Dolly Parton's piercing treble with the pablum strum-strum of a dulcimer behind it. Maggie found a tape player in the back hallway sitting on the floor. How long had it been playing? Days? Weeks? Maggie punched the Off button.

Her mother followed, dragging the broom, her eyes unblinking, mean. "You cannot abide it!" Her voice accused, dripping venom. But that was nothing new for Maggie. Sarcasm had colored her mother's communication from as early as she could remember. This, at least, was a woman she recognized.

"It's driving me crazy," Maggie said, then laughed hearing the joke.

There was no laughter from the dragger of brooms. "Devils cannot abide a happy sound."

Maggie tried inching up on her, hands out like the paintings of Jesus. "Come on, now. Let's sit down." *Shuffle the little children*, as her mother used to say.

All went well until Maggie made actual contact. She'd gotten no more than two of her fingers on her mother's elbow and suddenly the woman was windmilling again, dropping the broom and screaming at her when— *Knock-Knock-Knock*—another voice sailed over top, "'Scuse me, Miz Dull?"

Maggie looked toward the open door to see a woman in white taking in the scene, staring at a woman in a lime green miniskirt fending off a crazy lady in crazy clothing in a crazified house whose every drawer and closet had been emptied into its middle.

A nurse, Maggie realized. White dress, tie shoes. Some sort of badge clipped off her collar. "Good morning," she said.

"Who the hell are you?" Maggie barked past her mother.

The woman's hand snapped up, index finger held high, stopping her cold. "There is no hell in this house." Maggie's mother rushed to the woman crying, "*Gory* hallelujah," reaching for her hand.

"Glory," the woman said, beaming. "Look at you, Miz Dull. You are up and about," then saying to Maggie, "I am Burnice Kling."

"I know her by her pearls!" Maggie's mother pointed. Sure enough, the woman wore an oversized strand of plastic pearls. Big ones over her polyester uniform.

Had the whole world gone mad?

Like biddies meeting for tea, their voices music-boxy, the nurse and her mother began talking at once.

"I have risen!" her mother crowed.

"From the bed!" the nurse filled in and the two began to laugh, her mother doubled over like a girl trying not to pee her pants.

The nurse patted the top of her back, speaking to Maggie. "I'm with the hospice program," she said. "Solace. I'm part of the home-visit staff."

"Home-visit! When is the last time you bothered to visit this home?"

Burnice Kling kept smiling. "I am sorry. I did not get your name."

"*My* name? My name is Maggie Dulé—Dull. I am Mrs. Dull's daughter."

Her mother began flailing again, yelling, "Do not visit! Do not drop by!" with Maggie saying, "Mother, I called, remember?" and the nurse pleading, "Miz Dull, this is your baby!"

As had always been the case, Maggie got the upper hand by making more noise than anyone else. She pushed Burnice's hands off, steering her mother toward a ratty plaid armchair that had been part of the Dull household since well before any children came along, all the while saying, "You're right. You're right, Mrs. Dull. I am not your daughter," which finally quieted the woman. Nurse Kling did not move from the doorway.

"I do not want to see my children."

Maggie got her mother seated, kneeling next to her, feeling herself every inch the stranger she was pretending to be. "So I gather. I tell you what, Mrs. Dull, I will keep your children away from you. All of them." Leaning on the "all." As if there were a host of adoring progeny hoping for a fairy-tale return.

Her mother's nose reddened. She looked past Maggie toward the nurse. "Where are the pearls?"

"She has them on, Miz Dull. They're underneath. I saw them."

Just like that her mother tucked over, pushing her forehead into Maggie, clasping two hands around her neck, "You're my angel."

There was that sting in Maggie's eyes again—the red hair—the ginger beer. She blinked the feeling away.

"Hang on, Mrs. Dull."

She loosed herself from her mother's fingers, going right to the nurse at the door. "Consider yourself fired, Miss—Kling was it? As in, fired-fired. I will be in touch with your supervisor the second you're off the premises."

The nurse seemed unfazed. She handed Maggie a card. SOLACE, it read. "Her medication is on the kitchen counter in a tray." Turning away, then turning back on the porch, "Your mama seems better today. Just yesterday, she was having trouble getting out of bed." The woman announced it as if declaring herself the gold medal winner in a baking contest.

She got halfway up the stairs, then turned one last time. "You might speak to her about whether she wants to stay home or come in to Solace. Either way, we are here to help."

"The salt burns their feet!" her mother crowed from across the room.

Burnice nodded to Maggie, maintaining her recipe-swapping tone. "Your mama was concerned about devils in the house. She'll be all right now. I'll leave my table cloth here—that's what you're standing on. It was my mother's. If you'd kindly fold it up, I'll fetch it later."

How was it the crazy spoke with such conviction? Maggie took a deep breath. "You will not set foot in this house again. I will see that your property is returned to you."

The nurse went sideways waving. "Goodbye, Miz Dull!"

Maggie's mother wiggled the end of one of her shawls like a hankie. "No room for the lazy!"

"No, ma'am."

Maggie damn near slammed the door.

She took a breath.

Her mother stared. It was unclear who she thought she was looking at. Which made the charade that much easier.

"Well, Mrs. Dull, how about we straighten up a little?" Maggie used the same tone she took with clients who were wondering whether to spring for the up-grade from shrimp cocktail to tuna carpaccio. But her mother began to sag. Maggie pushed a pillow under her neck. She lifted her swollen ankles one at a time to place them on a footstool.

"Jesus!" Maggie heard herself say the word. It was an exhalation, not a prayer. She sat back on her heels, then sank all the way to the floor, leaning her back against her mother's chair, toeing off her heels, splaying her legs wide, listening to her mother's breathing drift into sleep.

She would have to gather up all the fabric. Bag the tinsel. And that rock salt, the glitter. It could take a whole afternoon to vacuum that up. Then find a handyman to deal with the stairs. Call the bank and the doctor. Oh, and the hospice. The hospice first thing. Get that damn nurse fired. Find out what to do with her mother. Meanwhile Amelia was waiting. No doubt there were carolers to book, caterers to confirm.

How in God's name could she wrap everything up in Crazyland in time to get back to work by Monday? On this of all ghastly weeks, with everyone in the United States of Pilgrim closing up shop for turkey-day, there wouldn't be a soul available anywhere to get things done.

Her mother shifted behind her.

Maggie surveyed the wreckage. Where to begin? She spied her purse lying on the floor. A small paper bag had rolled out covered with premature Christmas theming, mistletoes and bunting. The beak and single side eye of a carved redbird poked up from inside as if hatching, as if trying to peck its way into this world, this house, this house of her growing up and leaving, this house of her mother, a wooden fledgling struggling to be born for the lover of redbirds who was snoring mightily now in a state thicker than sleep.

Where Clouds Are Far Behind

August Early
Afternoon

Mr. Early found himself in another vestibule there at Solace. Not with glass doors like at the hospital, but with a normal knob door like at a house. There was a row of wall hooks for coats. Somebody had set an old feed can in the corner to hold umbrellas and a few carved walking sticks. Wallpaper running the length of the hall reminded him of his grandmother, painted vines rising in row after twining row as if they were real ivies growing up from the floor. Before him stood a high counter of speckled plastic, modern and out of place in the wood and vinage.

Theo hadn't made it yet. No surprise. He'd caught her telling the boys who hefted her into the ambulance, "Keep that lead foot off the gas now. I want you to drive normal."

Sure enough, when they did pull into the driveway, it was slow and quiet. No sirens, no lights, the ambulance easing over the curb like they were carrying a truckload of eggs, which Mr. Early appreciated. Though she never spoke of it, he knew Theo had been afflicted with aching pain for some months now. He could see it in her eyes, the way she seemed to be looking back and into her own body, pondering, most like, the troubles she was feeling.

They were young fellows, the two boys who came swinging out from the ambulance—the one, tar-haired, maybe looking to be of Cherokee blood, the other as freckled as a dirt-speckled rock. They banged open the back door, plating Theo out sideways like a tray full of food, then raising her up to table height on a wheel-bed. One of her hands came out from under the blanket they'd given her, waving feebly until the boys raised her head up to where she was sitting and could nod as he came into her view.

She looked tidy enough. He'd gotten her hair back in a clip. It was entirely white now with a few spots gone from her head which he knew never to speak of. He'd held the mirror for her to put on her lipstick. Red. *Too red,* he thought, with her skin gone see-through pale like a tadpole, but he saw it made her feel better to do.

Along came a man in an odd hat, bright-colored and disc-shaped like a summer placemat. The boys piped up. "Early," they said.

"Welcome to Solace." The man spoke with an accent from a far-away part of the world. "Call me Isah." He shook Mr. Early's hand, spinning the wheelbed around to head it straight inside. "That's my Christian name. Don't bother with the rest. Isah will do." He was sharp enough to jump the gun with Theo, leaning over to reassure her, "Your husband can do all the paperwork," divining somehow that Mr. Early had the Blue Cross with him, which he surely did. He kept it in his wallet at all times now.

Mr. Early could see his wife taking in the ivied walls. "Oh, yes," she murmured in her Sunday voice, as if this were Isah's home and it was up to her to acknowledge the pride he must feel in owning such a fine place to live.

"Here we are," Isah said, "5-B." That was the number outside the door. As she rolled into the room, Theo dropped her words of politeness and fell altogether silent. It was clear she was impressed. Truth to tell, Mr. Early was too.

The room was mostly pale blue which was Theo's favorite. The bed had handles with crib bars like the beds in the hospital, but there was a quilt there. Not as good as her own stitching to be sure, still it looked home sewn and neighborly. Alongside ran a window so that, once Isah got Theo into bed and settled with the quilt drawn to where she could reach it, she didn't even have to turn her head to get the view of the houses across the way and beyond them the Blue Ridge.

Isah told them that things would be quiet since Solace sat on a dead-end street. The only traffic was folks who lived there coming to and from work. Theo did not turn her gaze from the window as he pulled up the crib bars. He told her to ring for help if she wanted to get up, showing them both the cord with the button and then sliding it under her hand. Nothing he said or did shifted her attention from the line of houses outside, each one the same size but painted a different color of yellow or green or gray.

Isah turned to Mr. Early. "Make yourself at home." He gestured toward a recliner chair exactly like the one in the hospital. "It's big enough to sleep in if you need to, okay, man? I got to get on to other things. You all right now?"

Mr. Early told him he was, shaking his hand and thanking him for his time.

Then it was just the two of them.

It was a pleasant evening. The best they'd had in many a time. They sat gazing out at the houses across the way, Theo in her bed, Mr. Early in his chair. The afternoon dimmed into evening. A single streetlight winked on. Then another. Pools of wet leaves steamed strands of heat off the sidewalk into the chilling air. Night clouds fingered over the darkening mountains.

Eventually the view froze into a stillness of houses and parked cars under the streetlights. Mr. Early stirred himself. There were things left to do.

He got Theo's attention to where he could unpack, her pointing and him putting things where she wanted. He asked Theo if they shouldn't make a list of what she might need from home.

She looked surprised. Maybe she had not thought how she would be staying and he would be going. But the girls were waiting for him. The twins. He saw her remember that.

Mr. Early got busy looking for a paper and something to write with.

"Goo-oo-ood evening." A middle-aged woman came striding through the door, white-yellow curls bouncing around her ears. She put him in mind of a palomino he'd seen, rare as they were, in a visitation of Mexican cowboys that rode in the Garnet parade one year, tricked up with silvered hackamores and hammered stirrups. She was like that too. Shiny. Alert as any horse would be high-stepping down a foreign street between lines of hollering children and waving flags.

"I am Mrs. Hipps, but I hope you will call me Dee Dee," she said, slipping a thermometer into his wife's mouth. "Welcome to Solace, Mrs. Early. I'm a supervisor. I'll be on until about midnight tonight." Theo could not reply with her mouth full. "And you must be Mr. Early," she said, all the while reaching under the quilt, touching Theo's hands and then moving down to hold onto each of her feet in turn. "You seem warm enough. You alright there?" The thermometer started beeping. She pulled it out and squinted. "That's fine. You're doing just fine. Now your supper will be here any minute." She turned to Mr. Early, "Did anybody show you around?" He wasn't sure what to say. By the time he was sure, she already had him by the hand, winking at Theo. "I'm going to borrow your husband for just a second."

Miz Hipps pulled him out, near-running him down the hallway to a big room at the far end.

"This is our Solace family room. You can use it any time."

It was the size of maybe two bedrooms. Crank-handle windows opened to a ring of pines Mr. Early could just make out in the gloom. A TV, bigger than his own, sat on the opposite wall. There were chairs and sofas. Miz Hipps said one of them was fold-out for folks as stayed over. Mr. Early wondered, if he didn't go home, whether he would have to sleep there on the fold-out and not in with his wife, but he could not find a way to ask about it.

"Come on. Come on." Miz Hipps flew down the hallway past doors with in them different sick people, mostly very old.

Something slowed her outside a room catty-corner from Theo's. It had in it a mountain boy who looked like Mr. Early himself in his twenties only maybe forty pounds lighter to be a shell of skeleton, nothing more. He lay in his bed, his face stringy-boned, his pole neck covered with dark brown patches like a pied pig. There were spots on his cheeks and forehead too. His leaky eyes slid from Miz Hipps to Mr. Early with one of them wandering off sideways on its own. Mr. Early couldn't think whether those eyes were seeing much of anything at all. It might be Miz Hipps spoke to him, but Mr. Early was hearing nothing for watching that one stray eye rolling around in the boy's head like a marble in a bowl.

"Come on, come on!" Miz Hipps led off down the hall again. She showed him the front parlor with a stand-up piano, then steered him into a place she called the Meditation Room. "You can bring in your Bible if you want to. It's just some folks need to *not* call it praying while they do just that."

The room was narrow like a closet. It did not have the usual cross or pews, only some pillows on the floor and a squat yellow candle burning perfume into the air. One round window sat high on the wall, pieces of colored glass making pictures, he could see, of nurses and a dove at the top.

"It's quiet," he said to be respectful. Miz Hipps allowed as how it was.

"We have lots of different people here," she whispered. "That's why there's not much church to it."

Miz Hipps took him to the kitchen last. She introduced him to the lady in charge there, a Miss Cherille, announcing that he was Miz Early's husband who was new in 5-B.

As tiny as Miss Cherille was, she stood tall in her work shoes. She looked like something out of a child's story book, her hair more like fur and cut the way his mama had always cut his, setting a bowl on his head and scissoring off everything that stuck out from the rim.

Miss Cherille put down her tray of acorn squash to shake Mr. Early's hand. She told him, smiling, that this was the roost she ruled. She showed him the part of the kitchen table he could go to and the part he could not because, she said, they had to keep that part medicine-clean to prepare food for those that were truly deep sick.

"Over here, where you visitors can go," she said, "I always keep a pitcher of water. Most days there's something to eat if ever you are hungry."

Right then and there she scooped up a plastic plate of cookies, each one shaped like a leaf with orange sprinkles, all of them regular to be store-bought, most likely of sugar. Mr. Early said, "No, thank you," before thinking because that's what he always did even though the cookies looked appetizing.

Miss Cherille tipped her head to look at him. "Early...?" she said. "Where're your people from?"

He told her Little Piney.

"I knew it. I knew it. I'm a Meade of the Dulaney-Meades down in Big Piney. I believe we knew an Early. A Letta-Jean Early raised the ponies."

"That would be my mama."

"Lord save us, my brother and I used to take lessons from your mama. How is she doing?"

"She passed."

"Aw, God love her. My mama too. Did you go to the Piney schools?"

"Yes'm."

"Oh, well, my mama sent us all the way in to Garnet for our school." Miss Cherille laughed. "Been in Garnet ever since. Married a MacLaine, but after Toby MacLaine feathered himself a second nest with that check-out girl over to the Kmart, I took my own good name back." She rared up like a barnyard goose. "Born a Meade, I shall be buried a Meade."

"The way you're going, you surely will," said Miz Hipps. The two of them laughed.

Miss Cherille held the plate of store-bought cookies out to Mr. Early. "Go on and have you some. A home nurse brought them in from the Bi-Lo." Miz Hipps helped herself. Mr. Early took just the one.

"I'll make sure your wife eats. Fix for you too if need be. You come on any time. Just remember to take that side of the table."

Mr. Early nodded.

Miz Hipps reached for one more cookie. "Don't you want to take that parka off, Mr. Early? There's some hangers in your wife's room. You know your way back."

He found Theo raised up in bed with a supper tray swung over her lap. She did not seem to know he was there. He watched her poke at the food like a chicken sorting dirt from seed. Holding her fork backward like a child, she squinted closer and closer at the tray until finally her nose touched the collards and Mr. Early had to wipe it off. She did not mind. He let her do as she pleased, unwrapping a small cup of juice and turning her plate around slowly to where she could get at the creamed corn which she dearly loved.

She took a bite or two.

"Theo?"

She did not respond.

"Theo?"

Mr. Early let go of her and took a step back. Then another. He wanted to see if she would notice, but she did not. Her face never came up from fidgeting with the corn, spreading the kernels apart on her plate, sniffing at them like a dog.

That's when Mr. Early thought he might could slip away to home. She'd never know he wasn't there or even where he was until morning, and by then he could be right back in his chair for her to wake up to.

He took another step back, watching. He wondered, should he tell Miz Hipps he was leaving, backing up now clear out of Theo's room with his parka still on, set to go. But, turning, he was brought up short in the hallway.

Coming out of the room across from Theo's was a spaceman.

A spaceman.

It scared Mr. Early so bad his heart liked to stop, jumping with a jolt and then hurting to where he could not breathe.

It was a spaceman in a space uniform like on TV only yellow instead of silver, a saggy suit with big gloves and boots and a curved mask Mr. Early couldn't see inside of for the light glancing off and the reflection of his own self moving watery across the front.

The spaceman was dragging a huge plastic bag, yellow like his uniform, a bag so heavy that he had to kick and pull at it to get into the hallway. He tilted his head, seeming to take a breath and then heaved, pull-stepping away from Mr. Early, yanking the bag behind him as he pushed out of sight through a door that said EMPLOYEES ONLY.

The room he left behind was empty, the bed sheetless.

Where was the marble-eyed boy?

Mr. Early knew without knowing what he knew, and the knowing made him so lightheaded he had to put his hand back to the wall behind him to sit down right there in the hallway.

"Mr. Early? Mr. Early?" He heard it the second time, looking up into Isah's face.

"You all right, man?" Isah asked, crouching now at face level. "What happened? Too much excitement?"

Dee Dee Hipps came running. "That's all we need!" She put his wrist between her fingers like he'd seen the nurses do with Theo.

Theo. My God. Theo. Had she seen the spaceman? Mr. Early looked toward her door, but sitting where he was, he could not see inside. *Please God,* he prayed, *please let her never set eyes on a thing like that.*

"What happened?" Miz Hipps was asking.

"I got a mite tippy," he said, doing his best to get up until they helped with both arms and he was right again.

Angels in heaven and earth below, he wanted out of that place. He wanted out that very second like a horse on the big scales. "I have to go," he said, pulling their hands off him, aiming for the vestibule and the parking lot beyond.

But Miz Hipps came after him. "You shouldn't be driving. We need to check your blood pressure." She snatched at his jacket sleeve while Isah pushed from behind. Together they got him turned around and seated in the parlor with Miz Hipps scolding him gently, talking about how they had their hands full enough without him fainting behind the wheel and sending himself and God knows how many others to the hospital to burden busy health care professionals like themselves.

All the while she was putting a band around his arm, puffing it up and listening with her earpiece. Mr. Early sat quiet. *Maybe I dreamed it,* he thought. *Maybe I dreamed the bed with no sheets.*

Miz Hipps said he sounded all right now, but just to be careful. It had been a big day bringing his wife in and seeing to her the way he had.

Mr. Early all but bolted, the spaceman with the plastic bag still fresh burned into the backs of his eyeballs like the opposite of a Santa come to give something nice from his sack. The very opposite.

Striding now to his truck, hearing its solid squeal as the door opened, feeling the sharp curlicues of the torn seat poking at his backside, Mr. Early wrenched the gear shift, punching now the brake, now the gas, hauling that truck, by God, out of its parking place, roaring away from Solace up one road to the next and from that to another, on and on until he got to his own road, to their home road.

He pulled into the driveway. The dogs ran alongside barking, not with alarm but with pleasure, having heard the familiar sound of the motor, baying when he jerked to a stop and running first to the passenger door, then back around to his own when that didn't open.

Do Not Withhold Your Coat

Pam and Walker Crowe
Afternoon

The morning dribbled by as Walker predicted with not a soul coming through the Mountain Man. That meant hours of re-penning faded price tags and moving a display of cut-from-scrap honey-dippers out from under the big carved goose into plainer view on a sideboard doily.

Was it any wonder that Hazel Gurley's face in the door some time after lunch might just as well have been the Savior Himself? Even as grim as old gravy, Hazel was company.

In she came, wheezing from walking. She had a patient with her, a frail man who made his way through the door with the help of two canes. One was homemade, the crooked branch of no special tree. The other, much shorter, ran straight and tapered, shiny black wood with what looked to be real silver at the top. Clearly the man had no sense of who anybody was or where he might be, but he was very good about touching things. He looked to Hazel first and, if she nodded *Yes,* he set his canes down to take things up very carefully. Mostly all he wanted was to pat the old tools in the corner, the worn hoe handles and pitchforks that city tourists took home by the carful in high season.

Pam loved a Hazel visit because Hazel would chat, and chat moved the day along. Walker loved a Hazel visit because women-talk generally meant he could prop back in a tufted chair next to the open side door and take a snooze. Not so today, though, because here was Hazel asking them both had they noticed the girl at the bus stop.

What girl? they asked.

The one at the bus stop. Had they not seen her on their way to lunch? Wearing a coat as if it were the November it was supposed to be instead of boiling hot?

They said they had not. They said they'd seen Larry Pine sticking his head out from the office over at the Esso—they still called it the Esso even though the sign had long since been switched to EXXON. Larry'd waved them over to say he'd heard the Second Time Around Shop was closing so they'd carried their sandwiches around the other way to go by, and sure enough the sign there said CLOSED UNTIL FURTHER NOTICE.

Which set Hazel off talking about the town and how could anybody make a living with the Bi-Los and the Rite Drugs coming in, so that the three of them lost all track of her original question.

The whole day went that way, one distraction after another. It wasn't until nigh onto 4:30 that Jonelle Hipps came up the street in a tizzy.

"Oh dear, oh dear!"

Tizzy was Jonelle's middle name. Eyes outsized by layers of eye shadow progressing from deep purple to a frosty white, she came straight to the counter where Pam was re-setting arrowheads inside the case.

"It's Beau McCallum. Poor man doesn't have enough to do keeping the Rexall going all by his lonesome when he gets wind—maybe a half hour ago, no more—he gets wind that that little girl who works for him—you know, the simple one?"

"Are you speaking of Cadence?" Pam and Walker both caught what was coming before it came.

"Oh, yes, Cadence, that's it," Jonelle rattled on. "It seems that she's been sitting out at the bus stop all day long."

"Cadence Greevey?"

"You know her?"

"Cadence is Verleana Greevey's girl. Verleana Pole Greevey—who works for us here in the shop."

"Worked for us," Walker corrected.

Jonelle looked stricken. "She is Verleana's girl, of course she is. What was I thinking? Honestly, some days, you can put one and one smack in front of me, I still won't get to two. What a pity, a child like that and Verleana with no husband." It looked like Jonelle would send her head clean off her neck, she was shaking it so hard. "That explains it. Beau said he came in early for inventory. He brought his lunch from home, so he never set foot out all day to see her. Mind you, I was in and out too, up to the Pay Less for a chicken sandwich and over to the post office, but that would all be going the other way."

Walker was sorting it through. "We went by there this morning. We didn't see her."

Pam was adamant, "We know Cadence. She was not there."

All the while, Jonelle was waving her hands, vibrating them like she had the tremors. "No, no. Come to find out, she wasn't at the bus stop the whole time. Apparently, she's been riding the bus to Garnet. To Garnet and back. All day long. By herself. Why? Because her mama's at Solace. Did ya'll know this?"

Pam shook her head, *No*, meaning, *Don't let this be true.*

Jonelle hardly took a breath. "Beau told me he got a call yesterday from a nurse or some such. Him with his own family to take care of, but they called him, because the child gave them his number."

Pam let out a little gasp and sank down on her stool.

"Now, this nurse told him that Cadence's daddy was coming down from the North to look after her. As far as Beau knew, she was safe in her daddy's hands. So imagine his surprise when he steps out of the store this afternoon, just to shake the mud off the mud mat, and there she is sitting all by herself."

"At the bus stop…" Pam barely got the words out.

Walker could see distress building in his wife's face. "What happened to her daddy?" he asked on her behalf.

"No one knows." Jonelle tapped her pointing finger back and forth on the counter with each syllable.

"Her daddy is Bobby," Pam said. "You remember? Bobby O. Greevey?"

"Who doesn't?" Jonelle rolled her eyes.

Pam felt so sick she needed to lean over. Had she been a personage of the Bible, she'd be rending her garments by now. Once again—once again in her foolishness!—the good Lord had spoken, crying out to her all day long through ordinary people, heralds and prophets asking her about a little girl, a *strange* little girl, begging her on His behalf to go to the aid of a child. Had she heeded His message? No.

Walker knew that look on his wife's face. He could almost hear her inner recriminations as she began to rock side to side.

Jonelle turned to him. "The poor child must have walked, don't you think? Walked into town with her coat and her purse and her money. She told Beau she got on the bus not once but three times! How does that make any sense?"

"Different buses, different routes," Walker suggested.

"With different drivers. Oh, that's good."

Walker was putting it together now. "She must have got on, paid her money and rode for a while. Long enough that a driver might ask where she was going..."

Pam had one of the counter drawers half-open, reaching for a tissue. She froze. "Solace." She looked at Walker in horror. "Solace. Hospice. Hospital. The driver asked her where she was going and she said, 'The hospital,' and he said, 'Which hospital?' but she didn't know."

"Oh, that's it." Jonelle's voice warmed.

Pam saw things clearly now. "He probably rode her in and rode her right back again. Because you can tell there's something not quite right, you can tell by her face. Any driver could see that. He probably asked her, did she know how to get home and she said, 'Yes,' because that child was taught by her mother to tell the truth, and the truth is, she knows how to walk herself home. So he opened those bus doors right there at the bench and told her to hie herself back up the mountain where she belonged."

"But she didn't," said Walker.

"She did not," Pam finally pulled out a tissue. "She tried another bus instead. Because her heart was set on seeing her mama."

Walker watched Pam dab at the corners of her eyes, praying to a God he wasn't nearly as sure of as his wife, praying for Him to spare her, spare them both her suffering over the suffering of others, real or imagined. Most times, it was imagined, but that never stopped Pam. Not since they'd gotten their own children up and out of the house. Ever since, she'd taken to worrying over the world as if the fate of every wounded sparrow was in her hands.

Jonelle went back to her head wagging. "Well, ya'll are making a heap more sense than Beau. He said that after he found her, Cadence clammed up on him. Even started to cry, which, according to him, is not her usual thing."

"Oh, Jonelle…" Pam wiped her nose. Her rocking side to side lurched back to front. "The fact is, Maggie Dull saw her this morning. You remember Maggie? She's in town visiting her mother. She asked about a 'strange girl' on the bus bench. And then Hazel Gurley came in saying the same thing. I paid them no mind."

"We didn't know," Walker pleaded with her. He could see those rain-clouds getting ready to burst.

"We should have known!" Pam was out-and-out crying now.

"I hear the child's mama went crazy," Jonelle said.

And just like that, like a faucet shutting off, the tears stopped. Pam's eyes locked on her husband. "Walker, we have done that child a disservice." She was already standing, pushing papers into drawers, grabbing her purse.

"Don't you say that, Pammy." He spoke as if Jonelle weren't there, coming over to her, taking her hand in his. "We've done a world of good for her mother. Kept her working all these years when we hardly do enough business to cover ourselves."

Pam batted his hand away. "Verleana Greevey has been our salvation, not the other way around! Her being here kept us from working ourselves into an early grave!"

Walker grabbed for her again, trapping her hand between the two of his. "We went way beyond the call of duty."

Here came Jonelle's hand covering the both of theirs. "You two are going to heaven for all you did, don't you forget it. The child will be all right. Beau said he gave her a packet of flower Kleenex and she loved it. The tears dried right up and out came a big smile."

Thinking on it summoned the rooster in Walker. He could feel himself rise up as if he had a chest of feathers, as if there was a bright red comb there on top of his head. "Where on earth is her daddy?"

"Beau says—she says —*he's* in the hospital."

"Oh, Lord," said Pam. "She's confused."

"Con-fused," Jonelle said, putting an emphasis on the word to mean, *She's a whole lot more than confused.*

Pam felt like she was spiraling into quicksand. Not that she was likely to experience quicksand, but she'd read about it, how things looked solid enough and you took a step and suddenly you were sinking and couldn't get out.

Jonelle thinned down her lips. "What a calamity of errors."

Pam gave Walker her tragic face. "We'd best head over to see Beau." She got free of his hands to clip her purse closed.

Walker was desperate. He spoke before thinking. "What about the shop?"

"For heaven's sake, Walker Crowe, on a Monday? The Monday before Thanksgiving? We won't do a cent of business. It was idiotic for you to insist on opening in the first place."

Walker knew right then and there to keep his mouth tight shut.

"Always thinking about money!" Pam locked the cash drawer and huffed past him. "Throw the deadbolt on the back door. We've got to see about Verleana's girl."

Walker felt the tide of their shared life rushing out, sucking the days to come in the wrong direction, away from simple hearth and home back out into an ocean of family obligation, the stormy sea he'd paddled across for decades to find, at last, a quiet cove, a child-unburdened porch where he and Pam—and no one else—could take their ease. No hope of that now.

Walker went to the back door. His wife went to the front. Jonelle stood in between, not sure who to follow, but calling out, "I believe Beau already took the girl home."

Pam stopped under the stag's head. "Then we'll go by her house. Probably nobody there to see she has supper."

Walker was buying time, turning off lights.

"You are going to heaven," Jonelle purred.

Pam pushed the front door open so forcefully that the Country Christmas Wreath which she'd only just mounted—a circle of rusted jingle bells and metal ribbons twisted out of old tobacco cans—crashed against the glass causing the OPEN sign to flip over to CLOSED on its own.

"I am not going to heaven, nor near any such place!" her voice rang out over the clanging. "God sends His messengers to me, one after the other, and I no-mind them like they was morning magpies."

Walker came running, even as she pointed three fingers to the sky, saying, "'Faith, hope and charity! And the greatest of these—?'"

Walker knew what she wanted him to say, but silence was his only way of speaking now. Of saying, *Stop.* Of saying, *Wait.* Of saying, *Have we not done enough?*

"—Charity!" Pam sang it out, "Not redbirds. Not bags of powdered donuts—charity!"

Pam held the door open, waving them out. "I am going straight to hell."

The bell wreath crashed again as the door slammed shut.

Home Is Where The Heart

Bobby O. Greevey
Evening

...is, thought Bobby. *At least home is where my heart is. Though why I bother...*

He was fit to be tied. He'd made do with scant spoonfuls of the tepid mash hospitals called food. Meanwhile the late shift had come on reducing all hallway bustle to the rattle of an occasional service cart. There was nothing to do, nothing even to look at but a surround of wallpaper—lavender and beige—and linoleum—more lavender and beige—all of it glazed with a rubberized sheen that guaranteed sponge-able surfaces. Now, *now* Bobby was feeling lonely. The phone call didn't help.

"Listen, honey," Paco said. Not insincere. Meaning the "honey." But inside the placating tone, Bobby heard irritation. "They're holding you for observation, that's all. The X-ray looked normal."

"Krystal is dead."

"I know. Our baby's gone." Finally some feeling in Paco's voice. "It was too much for her, the long drive, the snow. I shouldn't have let you take her."

Bobby did not trust himself to speak. Here he was in the hospital, for Christ's sake, and Paco was worried about the damn car.

"Think of it as vacation. Lie around. Get waited on hand and foot. Play the near-death thing—which the doctors say it wasn't, by the way—play it for all it's worth. But if some hunky RN offers you physical therapy, babe, it's extremities only, got me? With one of the girl nurses."

Still Bobby didn't laugh, so Paco tried his lawyer voice. "You'll be gone by morning. There isn't any point in my rushing down. You okay with that?"

Bobby said he was. He thought he was. He was doing his it's-only-a-flesh-wound routine to the point that he had himself fooled.

"By the time I got there, you'd be in Pineburg or Pineville—"

"Piney. Little Piney."

"—whatever—and I'd have cancelled clients. Which reminds me: the garage keeps calling. Some problem with your schedule. Can you call them? Tomorrow of course. Does your head hurt?"

Bobby said, "No." He meant *Yes.* He didn't want to tell Paco how he really felt. Like an orphan in some World War II movie, a tragic boy from Dresden or Bucharest, plucked out of the bomb wreckage, lying on a bare white cot in a strange refugee camp with a deep intuition that his entire family had been wiped out and that he was alone. Alone.

Paco was supposed to pick up on that. He was supposed to hear the bravery in a little boy's voice and say, "Hang on. I'll be right there…"

Mercifully, Bobby had the room to himself until some time after Paco's begging off when an emaciated woman was wheeled in. She looked like the specter of everything he never wanted to become, a bent, sexless frame covered with skin.

"Temporary," the aides said. Bad weather had filled every spare bed.

The poor thing was conscious. She nodded to Bobby. Then a sheet with an interlocking pattern of lavender lightning bolts got pulled screeling between them on a flimsy metal track. At least Bobby didn't have to look at her, but he could hear every tiny shift on the other side of the curtain, each sound a testament to some imagined detail of hospital discomfort.

Bobby turned on the television to distract himself. Re-runs spooled: *Hee Haw. Mutual of Omaha's Wild Kingdom.* He and Paco used to watch mindless TV together back when they were dating, back when it was okay to be unserious. Before they decided to share the joys of mortgages and car payments.

Paco was right, of course. He couldn't very well cancel clients. Cancelled clients meant cancelled checks. Between the two of them in a brand new house, they had precious little left with which to pay for their Christmas get-away, the gay-friendly bed-and-breakfast Paco had found, some winter refuge up in Michigan known for cross-country skiing. They'd do maybe an hour of that, just enough to earn themselves endless hours in front of a fire with toddies and blankets. They'd both been pulling long hours. They needed a break.

Bobby eyed his dinner tray. A trio of disposable serving cups wrapped in plastic had rained droplets of condensation to form mini swamps and deltas in the cooling food. Couldn't someone take it away? Where were the orderlies?

A sharp rapping made Bobby's heart jump. If only he could see around the wretched curtain to the door.

"Mrs. Weissman? I'm Doctor Davis. I will be your anesthesiologist tomorrow. Your family asked me to come by and check on you. Do you mind if I sit down?"

Bobby heard chair legs scraping on the other side of the sheet. He kept the TV volume low enough to catch something about a "procedure." The doctor seemed to be suggesting, dancing around it, but getting the gist across, that Mrs. Weissman's chances weren't the best in the world.

And then the guy was wrapping things up, the chair scraping again. "Trust in the Lord Jesus," he said, "as will I, as will everyone on your surgical team."

Whoa, Bobby thought, *is this a Bible hospital?* Nobody'd asked about his spiritual affiliation when they checked him in and thank God, because he was a poster child for the lapsed. He and Paco worshipped at the Church of Lattes and the Sunday Paper.

"Embrace your Savior, Mrs. Weissman," the doctor said. "He'll be right there beside you."

And then a tumult erupted. From the sound of it, people crowding into the room from the hallway. Lots of them. Lots of "Hey, Mama's and "There you are, Mommy's." Someone pulled the sheet-curtain back and peered around at Bobby, a heavy-set man in a reindeer V-neck. Had Christmas come early?

"Good evening, brother."

Bobby nodded.

"We disturbing you?"

Bobby shook his head and pointed to the TV as if he couldn't hear a thing. As if he weren't hanging onto every word.

"God bless you, son." The man pulled the curtain back into place.

A woman's voice, youngish, gushed good will: "Mother, we are so blessed to have Doctor Davis come in at this hour to talk to you about your surgery."

Still no word from Mrs. Weissman herself. The doctor's voice chimed in, "Before I leave, I wonder if we might say a word of prayer together."

There was some shuffling. People must have stepped in toward the bed because their shapes disappeared from the curtain.

"O Lamb of God, that takest away the sins of the world, have mercy upon Mrs. Isaac Weissman here tonight. Grant her peace in her heart as we care for her body, commending her spirit to Your everlasting love. In Jesus' name, Amen."

There were lots of "Amen's. Then a host of "Thank you's!". The doctor took his leave.

A man spoke up, maybe Mr. Reindeer Sweater, announcing that they would be in the cafeteria. "Goodnight, Mother Weissman." Footsteps receded in the hall. Then, nothing.

Bobby waited.

"We're doing what we think is best, Mother."

Finally a new voice came, part snarl, part burp: "Leave. Me. Alone."

"Mother."

At greater volume, "Get the hell out of my face!"

"That's the Devil talking, Mother."

The voice rose from unnatural bass to baritone: "It's your father screaming from his grave!"

There was a rustle of sheets or a blanket. "Come on, Mother. Lie down. We love you. Jesus loves you."

The mother's voice, hoarse, lost its oomph: "My hand to God. . .!"

More rustling.

Bobby held himself still, gaze locked on the TV screen.

The woman said a stiff goodnight to her mother.

A chair scraped.

A bag rustled.

Shuffle shuffle.

Tromp tromp.

Silence.

Bobby held himself absolutely still. Nothing stirred from the other side of the curtain. Was the woman awake? Maybe she was holding her breath, listening the way he was.

He tried to watch TV. A commercial flashed by featuring a snappy red pickup shot from every angle like an action sequence in a movie, but he couldn't keep his mind on it because his feet were blocks of ice. Maybe the accident had damaged the part of his brain that controlled body temperature. Maybe he'd freeze to death right there in the bed, but nobody would know because he was too busy being a tough guy to ring for help until it was too late and he'd pass out or fall asleep like the guys who froze to death up on Everest and they'd find him in the morning gray-dead in the bed, maybe sliding out a little with one arm dangling, rigor mortis preserving his last gesture as he reached for a telltale alarm button lying on the floor.

Bobby wormed down into the single blanket they'd given him, curling his feet up to his butt. *Go to sleep,* he told himself as if he were his own mother, *Go to sleep...* when he heard a noise, much too quiet, much too close. In a heartbeat, he shot his body around, twisting in time to see clawlike fingers cribbled around the sheet curtain, pulling it back as, oh so slowly, the grizzled hair, then temple, then wide right eyeball of Mrs. Weissman came into view. Just that much. The one terrible saucer eye staring at him.

"Ah, God!" he clutched his blanket, flinching up and backwards to the far side of the bed.

She used the sheet as a veil, holding it over her face, then getting her two eyes, her nose into view. "Run for your life!" she hissed.

She came around the sheet now. Her skinny-sick right arm trailing an IV line, she shuffled up next to the bed—*his* bed, for God's sake—and leaned over him to whisper, "They're going to kill me."

Bobby was instantly out the door yelling.

Nurses came running, shaking their heads in disbelief. "We gave her enough to flatten a horse."

Bobby could see it all from the hallway. The woman fought, eyes open but blind, like a show he'd seen on TV about sharks, how you could kill one, but it would keep swimming because apparently sharks had brains in their spines that kept them moving, alive or dead, zombie sharks with dead eyes whose tails kept them going forward toward nothing. That was Mrs. Weissman. She was fighting for her life and she was not going to make it. In the morning they'd slap her onto an operating table with Dr. Bible Thumper quoting scripture over her drug-coma'ed body and the family out in the waiting room in a prayer circle. Praying for her when she didn't have a prayer.

But it wouldn't be Jesus calling her home, Bobby thought. It would be Isaac. Wasn't that the name? Mrs. *Isaac* Weissman? Surely her husband would elbow Jesus out of the way. Surely he'd be there to welcome her to the other side, to the place where his people, their people, their blood people, welcomed the dead. Surely Isaac was waiting for his bride.

They tied the woman down in her crib, hands and feet, explaining the restraints to her as if she could understand. Adam, the nurse in charge, pumped a syringe of something into her IV line. After a minute, her breathing steadied. She stopped moving.

Bobby didn't move either, plastered to the far wall of the hallway, looking into the dark room from the bright light outside.

Adam came out to him with a that-was-a-close-one grin. He was a tall guy, maybe in his thirties. African-American. Lean. Probably a jogger. He'd been on when Bobby arrived the night before. He was on again, and thank God, because Adam was a brother in every sense of the word.

"That should do it," he said to Bobby.

"I'm not staying."

Adam stopped in his tracks. "Look, we've got a quiet room down at 14-C. We could put you in there."

"No. I'm checking out," said Bobby, "I'm going home."

"You can't check out. A doctor has to do that."

"That's not true." Bobby smiled. It came in handy, living with a lawyer. "I *can* check out. I have been given no medication other than Tylenol. I am not a danger to myself or others. I am leaving this hospital." He walked right past Mrs. Weissman to the closet. His suitcase was there. So were his pants, his shoes, the blood-stained shirt.

Adam came in after him, "You're going to have to sign a release."

"I'll sign anything you want."

Which Bobby did. They pulled some poor resident out of his catnap to get an official non-approval. He warned Bobby about leaving the hospital too early. Bobby said he understood. He signed sheaves of papers including one acknowledging that he'd refused a wheelchair.

Adam asked where he would go. Bobby told him Cincinnati. Adam asked, "How?" and Bobby said, "A rental car." At which point they both laughed. Fat chance in Smallville, USA at that hour. It was the middle of the night, for God's sake. By then they were buddy-buddies. Bobby asked for his suggestion.

"The only thing I can think of is a bus," Adam said.

Buses made Bobby nauseous. He hadn't gotten near one since he was a kid, but come hell or high water, he was going home.

A volunteer at the entry desk called a cab, her eyes lingering momentarily on the blood-wrecked shirt under Bobby's jacket. He could have put on a clean one. He didn't want to.

Waiting outside felt good. Great in fact. The cold air was bracing. Bobby pictured himself standing there, his breath clouding back into his face, the patch of gauze on his head looking kind of cool. Like he was a lowlife in some gangster caper, the type who'd wear a cocked fedora and have a cigarette hanging out of his mouth.

He was seeing the whole movie now. Him easing into a beat-up cab. The driver noticing him wince in the rearview. Maybe feeling a little sorry for him. Maybe suggesting they stop for a cup of coffee, a slab of pie. Maybe sitting in a diner watching the streetlights wink off as dawn came crawling up out of the gutters onto the snow-banked streets, Bobby dazzling the driver with tales of his exploits.

The cab came alright. But there was no pie in the deal. No coffee either. Bobby was driven through what was clearly the wrong side of town, past a stretch of neglected strip malls to the bus station at the far end. He handed the driver a wad of bills—*Keep the change!*—wheeling his bag around a row of bums slumped at the curb.

Several hours later, rumpled and bandaged like a returning war hero, Bobby climbed aboard a Greyhound, claiming two seats and settling back to suck down hours of fetid, diesel-soaked air. His stained shirt itched him, but he wasn't going to change. He wanted Paco to *see* when he opened the door. He wanted him to grasp in an instant the whole hideous journey—to take in the dried blood and florid bruising, to breathe the stench of cramped people on a cramped bus—and then to fold him in his arms. To ask him, finally, "Are you all right?"

Absence Makes

August Early
After Suppertime

Mr. Early was late for supper. "Better late than never," Miss Susan said, holding her screen door ajar. Always the sharpness to her voice. It was no wonder she and Theo were friends.

The twins had stayed with Miss Susan Neville the last couple of nights just as Theo had planned. So that he could come and go. So that they could get on with their lives. Truth be told, Mr. Early wanted to see them every minute of every day, but it confused his mind. To lose their mama and now their gramama. He had no idea what to say to them. And Miss Susan was such a body of busyness when he was there, always doing for them, having them to finish their milk or wiping their mouths or fixing their socks to go with their dresses. It was hard to get a word in.

Mr. Early could barely get his boots off what with the girls grabbing for him, Sue-Sue nigh on to yelling that Miss Susan had done her hair a new way and did he like it.

He said he did, though he didn't remember the old way.

Serena was quiet as always. Since her baby years, she'd had Sue-Sue do the talking for her. Serena made him nervous, the way she looked at him.

Both girls were on their best behavior for supper, bathed and dressed in summer play clothes. They did not ask about Theo at all. Mr. Early thought Miss Susan was behind that, telling them not to trouble him in his trouble. But he wanted them to ask, because it was harder when he had to speak first.

She fed him a good pork chop with applesauce and noodles, getting up and down from her chair. Late as he was, she'd held the girls' supper to eat with him. They allowed as how it was a good meal.

Then Miss Susan had them go into the front room on the couch. "Go sit," she told the girls. She retired to the kitchen. Mr. Early could hear the running of sink water, but no splashing. He imagined her standing at the door listening. He knew she did that for his wife so that she could say later, or at least know in her heart, that she'd done the best she could for Theo's babies.

Mr. Early sat with his girls, Sue-Sue to his left and Serena to hers. Their jig-addled legs bounced up and down on the seat cushion.

"What'd ya'll do all day?" he asked, completely forgetting school.

"School," they both said.

"That's good. And then you come home?"

"No. We come to Miss Susan," said Sue-Sue, setting him straight.

"That's right." He looked at his shoes and their shoes and how tiny-small their feet were and then there was that water in his eyes again. There was no place for him to look that made it better.

Serena fidgeted on her side of the couch, raising up enough that she could reach over her sister to touch his ear.

"Your hair needs cutting, Daddy. It's sticking out like feathers on a old hen." Both of them laughed.

When would he tell them it was Grampa, not Daddy?

Theo would say, "Never," but he saw they were growing. Any time now, some child on the playground would ask them, "Ain't your daddy kinda old to be your daddy?" or "Ain't your mommy really your gramommy?" and the whole thing would come spilling out. It wasn't their fault about their real-true mama. It wasn't anybody's fault. But Theo didn't want them thinking their own mother had chosen the drugs over them. Which she had. But Theo didn't want it said.

"Don't jump on the couch," bossed Sue-Sue.

Mr. Early patted the hair down around his head. He supposed he did need a haircut. Theo'd managed the last one, sick as she was. Out on the back steps, as always. He'd come away feeling naked since his wife's eyesight was none too good by then and she'd cut him a little close.

"Don't jump on Miss Susan's nice sofa." Mr. Early tried to sound mad, but he couldn't. Serena settled herself half in Sue-Sue's lap.

"I saw your mama today." He kept his eye on the middle of the hook rug. "We took her to a nice place they call Solace."

"When is she coming home?" asked Sue-Sue in her bossy voice.

"Well, now, your mama says she can't come home just yet. 'Cause she doesn't want to be bothered cleaning up after us. So she's going to stay there for a while."

The girls seemed to be pondering their all four knees.

"She don't want to come home." said Sue-Sue. It wasn't a question.

"No," he said, "That's not the way she told it to me. She says she *wants* to come home. But comin' home's a trial when you're sick." He picked at a stain of pork chop on his trouser leg. "Your mama ain't like everybody else. She has her ways and this is one of them."

Serena spoke up without bouncing. "Miss Susan says she is going to Jesus."

"To the angels," Sue-Sue corrected. "Is that true?" Both of them looking up at him, then looking to see what he was studying in the rug on the floor. It seemed like no one was breathing, not even Miss Susan hanging behind the kitchen door.

"We're all a-goin' to Jesus some day," he said. "It's no use to wonderin' why. You know from Bible school: 'The Lord works in —' what?"

"'In mysterious ways,'" said Sue-Sue, tapping her two hands on the sofa cushion for emphasis.

"'Mysterious ways...'" echoed her sister.

"There's nothin' for it, girls. There's nothin' for it."

Mr. Early wanted to be out of there so bad he could taste it, bitter in his mouth with the traces of sweet apple and pork juices. He could feel his boot heel on the door jam, hear the screen door slapping shut, his crunch stomping up the gravel drive, maybe slinging his Winchester and veering off into the woods, maybe heading deep in to one of the blinds up Brushy to wait—wait for a buck to cross into his sights and then think, *The Lord giveth and the Lord taketh away,* all the while moving the rifle as smooth and as steady as you please, thinking, *Now, Now Now,* knowing he had a clean kill and then, in the next moment, for the hell of it, for the sheer hell of it, thinking, *No.* He would let the damn thing go, that's what he told himself. He would re-set the safety down off the shot. He would let it go because on this night the Lord would give, but the Lord would not take away, and he would be the Lord, squatting all night among castoff leaves and low laurel, squatting in the one place any man would want to be, the moist skins of the galax reflecting, finally, a coming dawn.

Of course he could not do any of that. Instead he had to sit in pure misery on Miss Susan's blossom-bouquet couch as the two girls hovered half on and half off the cushion without much expression on their faces.

"Can we see her?" Serena asked as Sue-Sue said, "When can we see Mama?"

"She's wantin' to see you." He knew he was telling a lie. Despite all the sycamore in Theo, there were things for which she could not summon strength. More important to her than holding her babies one more time was their holding the notion of a mama whole and hale, a mama they could be proud of. After all she had gone through with her only child, that was the Theo she wanted them to remember.

"I will take you there. Not tomorrow 'cause you got school. But maybe after."

He stood, saying it was bedtime. They all three forgot the rule about Miss Susan's couch, because both girls jumped on it, arms raised, to play the old game. They were still small enough and he was still strong enough, one wrapping her arms tight around his neck, legs around his waist from the front, the other hanging on from the back, each with a face to one or the other of his ears and squealing, "Git up, y'old mule! Git up, Daddy!"

Mr. Early turned this way and that, trying to swing them off which, when they were littler, he could do. Now with them growing, they could ride him all day. They had his mother's legs, the long legs of born horse people. *Good for balance,* his mother used to say. Good riding was all about balance.

But it turned out daddy-riding was all about tight-on clinging. Mr. Early had to remind them every so often not to cut off his air, gripping his neck the way they were as he swung them down the hallway to the bedroom Miss Susan had made up.

And there, sure enough, was Miss Susan coming out of the kitchen from behind, showing him by her perfect timing that he'd been right about her listening.

"Get on offa your Daddy," she proclaimed, but tolerating the ruckus.

Then came the business of putting the girls to bed. Mr. Early made a joke of it, pretending to fall, rolling on them with just enough weight that they gasped laughing and had to let go.

"Shoes!" He used his papa bear voice which made them stop wiggling. Their all four feet went straight into the air.

"You're big girls now." He was roaring, hands on hips. "Get them shoes off!" They reached up and pulled their shoes off without lowering their legs, throwing them to the floor with four thumps——one, two, three, four.

"Whose house is this to make such a mess? Your'n?"

"No sir!" They had to bury their faces into the quilt for laughing.

"Get them nighties on!"

Miss Susan came up next to the bed, undressing and re-dressing the girls with him sitting watching and them acting like babies and having her to dress them until she got impatient and told them to help.

She led them in their prayers, the same sing-song words he'd said at their age: "…If I should die before I wake, I pray the Lord my soul to take."

Here they paused. "Bless Mama and Daddy and Miss Susan," said Serena.

"And Mama," said Sue-Sue.

"And Daddy," said Serena.

"And Mama," said Sue-Sue again with just the hint of a smile coming.

"And Daddy," said Serena with her a tiny-smile coming too, until Miss Susan said, "That's enough now."

Mr. Early could tell they weren't ready for sleep. They reached up for a neck hug, bouncing from knees to bare feet on the mattress, until he had to tell them to be good now, because Miss Susan was a saint just to let them stay with her.

And they were good girls, wriggling into the parts of the bed that suited them, grabbing and punching at pillows, both of them turning away from the light as he switched it off. Sue-Sue had her Bun-Bun. Serena had Flo. Must have been Theo had packed them along with the shirts and socks and sweaters she'd put in the twin princess suitcases. When had she done that? When had she known?

Mr. Early eased himself out behind Miss Susan who closed their door. She seemed of no mind to do much talking.

As always, Mr. Early thanked her for supper, for taking such good care. He asked her, was there anything she needed from him.

She told him to tell his wife—to be *sure* to tell his wife—that her girls were just fine. She always spoke of them as Theo's girls.

The night was a hollow stillness of no moon. Mr. Early walked back the fifty yards or so to his empty house. Empty except for the dogs circling and whining until, noting his quiet, they hushed up and quieted too.

He could not get used to the nobody in bed next to him. All he could do was lie and wait for night to swing itself back into morning, for the dogs to stir, for the sun to rise and tell him to get up and do, as if there were something that could be done.

TUESDAY

November 21, 1989

A Stitch In Time

Maggie Dull
Early Morning

Ropes of cigarette smoke curled out of her mother's nostrils into the chill. *Smoking herself into the grave,* Maggie thought. They were out on the side porch wrapped in blankets. Around them, at the edge of the yard, trees loomed like dark sentries determined to block the morning light.

"What was your name again?"

"Maggie."

"Ooooo, Margaret," her mother cooed. "That was my daughter's name."

A short laugh erupted, a snort really, so that Maggie had to spit her coffee back.

"Is that right?" Maggie stretched each vowel, her drawl a caricature, the parody of a self-appointed Samaritan dropping in on an ailing neighbor. "You say that *was* her name. Has your daughter passed?"

"Past caring about. Abandoned me long ago."

"No!" Maggie emulated surprise. "What kind of a daughter would do that?"

There was no answer.

Freedom's just another word…

Where was the sting? Maggie should have been smarting, but she wasn't. The whole thing was liberating, really: she and her mother finally having a heart-to-heart, because this wasn't her mother, she wasn't her child.

"Tell me, where did the name Margaret come from?" Margaret seemed such an old-lady name, so not the Jessica or Willow of Maggie's grade school classmates. She'd always assumed it came from some Dull relation.

"Margaret Hamilton," came the answer.

It didn't ring a bell.

"The Wicked Witch."

Was she talking *Oz?* Maggie managed to keep her face straight. "You mean of the West? You named your daughter after the Wicked Witch of the West?"

"Not the witch! The actress!" Her mother leaned in, conspiratorially, "She was no glamour puss, you know."

"The daughter or the witch?" Maggie asked.

Or both, she thought. *Ouch.* Here was the sting. The low maternal opinion to which Maggie had adjusted over the course of her entire life sank even lower. Apparently the woman had pegged her as both wicked and unsightly at birth.

Once again the sphinx-formerly-known-as-her-mother offered no answer. Her eyelids closed, one, two, out of sync like a broken doll's. Maggie was already used to the end-days rhythm of it all. One hour Chatty Cathy, the next, gonzo, head tipped over in mid-sentence, out like a light.

Sure enough, her mother was snoring again.

Hallelujah. A respite. It had been a long night of bagging and folding and vacuuming punctuated by maddeningly slow ramblings about the house, both physical and metaphysical, with her mother pointing out the supernatural purpose of the mess. How tinsel scared off flying devils. How snacks placed carefully by the fireplace tempted angels, who surely landed on rooftops to make their appearance via the chimney. Apparently her mother had them confused with Santa.

"Can't they walk through walls?" Maggie'd asked.

There had been no answer then. There wasn't one now.

Which left Maggie a blessed, glorious stretch of No Mom's Time to sip her coffee. Thank God the old girl kept some caffeine in the house, though judging from the matte finish of the grind, it packed a measly wallop. The brand was Maxwell House which Maggie didn't remember from the old days. Her mother always swore by Hills Brothers. Maybe that nurse had put the can in the fridge.

Maggie stared into a patch of beech trees beyond the driveway. Not a branch twitched. Not a leaf fell. The trunks, undressed of their summer, merged to a tissue of slate in the dawn light. Three crows had stationed themselves out on the road, a funereal tag team working the line of gravel for stray garbage.

Maggie'd forgotten how much she liked a porch sit, particularly as day broke. How long had it been since she'd stopped for a second? Her life had gotten so crazy. *Crazy.* The word made her smile. *Frantic,* maybe, but *crazy* these days meant something else.

Take the whole pearls thing. Her mother waking up in the night sometime between dealing with tinsel and rock salt, pointed at Maggie like a soon-to-be-slashee in some B horror movie and yelled, "Where are the pearls?" with Maggie asking again and again, "What pearls? Where?" until her mother pushed her hands away and said, "Where else?"

Where else. Zen *koans* had become her mother's preferred mode of communication. The irony being, it was so very Palo Alto. In Northern California, the cryptic was considered magical, full of meaning precisely because it was devoid of meaning. Maggie lived in a world where emptiness signified potential and potential was all, trumping the disheartening limitations of the real. She couldn't be more out of phase with it. Indeed, Maggie was a reality gal through and through. That's why she made such a good living out there. She flourished among the vague.

Maggie found the pearls—where else? In a red leather box at the back of the bedroom closet. She remembered sneaking it off the shelf as a girl to finger its contents, flaunting her mother's directive to keep her mitts out of there as if what lay within had some value.

How wrong could she be? The pearls inside were standard issue for women of her mother's generation, particularly women of no means. Too large, too round. Strung on string, not gut. But they had the desired effect. The minute Maggie got them on, her mother calmed down. Maggie had been wearing them ever since.

She glanced over in time to see her mother flicking a cigarette lighter up close to her face where there was no cigarette, a jet of flame shooting past her lips and nose, instantly torching the fringe of gray hair where there once were bangs.

Maggie jumped, screaming "Mother!" snatching up her blanket, even the blouse off her own body, pulling it from its buttons and rushing toward the burning woman, throwing everything she had at her mother's forehead, blouse and blanket, even lifting the hem of her skirt, to smother the smolder. The lighter went flying, as did Maggie's coffee. Her mother pawed her off, trying to breathe, trying to see.

"Jesus, mother, you're going to burn the house down and us with it!" Maggie gently pulled things back to take a look at the damage.

"I am not your mother," her mother hissed.

"My mistake." Maggie went on examining her. The hair was singed off at the top, of course. But only at the top. The skin was pink, a deep pink. Perhaps they would get away with nothing worse than a bad blister. Maggie stepped back to get a better look. The woman-formerly-known-as-her-mother glared daggers.

"Mrs. Dull, can we make a deal?" Maggie got busy rooting around in her mother's bathrobe pockets. She pulled two lighters from one, three from another, the cheap, plastic kind sold in packets of ten. "If you want a cigarette, ask me and *I* will light it. Okay? Promise me." Coaxing the woman to her feet and starting her back inside, glancing to see if there were any passers-by gawking at a woman in a bra guiding an elderly crone with a blouse on her head, thinking, *I've got to sterilize that burn.* Thinking, *Maybe we can do some sort of turban thing to hide the bald spot.* Thinking, *There is no way I can leave her alone again. Ever.*

Her mother put her hands up to where her bangs used to be. "She burned in that house."

"Who's that?" Maggie was settling her onto the living room couch.

"Old Miz Eargle."

Crackle-crackle-crackle. Maggie was instantly back there, standing in her parents' bedroom, watching her daddy in his boxers looking out through the window to the trailer inferno beyond.

"You told me nobody died."

Her mother shook her head *No, No* and *No* again. "All they found was the skull burned clean. And teeth, the false ones, melted by."

Over the next snooze hiatus, Maggie scooped up every hidden flame-thrower she could find, not only lighters and matches, but all instruments of potential self-destruction, too-sharp scissors from the bathroom, most of the knife set. She even found a hatchet in the laundry room. All were collected in a basket and deposited in the trunk of the Tracer.

Her mother slept on. A blister was forming at the edge of her hairline. Maggie got some ointment on it and a Band-aid.

Next she flew through some calls.

She skipped Viktor. Never mind that he was home with the wifey. Even if he'd been on a business junket holed up in some hotel with the phone lines wide open, she wouldn't have called. *Nothing left to lose.*

She woke Amelia of course. It was an ungodly hour on the coast, but too bad. Maggie wasn't sure when she'd have another shot. She could hear the boyfriend griping in the background. Let him. He was sponging off Amelia anyway. God knows what they'd do with an extra 5K in the larder.

Groggy, Amelia ticked down her to-dos. There were the usual snafus: bartenders upping prices, custom décor running behind. Maggie spoke in deadlines, drilling down contingencies, making Amelia repeat everything back. She said to fax the bullet points to her so that they could literally work from the same page.

"Fax where?" Amelia asked.

Maggie felt like her head was going to explode. Where indeed? Would she have to drive in to Garnet? Who would stay with her mother while she did that?

"Just call me back at the end of the day." Maggie hung up in mid-good-bye.

She needed her own to-do list. That would help. Write down the nine million shake-down calls she had to make before her mother woke up. Plus the bank, the lawyer—Maggie assumed there'd be one. Was there a will? What about power of attorney? Within seconds she'd filled a sheet with mostly question marks, all the while thinking both, *I have to get back,* and, *I can't leave her.*

The Early Bird

August Early
Morning

Mr. Early sat on the front steps. He knew he had to go in to Solace, but it tired him, just walking from the kitchen to the porch. The stoop was as far as he'd gotten.

The dogs were swirling. The wagging of their tails, rumps a-shimmy, propelled them in circles, circling into each other's circles, heads always turning so as to keep him in their view no matter which way their bodies went. As much as they liked his patting, not one would stop for it, so he had to keep his hand out for them to run underneath. When one came close enough, Mr. Early thumped him or her along the ribcage or haunches, or swiped at a last feather of tail.

Shirley, in particular, leered at him with happy eyes. Catherine had found her some thirteen summers ago when she wasn't but thirteen herself. Years before the drugs and degradation. Before God took her, or banished her, maybe, sending her off to where the unrepentant go. Mr. Early had never been able to put them together, Catherine of the hollow eyes and her younger self, Daddy's girl, the woods-wanderer, poking around behind the Mountain Man to find a pie-spotted puppy panting under an old washing machine nobody'd hauled off to the dump.

It was Catherine who named her Shirley. Curly Shirley in full. The one dog they had to shave, her matting would get so bad. How she hated it, ears flat, eyes rolling in misery, but there was nothing for it. Her hair could ball up something awful. When Catherine took to fretting at Shirley's fretting, he'd tell her how Shirley was a lucky dog to get her puppy body back, all sleek and bug-shivery out from under that fur, while the others had to slobber with the heat. That's what he'd tell Catherine to make her smile. Back when she used to smile.

The morning brightened, the sun stepping the tree shadows back where they belonged. Mr. Early sat so long that the dogs began to lose interest, tilting their heads to the side grass, watching a winter beetle bumble across downed leaves, hoping, he imagined, for a bird to hop in and eat it. Precious few birds appeared that time of year though. Just some crows going tree to tree, checking the ground below for easy pickings.

Come home, he thought at Theo, closing his eyes. But then here came her face with the Coca-Cola mask, so he opened them again.

For the rising and setting of a million suns, for the ice freezing over and the dust covering every inch of the earth, Mr. Early wanted to stay there forever like the old washing machine out back of the Mountain Man waiting to be taken to the dump. Anything but go back to that place.

Shirley lay up under the shagbark, belly to the warmer earth. Mr. T. and Bridget had dropped to their sides, eyelids twitching with the last of the sweat bees settling there.

Mr. Early wondered what the dogs would do if they ran into a spaceman coming out of a bedroom, eyeless, dragging a double-hog-sized plastic bag.

Then he was heaving himself forward, staggering as his legs caught up with him, tramping toward the truck like the Devil was behind him with a big green stick. Shirley nigh on flipped herself over as she roused. All the dogs came rushing. He gunned the motor, catching sight of them in the rearview as they charged behind, then slowed, tails drooping. He would not stop to shut them back in.

The hind end of the truck slipped as he punched the accelerator. Where the gravel split off, Miss Susan would surely be watching from her window, no doubt standing all morning waiting for him to pass. He hoped she'd turn into her very own pillar of salt there, waiting for him to come home like a weird, dry snowman. It took his mind off things, picturing her crusted over as he drove down the mountain, looping off the bottom flank of Little Piney toward Big Piney and on into Garnet.

Not As The World Giveth

Cadence Greevey
Morning

"We're going to Solace, not comfort," Uncle Walker said.

"Solace, not comfort, Solace, not comfort." Cadence practiced it the whole way riding in the Crowes' car which was much bigger than her mama's. It had the tan, slide-y smooth seats she liked. She also liked how Uncle Walker held her hand to take her in the front door.

It turned out Solace was a house like any house only bigger and fancier than most. The walls had paintings of vines going up and down them which amazed Cadence since those vines looked alive.

In the hallway, Uncle Walker shook hands with a big-big man who had drawings all over his neck and fingers and probably all over his whole self under his clothes. His long, black moustache hung so low-down that Cadence thought of swinging on the two ends like ropes off a tree branch which made her smile without telling anyone why. The big-big man said his name was Bear. "Like a real bear," he said, "but a nice one."

Uncle Walker told Cadence to mind the bear man. "You stay put 'til we come get you. And no more buses, young lady." His voice was serious. "I have to get back to Auntie Pam, but you know where we are. We're at the Mountain Man, you remember?"

Of course Cadence remembered. It was just that she had her mind on other things like *Solace, not comfort* and swinging on the bear man's moustache.

Just like that, Uncle Walker was gone. The bear man told Cadence that her mama was second on the left. Then he was gone too, so Cadence had to find her way on her own.

She figured out to walk down the middle of the hallway. That way she could look in any door to see first whether it was her mama in there and if it wasn't, to keep walking until it was. That's how she found her, lying down flat sleeping, even though there was a La-Z Boy right next to the bed.

Cadence sat, waiting for her mama to wake up. *Speak when you are spoken to,* that's what she'd learned. She did not even take her jacket off until the bear man came in and showed her where to hang things up. He moved real fast, his eyes everywhere in the room, hanging plastic bags, making things beep. He said her mama had had a rough day.

Cadence thought to be helpful. "You need you some pails and a washcloth. That's how she likes it."

The bear man, at the door, turned full around to have a look at her like they were meeting for the first time. "We'll see," he said. Really looking at her. "Be a good girl now and stay right here." Not unkind. Like talking to a dog. Like talking to Hershey.

So Cadence stayed put. She could hear sounds in the hall. She could hear her mama's breathing—not quiet breathing, loud breathing. Cadence bent down, eye to bedrail, to get a closer look. That's when she saw—*oh my goodness*—the tie-ropes. Or, not ropes. They looked like dog leashes, short ones. Made of the same flat, shiny stuff that was Hershey's leash. Thick. Strong. They were wrapped around her mama's wrists and clamped to the rail with complicated metal buckles that had sharp teeth. Cadence didn't think she could figure how to undo one even if she took it in her mind to try, which she did not, because she knew she wasn't supposed to without being told.

She touched one very lightly. It was smooth like Rabbit. She had to pat it only the one way or it felt prickly on her fingertips.

It was amazing being that close to her mama's face. She could see all kinds of things. Spidery blue lines running under the skin of her side-neck. Faded freckles on her chin. Pinchy grooves running off the bottom of her ear.

It seemed like just the right moment to speak up about her daddy quick before her mama could wake and be upset the way she always was when Cadence talked about him.

"Daddy's in the hospital."

Her mama kept sleeping.

"I thought he was in here with you, mama, but Uncle Walker said that Daddy's in another hospital because he was in an accident."

That's when Cadence got into trouble. She could feel herself slipping, but every time she said something and waited and nothing got said back, she thought she might say a little more, just a little more. Pretty soon she was saying too much.

"Daddy was coming to see me, Mama. He called the day you went to the hospital."

She waited. Nothing.

"He's called me every day, Mama. Every day since the day he left for my whole life. You didn't know it 'cause he called when you were sleeping."

She knew it wasn't true and that it was wrong to say things that weren't true, but she wanted to anyway. She got lost in the telling.

"Did you know, where he lives in Cincinnati, it's a big snow every winter? I know from visiting that one time. So much snow there's a wall of it that keeps anybody from getting out, because there's just one door to Cincinnati, a little one that's frozen shut. So it's hard for Daddy to come visit me. Plus he's got his job at the garage which is like they keep him on a leash. That's what he told me. He said he's got a boss that keeps him on a leash like Hershey. A long leash that lets him go home, but he can't get as far as the snow door to push it open and come check on his girl."

It was fun, getting to make things up without being told to hush.

"But, Daddy, he's wily. You remember, Mama? And Paco too. So last night, didn't the two of them get to cutting that leash with a special scissors Paco has—fat scissors with teeth. They cut and cut until they cut clean through."

"Then they didn't start the car, they pushed it. You remember when Daddy pushed the station wagon down the hill once to get it going? That's what they did. They pushed his car, which is called Krystal, with Daddy steering and Paco pushing until Krystal got going and Daddy could drive real fast to bust through that frozen door—boom!—and on down the road to see his girl."

Cadence laughed.

"He was going too fast in the snow, Mama, 'cause he wanted to come see me so bad and that's why he got in an accident."

Cadence watched her mother's face for signs. If it had been any other day, she would never have gotten to say such things.

"Uncle Walker says that Daddy's in a hospital like you, but he gets out today. Or maybe tomorrow. Some time. And then he's coming home to check on his girl."

Her mother sighed a big sigh that made a bubble come up between her lips. It popped. Still she did not open her eyes.

After a while of waiting, Cadence pulled out her Magic Markers and the Big Tablet Auntie Pam had packed special in her bag. She drew a picture of the frozen door of Cincinnati and her daddy in Krystal as close as she could remember, with Paco pushing it from behind and a long, long road winding from there around the whole piece of paper with, at the end of the road, their house in Little Piney and Hershey still alive barking at the door.

Where There's A Will

August Early
Mid-Morning

Right as he was coming off Old 51, Mr. Early saw the Kmart sign high above the trees and had what Theo called a bright idea: Why not pull in and see if they had something special for her? She'd get after him if she thought he'd spent too much money, but if the price was right, she might to brighten for a little something new.

His spirits rose coming in. The Christmas decorations were going up. Not the Santa display yet, but two plump ladies in red Kmart shirts were throwing tinsel over a big plastic tree while a man in coveralls, who looked to be from a part of the world where snow was never seen, crouched at the front window painting in a blizzard of flakes the size of his head.

Mr. Early took a buggy out of habit, even though he planned to buy something small. He walked up and down every one of the aisles: Appliances. Bedding. Lamps. Women's Clothes. He knew he couldn't pick Theo something to wear if his life depended on it. Nor jewelry either, though he'd tried a few times and Theo had been polite. What she got given, she was careful to wear once, each thing, so he had no way of knowing what pleased her.

"Move it, old man!" A pack of teenagers with a buggy of their own, some riding, some pushing, came barreling at him wearing shelf-swiped elf hats, price tags flapping in the breeze. Mr. Early jumped to the side as their buggy slammed into his—"*Wreck* you, asshole!"—and they careened on down the aisle with one of the plump store ladies jogging flatfooted behind, waving a box of tinsel and yelling, "I'm calling the cops!" as they rounded the corner.

Mr. Early wished he could be the policeman she called. Wouldn't he give them a dressing down in that squad car, cuffing them, squiring them to the courthouse for booking and one hell of a fine. Maybe even some jail time.

He righted his buggy. Choosing only aisles that were empty of people, he steered himself into what looked like the Summer's-Over section. There on a sale shelf was a plastic pitcher of swirly green, a color that was wrong for winter, he knew, but he took to it, to its cheerfulness. He thought maybe Theo could have her water in it instead of the small one they'd given her which was brown and none too pretty.

But then, maybe a cup to go with it, he thought. And there in the next aisle, the Baby aisle, he found a cup or a glass, he didn't know which, because it was plastic. It had two layers around it with, in between, dark blue water. Real water, sealed off but sloshing, and inside little cutouts of shells and starfish that must have been plastic too, because they were just fine in the water. You could turn the glass sideways so that the shells floated all the way around the glass. Or you could turn it upside down and watch everything swim to the lip and not pour out.

In the check-out line, Mr. Early spied one last thing. It was a pen called Write-Brite. The sales girl showed him how to click it for a light to go on that made the whole thing glow. He wanted it for his wife right then. He did not even look at the price.

Bagging everything, the salesgirl said, "They sure are pretty," which made him feel more confident.

But out in the truck, with his presents sitting next to him on the seat, Mr. Early could not bring himself to turn the key. It was a perfect day. Hot sun. He didn't have but his parka on and that unzipped with the windows rolled clean down.

"Get the lead out, La-Z-Boy!"

Across the street through the windshield were two telephone repairmen. The one yelling rode high in the bucket of a crane hoisted above a SouthTel utility van. He was ex-city: too-long hair, graying curls sticking out from under a too-new cowboy hat. Below, his buddy rolled a big orange canister around their vehicle, blocking off traffic even though there was no traffic to be seen. He was younger by half. He looked military, with a close-shaved head, un-capped, and spotless navy pants.

They wore the same safety vests, only the one in the bucket, the older one, had taken his shirt off underneath. All shirts in fact. So that he was nothing but farmer tan, or SouthTel tan, with his vest strapped right overtop his bare chest. *Those arms do some work,* Mr. Early thought.

"Come on. I ain't got all day," Mr. Bucket slapped hard on his utility belt, raking the buckle around to the side so that whatever he hit was hanging off his butt. Damn if it wasn't a radio of some kind because here came a song that sounded something like a commercial for beer maybe. It had a beat, slow like honky tonk, but it wasn't country. Mr. Early could hear it clear across the street. Something about *one love* and *getting together* and *feeling alright.* It was catchy.

"Turn that shit down, man! You're gonna get us fired." The young one kept fiddling with his orange canister, widening the safety zone around them.

"Bite me, La-Z!"

"I'm serious, I need this job."

"You think John Henry Supervisor is going to give up his turkey vay-kay to spy on us? No way, José."

The older guy was lifting something from the crane bucket now, all pinks and oranges. An umbrella, it was an umbrella, a long one, girly, with a handle. He got busy jamming it into a homemade rig—Mr. Early could see it— twine lashed to the side of the bucket that made a cradle into which the guy twisted the pearl end of the umbrella and then opened it. *Phwomp.* Candy-colored butterflies and kitty cats ran around the rim. The man was singing with his radio, even dancing a little. Not much, just enough to bounce the bucket. He skewed the umbrella, changing its angle to create—

Shade!

This is a clever man, Mr. Early thought. *The SouthTel muck-a-mucks don't provide him enough cover, he engineers his own. He borrows the wife's umbrella or steals the girlfriend's and now he's got himself a little relief from the elements.*

Mr. Bucket clapped his hands. "Let's go. Hup!"

The younger one, positioned directly below him, tossed something straight up and fast. It was a glove. A work glove. Heavy. Dirty. Shedding as it went. "Hup!" Here came a second glove. And then the man in the bucket was tossing them around and around in circles to himself, hand to hand. One two, one two. In between tossing one and catching the other, he even swiped the hat off his own head and added that to the mix, saying, "Hup!" again.

"For Christ's sake," said the younger, but he never took his eyes away.

"Someday I'm gonna do this with tools!" the guy crowed.

"Not with me down here you're not."

One-two-three. The gloves and hat were caught neat. All three got put on in a flash, the back of one glove mopping sweat from around the guy's neck.

Mr. Early heard pulsed whining as Mr. Bucket got busy now, working a panel of controls, jerking his air chariot around in the sky forward-back and side-side, maneuvering that sucker in toward a tangle of electrical wires *that could kill you just touching one,* Mr. Early thought, and there the man was with his open umbrella, brazen, squeezing himself stop-start among the city's power lines, no expression on his face, just the look of someone doing his job, his buddy looking on from below.

Mr. Early had seen enough. He cranked up his truck, shooting himself out onto the empty road, roaring past the repair men toward Old 51, heading up the mountain, not down.

It took him half the time to get back than it had taken him to go, accelerating into the driveway without any mind to the gravel he was kicking up. He hoped he'd stirred enough dust to where Miss Susan couldn't see who it was coming, since she'd know he hadn't been gone long enough to see Theo.

He didn't care. He didn't care with the dogs barking their wild happiness at his return, Rocky and Shirley and Bridget and Mr. T. tearing toward him from around the barn and then getting lost in the brown plumes as he sped by. He did not so much as tip his foot off the gas. They'd have to have sense enough to stay out of his way. Which they did.

He snatched up his Kmart bag, stomping on past the dogs straight through to the back of the house. His house. Theo's house. They'd picked the room farthest from the road to sleep in, the shadier one facing a stand of sassafras. Even this late in the morning, the sun was only beginning to warm the bed. He tossed the bag on a stool just inside.

I am failing you, he thought.

He walked back and forth several times.

I am failing you.

He caught sight of the twins. The picture of them as babies on their bellies, turned toward each other with big smiles like they were looking in a mirror and seeing themselves. Their mother had taken that picture in the early, happy days and given it as a present in a silver frame.

Theo might like to have that, Mr. Early thought. He put it in the Kmart bag with the pitcher and the cup and the pen.

He stood staring out the bedroom window.

She will not come home, he thought.

Out back, Mr. T. sat in a bar of sunlight. Looking at him, Mr. Early could feel it, how his fur would soften the tickly winter grass beneath. He watched the dog sniff-sigh in a rapture of rising warmth, the sweep of fine hairs around his eyes and nose etched in light.

What will happen? he wondered. *How will the days be?*

He could see the image of Theo's brow furrowed even in sleep. He was sick to death of the way her face kept coming to him, sick of the sickness and sick of seeing her that way.

He slammed out the back door. The yard needed clearing. It was his job to pull the old vines, trim the laurel and cull any seedlings, because snakes and bears liked the cover and he didn't aim to make their sneaking up on him and his loved ones any easier. Besides, new growth changed the tenor of the woods. New trees crowded out old trees and he liked old trees. He knew how to work it so that each year things grew up just right.

It was a job any knowing man held off until spring, but Mr. Early was compelled to do it now. He tore things out by their roots, piling up strings of withered sweet-pea, dead hemlock and new poplar. He got busy enough to where he lost track of the presents and the Kmart bag, of the house and the dogs. Not Theo's nor the girls' nor nobody's face came to him after a while, until there was nothing but just the pulling and the piling and the pausing to strip down to his T-shirt with the sweat.

Later, he told himself, he would take the girls for chocolate dips down at the Rexall. Miss Susan might say it would spoil their suppers, but he would do it anyway, no matter what. He would take them for ice cream.

And if they asked, he would tell them that she was better. Like he'd been to see her. If they asked some more, he'd tell them, "Maybe tomorrow."

"Maybe tomorrow you can see her."

Maybe tomorrow.

As Pretty Does

Maggie Dull
Noon

The representatives from Solace arrived on time as promised, pulling into the driveway above the house at 12 o'clock sharp. Maggie watched them from the side porch, two women, tottering a bit in the gravel. They paused, as folks often did, to take in the view. With the leaves mostly gone, you could see through the web of branches clear across to the blue ridge of the Blue Ridge like looking at water through a screen.

Maggie came around front to greet them.

"Lana Hendren," said the one in front, extending a hand. Maggie's initial impression was good. At least this woman knew how to dress. The suit was maybe five or six years old, but a very good make. Jill Sander or a knock-off. The ochre complemented the woman's complexion, popping like rain-soaked summer squash against the darkness of her skin.

"Miss Hendren," Maggie said.

"Ms.," she corrected. "RN."

A professional, thought Maggie. *What a relief.*

The second woman was another story. Business-like, to be sure, but... It wasn't so much the ill fit of her clothing, purchased way too long ago in a size that should have been relegated to dim memory. No, it was something in the purse of her lips, in her dark eyes, lightless as mud. *This is one sour individual,* Maggie thought, as the woman introduced herself. "Hazel Gurley. Home-visit. Call me Hazel." She aimed that last remark not at Maggie, but at Ms. Hendren, conveying in her barbed tone a world of contempt for the world of pretension. With no invitation, she opened the front door, striding straight in to find her patient. Ms. Hendren remained on the porch with Maggie. Clearly it fell to her to speak with the "difficult" client.

At Maggie's nod, she sat, not hesitating for a moment even as she took in the rain stained surface of the patio chair onto which she was placing her perfect poly-blend skirt.

She spoke like a kindergarten teacher meeting a harried single mom. "I'm very pleased. Apparently this is the first time your mother has been out of bed for, let's see—" checking her clipboard, "—at least a few days. Is she complaining about pain?"

Maggie did not let her look down again, "Are you saying that she's improving?"

Ms. Hendren paused. "I'm saying she *feels* better." The phrasing precise.

"Does that mean actual improvement?"

An arresting gaze, the taking of Maggie's measure: "We see periods of relief like this, periods of increased vigor. They are not likely to indicate a change in the natural course of the disease."

"I see." Asked and answered. Her mother would not live longer, but she might live better along the way.

"As far as home visits are concerned, Miss Gurley will be filling in for Ms. Kling— "

"I want that Kling woman fired."

Ms. Hendren said nothing.

"I want her to lose her job."

"I understand."

"It wasn't professional."

"I understand."

"I don't think you do." Here it came, the dudgeon, the heat rising up the back of her neck. Maggie stood. "I don't think, looking around this house which I spent all night cleaning after getting off a plane from the West coast, I don't think you can imagine what it's like to step into your childhood home and find yourself on Lunatic Lane with your own mother as official tour guide." Maggie started pacing behind the chair. "She got it into her head that the Devil was coming to get her and here your employee—supposedly her caretaker, the person we are paying to safeguard someone clearly out of her mind—this woman starts throwing rock salt all over the house. Why? Because it burns devil feet or hooves or whatever. That's what she tells my mother. That's what my mother tells me. I mean, for God's sake, exploiting a dying woman's dementia! The place was a disaster area. Food by the fireplace because my mother's got angels confused with reindeer!"

"That must have been upsetting."

Maggie was having none of it. She would not be dialed back by hollow tones of professional empathy. "Ms. Hendren, I live in Northern California. That means I'm used to spiritual theatrics. The place is filled with hoo-haw types wearing neo-Hindu frou-frou, sporting healing amulets and magnetic crystals. So you and your organization are damn lucky it was me walking in here yesterday, because somebody *not* me, somebody less open-minded, and your entire organization would be in court this morning."

The nurse began re-buttoning her jacket. "Here, in the mountains—" she began.

"Oh, please don't run that romance-of-the-mountains number on me. I grew up in this neck of the woods."

"As did I." Now Ms. Hendren was standing. She looked straight across at Maggie. "Like you, I call this home," each word beveled to extreme politeness. "That helps me appreciate the things that have not changed since you and I came up. Folks here still believe in second and third and fourth chances. Ms. Kling will be counseled. She will be reassigned to another setting. Not a home setting. In-house at Solace where she will be closely monitored."

"In my world it's Strike One, you're out."

Neither made a move, eyes locked.

"Further concerns about Ms. Kling should go to her supervisors. I can give you their names. I am here for the patient."

"So am I." Maggie scowled, but inside, in a remote corner of herself, she was tipping her hat. *Damn, this woman is a cool customer.*

"My mother can't be left alone. She needs to be admitted to the hospice facility pronto. Isn't that the deal?"

"Yes. When it's time." The tone wasn't challenging, just factual.

"It's time."

"Her doctor will have to determine that." Again, laying out policy, nothing more.

"That's this Narduli character?"

"Dr. Narduli, yes."

"How soon could that be?" Maggie knew how she sounded. *Ding Dong, the Wicked Witch.* Exhibit A for the Me Generation, feathers ruffled at the inconvenience of a dying parent. But that wasn't it. The train was about to run off the goddamned track. Somebody had to take the wheel.

Miss Hendren's voice retained an uncanny note of deference. "I will call his office."

"Today?"

"The call, yes. But admitting her depends on when beds open up."

"Fine. Let me know how I can help move things along."

All the while Maggie's mind was running in parallel thinking, *I could work with this woman in another life. Maybe health care consulting. Dulé-Hendren, Inc. She'd cover medical, I'd do logistics: the party planning side of terminal illness.*

Home-Visit-Hazel returned to the front porch. She said nothing as she scribbled on Ms. Hendren's clipboard.

"Everything all right?" Maggie asked.

"Fine." There was nothing in the woman's expression to indicate how fine or not-fine things really were. Her eyes did not come up. "What happened to your mother's forehead?"

"Oh, she got hold of a cigarette lighter. I've cleaned them all out of the house now. There's a little blister. Will it be all right?"

"Fine." That was all Maggie got. Home-Visit Hazel kept writing, pressing down hard with a ballpoint pen.

Evaluation flowed through Maggie as coolly as observation. She did not like this woman. She didn't like the thought of her anywhere near her mother. And that surprised her. If justice meant tit for tat, then her mother had certainly earned a whopping dose of clinical severity, but for reasons passing all understanding—or *blasting* all understanding, as her mother used to say—Maggie didn't like the idea.

"Ms. Hendren, I appreciate your bringing Hazel by to meet us, however, I'd like to suspend home visits for the next few days while I'm here."

Eyes went to eyes and everything was communicated. Home-Visit-Hazel looked no more disappointed leaving the place than she had coming. Lana

Hendren maintained her kabuki of sympathetic listening, absorbing Maggie's theater-of-pressing-engagements while nodding judiciously as if to say, *We are all women with places to go and people to see.*

Their goodbyes were cordial, any unpleasantness attributed, by all parties apparently, to the difficulties of terminal care.

Maggie watched them go. *All right, Mother Dull. It's you and me against the world.*

She went back inside to find—thank God—her would-be arsonist keeled over, sound asleep.

Misery Loves

Bear
Shift Change

Bear looked up from the Admit desk at Solace. Dee Dee Hipps late? That was a sight you didn't see every day considering Dee Dee herself was known to be severe with those who kept *her* waiting. Not out of meanness, mind you. Anybody who knew Dee Dee knew she didn't have a mean bone. No, because it wasn't right and Dee Dee Hips was a stickler for doing things right.

Bear decided he'd cut her some slack, but not before he jerked her chain a little. "Cluster F!" he announced. He made a racket stacking charts and crumpling post-its.

"Wash your mouth out, mister."

"Well, it's been a heck of a day." He leaned hard on the "heck."

Dee Dee was having trouble getting her arm out of her jacket sleeve. "It's a wonder I'm here at all. They were short somebody at the Pay Less, so Curtis-Michael had to go in. I couldn't find anyone to watch the baby. Finally, I called his mother, Jonelle. Do you know Jonelle Hipps?"

Bear was more intent on signing out than paying her much mind. He said "Humph" in a way that could mean *Yes* or *No*.

"Big Piney's own Big Mama. Of course, you know where she was. Down at the Mountain Man jawing with her buddies."

Bear reached for his coffee cup, taking the last swig. "You got her to look after Carleton?"

"Said she was happy to, though Lord knows why, what with his whining, no matter you look left or right at him. She says Curtis-Michael was the same way." Dee Dee was over in the front closet now, jamming at things trying to squeeze her jacket in. "Who's on call? Tell me it's Narduli."

"Nope."

"Abramowitz?"

"Holiday week," he said. "They got a sub. Avilla Toth."

"A-wha-wha-who?" Dee Dee shoved the overflow boxes of gauze over just enough to wedge her jacket in between. "Bear, we have got to find a proper place for these supplies."

"Toth. Like Oath."

"What kind of name is that? Boy or girl?"

"Girl," said Bear. "She's a light weight. You know, scared to"—Dee Dee joined him—"call the shots."

He reached back and low-fived her as she came around the desk. How was it they did so well together? She, churchy; he much happier on his Kawasaki racing full throttle down a stretch of wicked switchbacks. Still, he got the biggest bang out of her. They'd honed a no-hassle way of working born of mutual respect that reminded him of the best of the corps.

"Like I said, it's a cluster—" he caught her look "—kerfuffle."

She laughed, checking the message board. "Talk to me."

"You want the bad news or the bad news? Burnice and Miz Dull: that whole thing blew up. The daughter came home and now she wants her fired."

"Who wants who fired?"

"The daughter wants Burnice fired. I sent Lana out there with Hazel to calm things down. We'll bring Burnice in-house."

"Good plan," Dee Dee nodded.

"But that leaves you short-handed. We've got Miz Early in 5B. And Miz Greevey—the one who came in yesterday—" Bear paused for effect. "She flipped."

"Oh, no."

"Banged herself up pretty good. We had to use restraints."

"Oh, dear."

"See what I mean? Kerfuffle. It took me three calls to get her a sedative with some kick. This Toth character wanted me to start with Tylenol."

"Does she have an accent?" Dee-Dee asked.

"Who, Toth? Thick. Like the Queen of England."

Bear had already started for the door when Dee Dee, up to her eyeballs in chart notes, waved his drained-and-stained coffee mug at him. "Do you see me wearing some I'M YOUR MOMMY badge?"

Busted. Bear swiped the cup out of her hand and went for the kitchen.

"Who's on with me?" she called after him.

"Well, that would be the other bad news. You've got the rookie."

Bear sympathized. It took them more time to supervise Kitty than do things themselves. Coming back by the desk, he slid his hand over Dee Dee's, not even breaking stride until he hit the front door. "Oh, and there's the Greevey girl—have you met her yet?"

"What do you mean 'girl?'"

"Child. Grown child. Her Uncle brought her in. There's some talk of the father coming down from up north, but I don't have any confirmation on that."

"You offered them child care with a full house?"

"I asked myself, 'What would Dee Dee do?'"

She gave him a look. "Take yourself on out of here."

Bear paused in the door, strapping on his helmet. There was no way in hell he'd actually wear it driving, but he put it on for show because Dee Dee insisted. "Cherille got the child fed."

"Hit the road, Mr. Kerfuffle, and let me do my job."

Bear caught the door as it was closing. "Oh, by the way, the child's not playing with a full deck..."

He heard Dee Dee's high-pitched, "Wha-a-a-t?" as the door came to. He was out in the parking lot at last, pulling his helmet off, shaking his hair loose in the weird warmth of the afternoon. He couldn't wait to kick the bike into gear, to stir the stale air into a breeze with some speed, with the roar of the motor and the blur of things sweeping past, to blast the world finally into motion.

The Darkest Hour Is Just Before

Kitty Pearl
Evening

Kitty felt flustered. Solace was full up, fourteen patients in fourteen beds. Bear said it got that way as the holidays came on. She thought Easter might be righter for the dying to make their way out of this world, but maybe it was harder to leave a greening place, what with the crocus coming and the dogwoods popping. Maybe winter helped a body loose its hold.

Kitty made her rounds.

Down the south hallway were their two AIDS patients, Mr. Church and Miss Tornauer. Of all the illnesses Kitty had to get up-close-and-personal with, this one scared her. She knew in her head it wasn't catching. Still, there was something troubling about the precautions they had to take, the gloves, the clean-up in full-body hazard suits, bagging and disposing everything as toxic waste. And then there was all the talk around it. The whispering at Bible study among people, coping, she guessed with a loved one so stricken. Coping, therefore, with all of the wondering about what kinds of lives led to such horror.

It was obvious that Miss Tornauer's life had been hard. Three of her front teeth, bared in morphine sleep, had disintegrated to something that looked like driftwood. Her skin, even her eyelids, had shriveled to old womanness and yet she was only twenty-something. Felled by drugs, by life on the street. Bear said somebody rich was paying the bills, but Kitty'd never seen a soul in her room except a probation officer who came by once. Out of pure kindness, not part of his job.

Kitty checked across the hall. Mr. Church was too weak to smile. He never let her do a thing for him, not straighten the sheet or move the pillow.

She tried not to take it personally. She reckoned he was shy of himself physically. Terrible how the illness could drain the man out of men to leave them blotched and shrunken. Kitty thought he must have worked in an office back when he was hale. A manager tooling around in a coat and tie, maybe over at State Farm or First Union. At least he had friends who came through, most of them younger, all of them men.

Mrs. Esposito was on the west hall. Ninety-six years old and dying of one of her cancers. She slept all the time going on three days now while her family came and sat, taking turns. That nice Mr. Esposito, her son, nodded to Kitty as she checked on things. She nodded right back. Nodding took the place of words, since neither spoke the other's language. Around the bed were several of his children—the grandchildren—just as well behaved as you please, smiling their daddy's same smile, watching Kitty for any instructions she might have. She held her palms up to her cheek and tipped her head over to indicate sleep. They nodded and did the same, each one holding one of Miss Cherille's oatmeal cookies. "Night night," Kitty said, pointing at Mrs. Esposito. "Night night," whispered the children, while their daddy put one finger up to his lips, *shshshsh-ing*. That was something they all understood.

Across the way, Milius Cornelius needed his bath. ALS had made him limp. Kitty was holding his upper body slung over one shoulder sponging his backside when here came Mr. Katz wheeling by the cracked doorway. Honestly, the man would not stay put. He had seemed not long for this earth when Dr. Narduli admitted him and yet here he was almost seven days in. That was a very long stay for anyone at Solace.

Mr. Katz was enamored of his wheelchair. Got folks to put him in early in the morning so he could make his own rounds between naps which he took sitting in the chair. He was sweet on the cook, calling her always *Miss* Cherille, calling her his girlfriend, parking his chair in the kitchen to watch her doings.

"Go on now," Kitty shoo'ed him. "Mr. Cornelius would not appreciate you nosing in here." She continued her gentle wiping as Mr. K wiggled at the tops of his wheels until he got them going forward, his ponytail of white hair backcombed and rubber-banded to look like an ancient Paul Revere.

He was nowhere to be seen when Kitty hit the north hallway to check on Mrs. Early. And thank God, because somehow Mrs. Early had gotten herself out of bed. The closet door was open. There she was rummaging inside.

"What are we up to?" Kitty tried to keep her tone pleasant, thinking, *Lord what if she fell?*

"I have to go," snapped Mrs. Early. She held a pair of shoes in one hand, clothes hangers in the other.

"No, you don't. You don't have anywhere to be." Kitty turned Mrs. Early back toward her bed. "Come on now. You're going to get me into trouble." She got the woman back up under the sheet, pried the shoes out of her hands. Mrs. Early lay stiff on the pillow, not meeting Kitty's eyes.

"You all right now?" Kitty got no reply. The face was blank, staring toward the window blinds. Kitty tried not to let it bother her. At least the woman seemed better, quiet, at any rate. Enough to where Kitty could go on about her business.

She came to Mrs. Greevey's door last. Burnice had told her once that you could feel some patients through the walls like heat through an oven door, that the ones with troubled spirits radiated that trouble out into the nearby air. Kitty took careful account of such wisdom. She believed that certain folks had special knowledge. Burnice Kling was one such. Burnice's sayings stayed with Kitty like words burned into a wooden sign.

Mrs. Greevey's room was hot with trouble. And, Lord have mercy, Kitty knew why coming in the door: the woman was tied down in the bed. Kitty had never seen such a thing before. Bear hadn't given her a word of warning about it, Dee Dee either. Testing her most like. Kitty knew they thought her too tender-hearted for Solace work. She would prove them wrong.

"Ca-denz?"

"What? No? I am Kitty Pearl, Mrs. Greevey."

Spittle-rattled, the woman made a sound that might have been speaking had she been able to summon the strength.

Suddenly Dee Dee was in the doorway behind Kitty. "Have you seen this before?"

"No, ma'am."

Dee Dee pushed past to the far side of the bed. "She banged herself up pretty good." Dee Dee fingered Mrs. Greevey's gown carefully off her shoulder. "Hold that, will you?"

Kitty could see a gash, red with swabbed blood. A sizable hematoma was coming up under the skin. Mrs. Greevey turned her head, eyelids only half open.

Dee Dee dressed the scrape. "Apparently she was trying to get out of bed, calling for her people—but not a soul came by, did they Miz. Greevey? Finally Bear caught her pulling her catheter out, climbing over the safety bar, I.V. and all. That's when we have to go for restraints."

Kitty saw canvas straps on each wrist. They didn't look tight, but they looked bad. She didn't like to see folks tie even their own dogs to a tree. She supposed it was the only way to let a wandery critter enjoy life outdoors. Still, in her mind, you owed it to a dog to put up a fence, give it the illusion of roaming to suit its nature. Maybe they could do some such for the rambling ill. Maybe put a fence at the door like the ones to keep children off staircases.

Dee Dee came around to Mrs. Greevey's front side. She carefully lifted her upper lip. "Oh, dear."

"Oh, dear," said Kitty as well.

Mrs. Greevey's left front tooth was broken off, the stump twisted in the gum. There was a good bit of dried blood on the inside of her mouth.

Another patient was calling. Dee Dee headed for the door "We have to clean that up. Keep her quiet and when I come back, we'll do it together."

Then Kitty was alone.

She fiddled, tucking blankets in, bending to line slippers up under the bed so that no one would trip on them.

When she straightened, Mrs. Greevey was bug-eyed, like she'd come upon Kitty as a thief trying to steal something in her house. Kitty felt her heart surge with the surprise of it.

"Ca-denz?"

"No ma'am, I'm not," said Kitty, turning to where Mrs. Greevey was staring and then starting, because there in the bedroom doorway was a girl, a big girl in a too-tight dress holding onto a ragged piece of gray-brown fur.

"Hello, mama," the girl said. "I brought you Rabbit."

Be It Ever So

Bobby O. Greevey
Evening

No sooner was he inside the front door than Bobby was throwing himself to his right, dropping bags and rattling the portrait off the wall before his brain could even tell him why. Something was flying straight at him. Something heavy, blunt, tumbling end-over-end. He was still moving as things shattered.

He heard Paco screaming, "Jesus Christ, what the hell do you think you're doing?"

Gripping the wall, Bobby looked over to see a baseball bat on the floor. The navy blue one. The one they kept in the hall closet. A line of navy paint arced along the faux-stucco overhead. The hall table lay on its side. The Stoddard flask, their treasure, was now a million pieces, scattered, strewn.

"What the fuck! You could have killed me!" Bobby stayed jammed into the corner in mid-dive. Paco stood equally frozen on the other side of the living room, his throwing arm still extended.

"What are you doing coming in like that?"

"Paco? I live here!"

"You gotta call! You gotta let me know!" Both yelling full force at each other.

Bobby didn't know where to put his hands. Glass was everywhere. "What are you thinking? A burglar's going to come in with a key?"

Paco crouched to eye level. "Didn't you hear me?"

"No!"

"All that scratching. I thought you were picking the lock. Didn't you hear me say I would call the police?"

"No! Jesus!" Bobby shook his head now, testing his neck, then shoulders, hands and knees to see if he was hurt. It was a miracle the bat had missed him. A miracle it missed the lancet by the door with its custom leading. He shifted his feet. Butterscotch shards surrounded him. There was no way he could get up. "You broke the Stoddard…"

Paco wasn't letting it go. "Seriously, what are you doing here? I thought you were in Pineburg."

"*Seriously?*" Bobby looked up from the wreckage incredulous. The man had gone loco. "Paco, are you dealing drugs out of the house when I'm not here? What the hell is going on?" His head was throbbing. Thirteen hours of bus hell, for God's sake and this was the Welcome Wagon?

Paco's voice was way too calm: "You want to close the door?"

Bobby went tit-for-tat: "You want to give me a hand?"

Paco got him up. Neither spoke. They went into solitary. That's what they called it when both parties tried to get a grip on themselves before more wrong things were said. Paco swept glass. Bobby gathered his bag, clearing the bat and righting the table.

"I'll do that," said Paco.

"*I'll* do it!" Bobby was seething.

Paco sat down heavy on the landing, holding the dustpan out so that its mound of incredibly expensive historic glass would not spill onto the carpet. It killed Bobby to look at him. The tight black curls, the otter eyelids. The charcoal etched around the rim of his lips. The perfect nails, pale over each brown finger, a color rich as river silt. Beside him Bobby always felt gluey, like the plainest of pancake batters with no fruit or spice.

"There's blood on your shirt."

"Oh, you noticed?"

Bobby brought a wastebasket up under the dustpan, tipping Paco's hand to spill its contents.

Paco didn't move. "Christ, Bob, I called the hospital this morning. They said you'd checked out. You didn't call me, so I figured you'd rented a car and gone to Pineburg."

"Piney."

"Isn't that what we said?" Paco took Bobby by the hand, pulling him down next to him on the stair. "Come here. What's with the Band-Aid?"

"It's a bandage. I have stitches. I told you that." Bobby was standing again.

"Stop!"

"Somebody's got to straighten up."

"Bob, stop."

There it was. The tone. The gentleness. A hint of the sound Bobby had engineered a sleepless, all-night horror-bus escape to hear. And now, hearing it, something in him snapped.

The wastebasket went up in the air. The overnight bag got swept off the coffee table taking candles and books with it. Then the bat was swinging every which way, crushing lampshades and exploding ornamental dishware before Paco could get him around the waist from behind—he was smaller that Bobby, but he was stronger—pulling his left arm down hard enough to bring the bat tip toward the ground, the two of them turning together with Paco saying "Stop! Stop! Stop!" this time with energy, with force.

Bobby did not remember scream-sobbing like that even as a child. Sniveling, yes. Stuffing back the tears when his finger got near sliced off with a hunting knife. But nothing like this. It sounded so weird that Paco actually let go of him. Bobby sank to his knees, convulsed, tapping the bat against the bandage on his forehead. Paco quick-pried it away. He grabbed a clean dish towel from the breakfront. Bobby used it to cover his face, muffling a new wave of screaming.

"Babe. You have a head injury," Paco's voice was always so measured. "You're probably on some wicked medication. You have to stop crying now, okay? It's only going to make you feel worse. Stop crying and let's get you to an emergency room."

Bobby shook his head *No,* with Paco trying to get him up, when the doorbell rang. Their heads whipped around like criminals caught in a home invasion.

"Oh, Christ," said Paco. "Can you believe it?"

He didn't open the door very far. Just enough for Bobby to see a teenaged boy holding—was that a pizza box? DOMINO'S. He saw the kid see Paco, then look past to where he was sitting on the floor bandaged, towel in hand, smashed stuff all around him. In a split second the kid's face went from boredom to intense focus.

"Wow." It was hard to surprise kids these days, but this guy was definitely impressed. Probably wondering if he should call the police.

Paco shrugged, ultra-cool. "Listen, you've got the wrong house. We didn't order pizza."

Bobby staggered up off the floor, well aware that he looked awful.

The kid nudged the door with his pizza box. "You okay, man?"

Bobby could have kissed him. Leave it to some Domino's boy to ask the sixty-four thousand dollar question. He spoke guy-to-guy. "I'm fine. We just had a little argument. You probably see this shit all the time." Poker-faced. A tough guy. Like he wasn't standing at Ground Zero of Domestic World War III.

"Okay. Take it easy!" The kid couldn't get off their front porch fast enough, high-tailing it for his Civic-turned-delivery-vehicle and then peeling out through the neighborhood.

Paco closed the front door neatly like a cocktail party hostess, the soul of decorum in the midst of high catastrophe. "I think we set gay rights back several hundred years. Now let's get you to a hospital."

Bobby was having none of it. "What are you going to do? Drop me off? You can't stand hospitals. God knows, you couldn't bring yourself to check on me yesterday."

Paco whirled. "You told me not to come!"

"That's what you say when you're in the hospital, asshole! You say 'Don't come' and then the person who loves you most in the world says 'I'm coming anyway.' I'm totaled in a blizzard and you can't take a day off work?"

"That's not fair."

"Admit it: you're terrified of sickness and blood and gore and mess and—God forbid—some simpleton being dumped on your doorstep."

There it was. Instantly the world went from inferno to tundra, lifeless, grassless, windswept for miles in every direction. Paco did not lift his eyes from his Adidas. The lawyer in him spoke. "I have been out front from the day we met about who I am and what I'm prepared to do."

Bobby came toward him, arms out, hands open, "What did you think? Did you think I was going to schlep her back up here?"

Paco held him off, every inch of his body saying, *Don't touch me.*

"Well?"

Nothing.

Bobby let his hands fall. "Did you think I would do that to you?"

"I don't know."

"You should know. We'll do what we always do. We'll talk. We'll come up with something."

"There is no something."

"How do you know?"

"There's nobody else to take her."

"We don't know that yet."

Paco began to pace a short circuit, three steps back and forth, back and forth. "Cut the crap, Bob. Cut the ever-loving, *We-Are-The-World* crap. You are her father. What the hell are you going to do? Send her to a home?"

"I don't know."

"Well, I do. That's why I'm here. That's why I've always been here."

Not with a bang. With a few words, heat-seeking straight for Bobby's heart. A line was drawn, not in space, but in time. There would only be before and after this moment.

Paco jingled the car keys. His voice was polite, impersonal: "You have to take care of your daughter. And I," one hand on the backdoor, "I do not. I am not prepared, I have never been prepared, I will never be prepared to be a daddy. Or a mommy."

He punched the button to open the garage, "Come on!"

"Paco?" Bobby stood in the doorway.

"You need a doctor."

"Paco?"

"What?" He was at the car now, frozen, one leg in.

"I promise. I will not bring her home." Bobby felt his heart shattering like the Stoddard.

"Get in." Paco sat himself down hard behind the wheel. He leaned on the horn. The noise was crazy loud. Painful. Bobby jumped from the steps straight into the passenger seat, twisting and pulling at the door as Paco jerked the gearshift, lurching backward, then, suddenly, jamming the brake down in mid-driveway. Bobby didn't know what to think.

Paco banged at the steering wheel with both fists, "You can't take care of a kid!"

"I know." Bobby's voice conciliatory.

"You can barely take care of you."

"Not to mention you!" Ah, God, how did broken hearts keep beating? Bobby's lips trembled like a boy's, but he kept talking. "Just give me time. I will handle this." Saying the wrong thing. Saying the right thing. His heart calving like an ice floe, its pieces drifting apart.

Bobby reached for Paco, straining against his seat belt, undoing it, Paco braking again, the car hanging half out in the street, Bobby taking Paco's face in his two hands to kiss him, Paco kissing back, really kissing, until he managed to set Bobby back enough in his own seat to pull out properly onto the road.

"I'm okay," Bobby sang out even with his head throbbing. "I don't need a hospital."

"Well, I do." Miracle of miracles, Paco was making a joke. "Besides, that's all we need—for you to sustain brain damage and end up staggering around the house like some—"

They both knew what he was about to say.

Bobby said it for him, "—retard?"

"Don't use that word. That's not where I'm coming from. Put your seatbelt on. We're going to get that head of yours examined."

Bobby sat back and watched the dopey houses in their dopey subdivision slide by. They'd chosen a decidedly downscale development because the price was right and everybody seemed up for maintaining lawns and fences and paint. Some of the neighbors had mounted sheaves of dried corn on their knockers. Mrs. Swan, predictably, had hoisted her nylon Thanksgiving flag off the front porch, a cartoon Pilgrim in appliquéd neons waving Hello.

"I'll call Russ on Monday." Finally, here was Paco. The Paco Bobby loved. Thoughtful. Courteous. Can-do. "Russ handles this kind of stuff. Does the girl have any relatives? Aunts? Cousins?"

Bobby looked down at his doughy hands. "Not blood kin. But there are neighbors. Or were. People who care."

They wove through a daisy chain of housing, identical tracts customized only by roof color and ornament.

Paco sighed. "We'll find a way."

"We will?"

"We will."

A way to what? Bobby felt the pieces of his heart eddying. Perhaps they would drift back together into a shape they once shared. He couldn't think anymore.

"After the hospital, can we do Chinese?"

Paco laughed. "You *must* have a head injury. You don't eat Chinese."

"You don't throw bats."

Paco took a minute. The road glinted in the headlights, slicked with motor oil and lawn run-off. "We're handling a problem client. A drug case."

"I knew it." There went Bobby's heart again. "Are we in danger?"

"I don't think so. I *didn't* think so. But I guess I had a whole story going in the back of my head about, you know, some kind of mob hit, when I heard you doing whatever the hell you were doing at the front door."

"You try getting a key in a lock when you've got brain damage."

"I tell you what, you do your best *not* to have brain damage and I'll take you for Chinese."

Bobby went from laughing to not. "Are we going to be okay?"

Paco looked over to see what he might mean. "Oh. Mob hits. No. Yes. I don't know. I've been watching too much TV. We're fine."

"'Cause if we have to do the whole witness protection song-and-dance, there's some amazing real estate south of here. A little spot called the Pineys—"

"Tell me you're kidding."

"I'm kidding."

He was. Bobby couldn't imagine being anywhere but right there, stuck at the light with Paco, on his way to yet another emergency room.

"I want mu shu."

Paco snorted. "Honestly, it's like duck droppings. At least let's do that Thai place."

"I want mu shu. Take out."

"Okay, okay."

Bobby tipped his head back against the seat.

It was as he had read. In severe injury, in the severing, for instance, of an arm or a leg, there was said to be no pain at all. Nothing. Just the gazing down and noticing that some part of the body was gone, an absence of struggle until the final sinking into whatever was next, coma or death or some forever changed version of life.

This is what they call shock, Bobby thought, even as happiness tucked around him like a soft blanket, closing out cold and dread and fear. Part of him was broken off. Part of him was gone. But which part? He was on his way with Paco to see a team of professional people, experts in crisis, all the king's horses and all the king's men. They would ask him the whole story, every remembered detail, then patch him up and discharge him. For take-out mu shu.

"Maybe on the way home," Bobby said, "We could swing by Domino's. Maybe pick up a couple of slices on the side."

Hell Hath No Fury

Cadence Greevey
After Supper

There was something wrong, Cadence could see it now. She wasn't half-way in the door when, "Ca-denz?" her mama called from the bed. Cadence could see a tooth was gone, a front tooth, broken half off with blood all around it. She had never seen such a thing on a grown-up before. She felt like crying.

"You got a boo-boo, Mama." She held out Rabbit.

"What have you got there?" A lady Cadence didn't know was kneeling by the bed. Praying, Cadence thought, and therefore someone nice. Plus she had a super-shiny, straight-combed, pink-white ponytail that made her pretty like a doll, one of the ones where, if you pressed a button in the back of its neck, you could pull a whole bunch of super-shiny, straight-combed, pink-white hair clean out of its head to be long and loose down its back or maybe rolled up and held with a straight pin pushed in just above its eyes for a hair-do.

"It's Rabbit that my mama gave me."

"Is this your mama?"

Cadence hated being in trouble. She tried to explain. "I am Cadence Greevey from Little Piney. I went for a walk because my mama sleeps all the time, and I found a room with a colored glass window in it like over at the Christ Mount, but this one isn't of Jesus. It has nurses in nurse caps and a white dove and lots of hearts floating in a blue sky with SOLACE as a word floating up there too. I can read as good as anybody and it spells Solace, I'm sure, which means comfort, that's what my Uncle Walker says."

Cadence had thought she would stay looking at the window for only a single minute, but that one minute turned into more while she ran her eyes up and down, tracing how the colored glass, broken into a million bits, fit itself into pictures that made one big picture.

"I like your hair," she said to the ponytail lady.

Suddenly, "Foof! Foof! Foof!" Her mama was yelling, pulling on the leashes that held her to the bed. The lady jumped up, not touching anything and yet—one-two-three—Cadence's mama went from lying down to sitting.

"You go on and let me handle this," the lady said. "Your mama's tooth is bothering her. I'm a nurse. My name's Kitty."

"FOO-OO-OOF!" Her mama started howling, so Cadence howled too.

Which right away brought another lady flying in from the hall—"What's all this ruckus?"—golden curls bouncing. "Look at you, Miz Greevey. You got yourself clabbered up."

Whoo-ee, she was quick rounding 'round that bed. Cadence watched her slide a finger into her mama's cuffed hand, circling it around inside the palm which might to have smoothed or tickled, Cadence couldn't tell, but it caught her mama up short.

"That's better, Miz G." The lady kept her finger there for her mama to hang onto. She looked up at Cadence. "You must be Miz Greevey's girl. I am Dee Dee Hips, the supervisor."

"Cadence Greevey from Little Piney."

"Nice to meet you, Cadence. Why don't you come stand over here by me." Cadence did as she was told. "You see this smile on my face, honey? I want to see it on your face too. That way when your mama looks at you, she'll know everything's all right."

"Like *I'm* the mama."

"Yes, indeed. Like she is your baby. Here." From out of her pocket, Miss Dee Dee pulled a tiny toothbrush wrapped in a clear wrapper. "I want you to open this and hold it 'til I'm ready. Can you do that?"

Cadence wanted to say, *Of course I can, I'm not stupid!* but she knew her manners. She tore the package carefully, holding the brush up clean for everyone to see.

"Now, Kitty, go on and fetch me a washcloth from the bathroom, will you? Run it under the cold water, wring it good and bring it here to me."

Nurse Kitty brought the washcloth. Miss Dee Dee pointed her down to the foot of the bed. "Lift up those blankets off her feet and I'll tell you how it's done." She smiled at the both of them. "My daddy worked his whole his life for the Garnet County Sheriff and he taught me something I will teach you: never fight *fight* with fight. You got you a mean drunk who doesn't want to see the inside of a jail? Take off his shoes and walk him backwards. That's all it takes. He'll be too worried about what's coming up under each step to make much fuss. Works like a charm. A cool washcloth on a bare foot will do the same thing. Go on ahead and try."

It put Cadence in mind of Sunday School, the picture of Mary Magdalene pouring water on Jesus's feet, seeing Nurse Kitty pat her mama's toes one at a time with the washcloth, then spreading it wide and wet-cool from the heel. That did the trick. Her mama tamed right down, hands dropping, eyes rolling sideways.

Miss Dee Dee took the toothbrush from Cadence. "Here we go," she said, brushing ever so gently.

"How," her mama said, meaning *Ow.*

Miss Dee Dee filled a paper cup. "Rinse for me."

Cadence saw it was clever, asking her mama to rinse since it was a lot to do, what with the cup and the washcloth, and so kept her mind off all that was troubling her.

Miss Dee Dee stroked one of her hands in its leash. "If it were me, I wouldn't like this one bit either, Miz Greevey. But seeing as how you keep falling out of bed, we're going to keep these on to keep you safe. All right?"

Cadence watched her mama run her tongue around her mouth.

"Tastes better, doesn't it? You sleep now. We'll see in the morning how you're feeling and where to go from there. Can we do that together? I'll crank you back." The bed began to tilt.

Nurse Kitty got busy re-tucking sheets and blankets. "Good job, Kitty Pearl," Miss Dee Dee told her. Nurse Kitty's face went pink as her ponytail.

"And you!" Miss Dee Dee swung on Cadence who all this time had been doing her very best not to get in the way. "What a good helper you are. Can I ask you to be my special helper again?"

Cadence said, "Yes, ma'am," but she worried, she would not know how.

"I want you to sit right here and help your mama go to sleep."

"Yes, ma'am." Cadence knew she could do that easy.

"When are your people coming for you?"

"Soon as they close the Mountain Man."

"Oh, I know all about that place. My mother-in-law practically pays rent she's in there so much." She and Nurse Kitty had a laugh. "It gets awful quiet here, sweetheart. Did you bring something with you to do?"

"My Big Tablet and Magic Markers." Cadence pulled out the drawing she'd made of Cincinnati with her daddy on the road to the Pineys.

"That's good, honey. You do some more coloring and I'll be back before you know it."

Then they were gone, Miss Dee Dee with Kitty Pearl in tow.

Cadence sat with her mama. She colored. She sat some more.

After a while, she didn't want to do anything except maybe take one more look at the half-tooth in her mama's mouth. She wondered, could she touch it just to see, would it wiggle? She wondered, if she did, would it come out altogether? She looked around. She listened. It didn't seem like anybody was there to see, so she went in slow with her pinky, thinking to slip it in under her mama's puffy upper lip when—"Hunh!"—her mama snorted awake.

"Hushy," she whispered.

It took Cadence a minute. "You mean Hershey?" She was too scared to look where her mama was looking, somewhere over by the door at a ghost dog maybe, coming in with blood-biting on his mind.

"Kiw!" Her mama's voice got louder.

"Kill?"

"Kiw him."

Cadence felt like she was sitting by the campfire on Brushy with Spidey Weaver telling tales of the Piney Phantom and all her classmates laughing, but her wanting to put her fingers in her ears she was so spooked.

Now her mama was crying. Snot ran from her nose. Cadence knew how much that could itch. She fetched a tissue to wipe it off.

"Kiw him. Sawwy." There were tears and tears and snot and tears. Cadence kept wiping. She knew "sawwy" meant "sorry."

"Sawwy."

"Don't cry, mama."

"Smew ode."

Hershey smelled old? As a ghost dog or as a dog-dog? Could you kill a dog for smelling old?

Her mama's tears had stopped. "Sawwy."

"Don't you worry," Cadence told her. "Hershey's in dog heaven now. A big giant yard of clouds where no dog has to wear a collar or get tied up ever again and there's always plenty of sunshine for naps and trees for shade and no matter how far they run, crazy running like any dog will do, they never get lost."

"Yawd?"

"A big backyard. He's gone home."

"Shome," slushed her mama.

Water pooled under her eyelids, making them flutter. Sleep came fast like fainting. After a while, she frowned, then started to snore.

Cadence kept herself close by the bed. For the first time in her life, for the very first time, she felt wholly and completely proud. Cadence, tongue-tied Cadence, Cadence the kids made fun of in school for getting her numbers backwards and her reading wrong, Cadence who never got to tell a story on campfire night—yet here it had come to her, a vision in her mind of the cloud-yard with Hershey running free—and she had been able to say it. A story, like a pasha on a hellephant. To help her mama sleep.

There was a sound in the hall. Cadence reached for the crib rail, thinking it to be Hershey coming back for the two of them, but it was only Miss Dee Dee passing by. "You all right, honey?" She disappeared, then reappeared, walking backward past the doorway to take another look.

Cadence froze. "Fine-fine-fine," she chirped.

Something on her face must have said that was true, because Miss Dee Dee took off again, "Nice work, baby girl! Gold star!" her voice floating behind her as she went.

WEDNESDAY

November 22, 1989

And Your Enemies Closer

Maggie Dull
Morning

The sun crested Brushy, focusing a single piercing beam directly into the bedroom window until Maggie had to squint, then close her eyes. Blind, one leg of her leggings halfway up, she hopped toward the drapes to pull them to.

"I don't know what's real!"

Maggie sighed. So much for the dream of a home workout. She hobbled into the living room to find her mother flailing on the couch as if the air were filled with wasps. "I don't know what's real!" She'd kicked the blanket to the floor rocking her way toward the edge of the cushion, clearly trying to get her feet beneath her to stand.

And go where? Maggie wondered. She kneeled, then half-lay across her, one hand gripping each arm. "Easy-*pleasy,* Mrs. Dull. Easy-*pleasy.*" Such Mad-Hatter aphorisms kept resurfacing, freed perhaps by the charade of pretending to be strangers.

Make something up, Maggie told herself. *A child sees monsters, you make something up!* She used her party-planner voice, a tone so bright it surprised her mother into momentary attention. "Mrs. Dull, anytime you see anyone or anything you don't recognize, all you have to do is ask, 'Are you real?'"

Her mother looked straight at her. "Are *you* real?"

Maggie laughed. "Real as rain." Another mother expression. "You see? That's what real things do: they tell you they're real. But if I'm a ghost and you ask me—'Are you real?'—I won't say a thing, because ghosts can't lie. That's the rule of ghosts."

Sheer nonsense—Where did this stuff come from?—but it seemed to have a calming effect. Her mother quieted, tugging at the gauze on her forehead.

"What's the matter? Does your head hurt, Mrs. Dull?"

"No, my heart does."

"Your heart hurts?"

Her mother pointed to her lower belly nodding very seriously. "Maggie?" She was asking, not addressing.

"That's right."

"That's my daughter's name."

"I know it is." Maggie couldn't help herself. "Your daughter who apparently was no glamour puss."

Her mother sat herself all the way back, smiling. "She didn't have to be. She was one smart cookie." The smile vanished as quickly as it had come. Her eyes watered. Her nose began to run. "My children left me," her voice shaking now with instant tears. "My daughter moved away."

Maggie reached for the tissues. "Why do you suppose that is, Mrs. Dull?"

Her mother snuffled and thought and snuffled some more. Then she pushed the tissues away, nodding, very solemn, "That's the rule of ghosts."

Heavens, was it pill time? Maybe one of her medications would steer the woman back in the direction of her right mind. *On the other hand,* Maggie thought, *this might be the most honest conversation we've ever had.*

She came around to sit next to her mother on the couch, re-tucking the blanket around the two of them, wiggling her bare feet in over her mother's slippers like minnows on a feeding frenzy. "Miss-uss Dull," she stretched the words out to buy time. "I wonder if it might not be time to move you to a place where you'll be taken care of better. What do you think about that?"

Instantly, up bubbled a string of giggles. "Oh, yes! We'll live high on the log."

Damn, if that didn't make Maggie laugh too.

"Let them eat steak!" her mother crowed, waving her two hands in a feeble version of *Whoopee* that sent her into a wheezing spell.

"That's cake, Mommy."

They both froze. The word had popped out before Maggie could stop it. She got busy wiping her mother's chin. "It's funny, Mrs. Dull. You remind me so much of my own mother. Would you mind if I called you Mommy?"

Her mother stiffened. "No!"

"Let's pretend," said Maggie.

Her mother shook her head back-forth, back-forth *No No No.* Maggie copied her, doing the same pouty *No No No,* then *Yes Yes Yes* until her mother played along, until she too was shaking her head *Yes,* evidently delighted to have been fooled into doing so. It was a ritual that went way back, Maggie averting maternal Vesuvius with every inanity she could call to mind, anything to keep the woman from blowing.

They cozied up together. Maggie pointed to a bright orange maple leaf lying just inside the front door, soggy, somehow tracked or blown in with all the comings and goings. "It's Thanksgiving tomorrow," she said. "Why don't I make us some turkey? Some mashed potatoes? Doesn't that sound good?"

"Boiled peanuts!" exclaimed her mother.

"You want boiled peanuts, we shall have boiled peanuts." Maggie wondered how in the hell she could pull that off. She remembered they came canned—it was probably a matter of heat-and-serve these days—but when in God's name would she be free enough to hit the Bi-Lo? It all came flooding back: the bank, the drug store, the as-yet-to-be-identified lawyer. She was kicking herself now. Why had she been in such an all-fired hurry to dismiss that nurse? Both nurses? She'd have to call the Crowes. Maybe they could come babysit for an hour or so.

Her mother, on the other hand, was beaming, reaching for the leaf, which Maggie brought to her, still dripping, to wave like a tiny flag. *Nothing like boiled peanuts to lift a girl's spirits.* Maggie took her mother's hand, the leafless one. "I make parties for a living. I'll make this really nice for you, Mommy."

Her mother frowned. She looked toward the fireplace, her face pinched with suspicion. "Where's the manna?"

Maggie knew what she meant. The Santa display, orange juice and sugar cookies that had been set out to entice the angels. Her mother brandished the leaf as if catching Maggie red-handed. "You ate it!"

"No, I didn't."

"Yes, you did!" Reaching and pulling at the pearls around Maggie's neck saying "I know you. You can't fool me."

"I suppose I can't." Maggie carefully unwrapped her mother's fingers from the flimsy strand of plastic beads so as not to break and scatter them.

"No more manna, Mommy. We don't need it. Any angel worth her wings will find her way right to you. But there's a redbird on the mantel. See it?" Her mother looked where she pointed. "I bought that for you. You love redbirds."

"I do?"

Looking into her mother's face, Maggie met a child she had never known, a girl, excited and making a little song now, waving her leaf flag, singing "Let them eat steak," her feet keeping time, her scorched head cleansed and Band-aided, her hands clapping mute around a blanket of which she could no longer keep track.

Do Unto Others

Cadence Greevey
Mid-Morning

Something about going home the night before had confused Cadence. Maybe it was because she hadn't actually gone there. Instead she'd slept at the Crowes' house since Uncle Walker said Auntie Pam said no more staying by herself. She was to stay with them until her daddy came, which Cadence agreed to only because they promised they'd drive her right back to see her mama in the morning. They gave her a nice dinner of corned beef and a fried egg and then she got to sleep in a high bed with bright white sheets and a "puff," that's what Auntie Pam called it.

But now, coming back into Solace, she got lost again. It didn't help that Uncle Walker dropped her off outside without parking the car. Then it was just her standing alone in the vine-covered hallway with all the doors that looked exactly the same.

Cadence walked into a room she thought was right, but it wasn't her mama inside. It was a lady with gray hair sticking off her head in all directions and some bald patches like a mangy dog.

The lady looked right at her and said, "August?" Then something changed in her eyes and she said, "No."

The lady had a suitcase on the bed, wide open with things hanging out of it and off of her. A blouse on top of her bathrobe. Ankle socks like a girl scrunched into heel shoes like a grown woman.

"I have to get out of here," the lady snapped at her. "My girls need me. I have to go." She was pushing on things, trying to get them in the suitcase, but some were still on their plastic hangers, bending so bad Cadence thought they might break.

The lady kept pushing, not looking up. "What day is it?"

That scared Cadence. She was afraid she might not give the right answer. "It might be Saturday or Sunday because they's no school today," she offered.

The lady looked like she was going to give her a spanking, slapping at the clothes and the suitcase.

Cadence tried to be helpful. "You could see maybe on TV about what day it is."

"I have to get out of here!" Cadence knew by her tone that *she* was the one who was supposed to get out of there, so she got out right quick, scooting back into the hallway.

There, thank heavens, on the other side of the hall, was her mama sound asleep in bed. Her mouth was almost closed now. Her lip looked better. There was no more blood, but coming in close, Cadence could see the tip of the broken tooth. She was fixing to get her finger in there when the nurse with the ponytail came charging into the room.

"You remember me. I'm Kitty."

"Yes, ma'am. Like the kitty-cat clock." Cadence pretended to be cleaning something off the side of her mama's mouth, wiping her finger on the blanket for show. Luckily, Nurse Kitty was too busy to notice, checking on the bag hanging by the bed. She said it was fine for Cadence to watch TV, just not too loud. She even turned it on before she left.

Cadence couldn't believe how good the TV was, much better than at home. She watched a kitchen show where two ladies dressed like Miss April Turner, the Weather Girl, cooked a Thanksgiving turkey and a special dish of whole apples with rice. Cadence had never had apples with rice, but it looked good with a gravy made from raisins. She wished she could learn to make it for her daddy, for him to take a big bite after driving so long to see his girl and say, "Oh my, what a delicious treat."

After a while, it was hard to watch TV because her mama started snoring. Loud, open-mouth snoring so that Cadence could see the broken place on her gum where the whole tooth had been. It bothered her since she knew no one had been there to wrap that tooth up and put it under the pillow for the tooth fairy to come.

Cadence slid her hand under the pillow, just to check, inching this way and that, feeling for a tooth and finding nothing.

Come on, Mama. Open your eyes.

She wanted to ask her what she should do. She even tried staring, though her mama always said staring wasn't polite. Like when Mrs. Lyons' little boy with the swollen-up forehead was in church, her mama told her to quit looking at him. "Unfortunate," her mama said. "That's what a boy like that is."

What if it was him with his tooth broke off? Cadence thought. *What would his mama do?*

It came to her. Oh, my goodness, how could she have missed it? Sitting across from her on the tray was a tissue box. And the tissue in that tissue box was white. White like a tooth. Cadence pulled out just one piece so as not to be wasteful, bunching it carefully into something that looked about tooth-sized.

Then, for a ribbon she folded a second tissue. She got out her markers, fat and juicy with color. Cadence chose the red one knowing it was, of all colors, her mama's favorite. She stained her tissue-ribbon by making little dots that blended into each other until the whole thing was red. Then she wrapped it around her tissue-tooth, holding it in place with one finger and crawling it, using the same inching of hand, deep under her mama's pillow.

"I found it, Mama, I found your tooth!" Cadence heard her voice too loud. She made herself whisper. "Sleep tight now and any minute—just like that—the tooth fairy will fly in here and leave you something extra special."

Extra special? How would that happen? Cadence was no fairy. She was only Cadence Greevey from Little Piney and she had nothing—nothing!—to sneak back under that pillow as a spirit come and gone, as a tiny Santa trading treasure for a tissue-tooth. There was nothing and nobody to help her now except the two ladies on TV saying, "Isn't this darling?" as they set up a table display of a puffy, paper sailboat on a strip of blue that said, in silver letters, GOD BLESS THE MERRY MAYFLOWER.

There's No Use Crying

August Early
Late Morning

Coming into Solace, there was nobody at the front desk. The sound of somebody pounding something rose from the direction of the kitchen, but no one came to say hello, so Mr. Early figured it was all right to go where he was going. He started for Theo's room, coming to it and then walking past, heading down the hall a ways to calm himself.

Miss Susan Neville had given him such a look of Almighty Judgment at breakfast. She knew he'd missed a whole day with Theo. She sat glaring as he told the twins their mama was doing fine, even though he had no way of knowing that. She had not bothered to get up from the table as he left.

At least he'd remembered to bring his presents. He kept the bag right on his lap as he drove.

She'll like them, he thought. *I'll tell her the girls picked them out.*

Mr. Early found himself standing stock still in the middle of the hall, gazing into a room at a woman he had not seen before. By the look of her, she wasn't dead, but she was surely out cold. Sitting by the bed was a big girl, both tall and plump. In her teens, Mr. Early thought, and yet wearing the kind of dress the twins might wear in the summer. Even with the TV on, the girl was leaning over the bed, her hand way up under the woman's pillow almost to her elbow. Plumping it maybe. Or maybe trying to lie next to the sick lady. Maybe her mother. Or her grandmother, like Theo. She was in an odd position.

Sensing he was there, the girl pulled her hand out, then nodded a greeting. That was when Mr. Early saw the cinches. Ropes on the sick woman's wrists clamped to the bed rails.

They tie you up like a dog, Mr. Early thought.

He could hear his mother saying, *Over my dead body.* He could see her horror of such things in a memory he had of her face.

They must have a good reason, he thought. The woman had probably gotten to cat-scratching the nurses. Or maybe, at the sight of some husband who'd run out on her and the big girl, she'd taken to throwing whatever she could lay her hands on. *Surely they don't tie you up for nothing.*

Mr. Early did not want Theo to see such a sight. He back-peddled to her door thinking to swing it to and block her view.

He found her standing half-dressed, jumbled up in her nightgown, a blouse up one arm and thick socks tucked into her good shoes. Her suitcase lay on the bed. She was busy mashing her clothes down into it with the hangers still on.

She felt him there, snapping her head around to say, "August Early, where have you been? We got to go!" Pumping down on clothes that would not wedge into the suitcase for the width of their hangers poking out either side.

"Go where?"

"They's taking people." Whispering like someone was listening in, "I won't get took."

"What do you mean, Theo?"

"A spaceman. I saw him. Yesterday." Theo was going back and forth two steps from the closet to the suitcase. She was tippy, but so mad Mr. Early was afraid to slow her down. "He takes people. The spaceman. Then he takes their things in a bag. I saw him." She slumped next to the mess on the bed, arms stretched over the suitcase. Her nose pinked. Mr. Early knew what that meant without ever seeing it in her face before.

"We have to go to church!" she said. "He cannot get me there!"

"It's not church day, Theo."

"Where's my hat? I can't find my hat!" She shook his hands off like Sue-Sue having a tantrum. Her eyes said *Do Something!*

Mr. Early began casting around for her church hat, knowing it wasn't there, saying, "Theo, it's not Sunday. It's Wednesday. You're all right."

"They's no school today, August. It's Sunday!" she said, bossy, angry.

"No, ma'am. It's Wednesday." He knelt down with her, taking her hand so that she had to look at him. He went in long strokes along her arm like he did Shirley's golden coat when she put her nose up under his hand for the feel of his touch.

"It's Wednesday?"

"That's right. It's the day before Thanksgiving."

Theo settled down. He peeled the blouse off from overtop her nightgown. "We can see about church come Sunday, but for now, we're going to stay right here." His hands told her to stand still, which she did, while he got her suitcase off the bed, pawing his present bag down into a corner of the sheets to make room.

"I saw a spaceman."

"Yes'm. I did too." Soothing her, pulling off her shoes—the church shoes. Her feet hung off the bed, each in a sock, like the girls' feet did every night.

"I believe he's the cleaning man is all," Mr. Early told her. "Extra cleaning, for folks who like things extra clean. But I won't let him clean in here."

He didn't see right away because it made no noise, but sure if he didn't look up to see tears. Not with any crying. Just tears coming down her cheeks, her voice woeful, saying, "Where *were* you?"

Mr. Early thought he might to go on ahead and die right then. His heart squeezed something awful, with him thinking all in a rush, What kind of man leaves his wife alone in such a place?

He had to hold onto her sloppy-sock feet for a minute, head bowed to her knees. Then he got to wiping her tears with his one finger. She paid him little mind. She did not seem to know the tears were there.

A lady came into the doorway. The way she walked made him know she was in charge. She caught sight of the suitcase. "Oh, Miz Early, are we at it again?"

She asked if he was Mr. Early, which he said he was. She said she was Burnice Kling and to call her Burnice. She was wide-bodied, much more so than Mr. Early himself, who was naturally stringy like all his people had been. She wore a white dress like the nurses on TV.

Being wide, Miss Burnice had to scooch herself in along the far side of the bed. "How are we, Miz Early?"

"Tolerable."

Miss Burnice held his wife's wrist looking at her watch. "The pain bothering you?"

Theo asked if it might be time for more medicine. Miss Burnice said that would be fine.

"You might want to be easing yourself this afternoon," she said to his wife, taking another look around the room. "They tell me you had a *big* day yesterday." She looked to Mr. Early. "She had a big day." Then back to Theo. "Kept wanting to pack your bags, didn't you Miz Early?"

"She thought it was church," Mr. Early explained.

"Mmmm-hmmm." Miss Burnice looked dead at him. Her "mmmm-hmmm" didn't mean exactly "mmmm-hmmm."

"I will be right back with some medicine. Here, put this under your tongue." She slipped a thermometer in and left the room.

Mr. Early got busy straightening Theo's things. He untangled hangers, buttoning what needed buttoning, zipping up the little suitcase, the one she'd gotten ready before the Holy Brides of Christ. He set it at the back of the closet, neat and tidy. He hung his jacket up next to her bathrobe.

The thermometer commenced to beeping. Miss Burnice came, the man called Isah scooting in right behind her with a tray of food. "You want help, Mrs. E? Maybe your husband can spoon for you." He opened the napkin, taking plastic from off the juice cup. Theo shooed him off as Miss Burnice took the thermometer from her mouth.

"Mmmm-hmmm." Miss Burnice read what she saw there, then threw the thermometer away, or at least part of it. She was gone before Mr. Early could ask what she'd seen.

"August," Theo said, any trace of tears gone from her cheeks. "You go find your own supper. Go on now." He did not know why she wanted him gone. Maybe she had no taste for food. Or maybe she was clumsy with the spoon and didn't like him seeing that.

Your wife knows how she wants it, chapter and verse. That's what Miss Hazel had said weeks ago on the porch. Mr. Early wished he could stay with his wife now, to tell her it was all right, to help her with the spoon. But she'd told him to go, so that's just what he did.

A Bird In The Hand

Cadence Greevey
Early Afternoon

Nurse Kitty came back, ponytail bobbing, with a man named Isah who carried a tray. While he got to unwrapping things, she told Cadence they had to see to her mother maybe eating something and would she kindly wait in the kitchen. Cadence knew her mama would not wake for food of any kind, but the kitchen sounded like a good place to go. It had been a while since breakfast.

"Can I take Rabbit for company?" Nurse Kitty said it would be all right. She pointed out to the hall saying, "Left, left, then right."

"Left, left, then right." Cadence went left. There were lots of doors that looked the same. Which one should she take?

A very old man came along in a wheelchair. He had a ponytail like Miss Kitty only hers was white-pink and his was white-white. He made his chair go with bent hands, the fingers all cramped together, but still he managed to push his way along. "Looking for the kitchen?" he asked as he rolled. "It's the last left, then the door on your right. Follow me."

He wheeled himself up ahead with Cadence following and thank goodness because it turned out the kitchen was a fun place to be. It had a table in the middle like on TV with lots of people there including a lady in charge, Miss Cherille. She was as round as she was short. Her hair was round too, curly like a lamb that made Cadence want to pat it.

"To whom do you belong?" Miss Cherille asked.

"I am Cadence Greevey from Little Piney. My mama is Verleana Pole Greevey."

"Well, Cadence Greevey from Little Piney, come in out of that door. You're gumming up the works."

Miss Cherille said she liked her dress and always to stay on one side of the table, because the other was for fixing for sick folks. Only the nurses could go there.

Without asking, Miss Cherille got to pouring Cadence some milk to go with two whole oatmeal cookies on a plate. Then she saw Rabbit. "They's no animals at my table," she said, which made everybody laugh. Cadence told her his name was Rabbit, but he was not alive.

"Well, if you're going to eat my cookies, Mr. Rabbit has to stay on your lap, covered up good with a napkin before you take even one bite."

Now, of all the things Cadence forgot which were so very many in school, she never missed saying grace over a meal. She liked the sing-song, so she bowed her head over the milk and cookies and Rabbit on her lap, weaving her fingers tight closed to sing her a quick blessing. Then she set to eating, breaking one little piece of oatmeal off at a time and mixing it with a swig of milk to make it mushy in her mouth.

There was some talking around her. Cadence paid it no mind. A very old lady two chairs over was taking chewed food out of her mouth and laying it back on the plate the way Cadence's mama would never have let her do until Miss Cherille took the plate away from her. The skinny man in the wheelchair, a beanpole like her daddy, didn't eat a thing.

And then there was the old man who came in right behind her. The short man. Plain. She'd seen him in the hall outside her mama's room, as frozen up now as he had been then, standing stock still in the kitchen door like a lizard thinking to blend into some rocks. He said something about being early. Miss Cherille got the man seated for his own milk and cookies.

Cadence ate her one-by-one bites fast now. She didn't want anyone to tell her she couldn't have both cookies, because her plan was to eat one and wrap the other in her napkin, which she did under the table so as not to be seen by anyone and them guessing what she was up to.

Nurse Kitty poked her head into the kitchen to tell Cadence, "You can go back to your mama when you're ready."

Was she ever! Cadence had the napkin-wrapped cookie in one hand, her empty cup in the other, hoping Miss Cherille might say what to do with it, but Miss Cherille was too busy so the short man, the early one, let her give it to him. Cadence said, "Thank you," on the run, heading quick down the hall before someone could see she had a cookie with her and call her back.

She found her way by going down the middle of each hall looking left and right until she saw her mama who was, of course, sleeping. The TV had one of the soaps on where ladies were getting ready for a holiday party. They wore beautiful dresses like the scales of fish flashing different colors. Each one had her hair done in a different shape of lightness and swirl like cotton candy.

Oh, how clever she was! Cadence knew her mama would say so when she woke up because, while the soap ladies got going to their holiday party, Cadence went ahead and cribbledy-crawled her hand back under her mama's pillow without her waking or even turning her head, turtling out the tissue-tooth and then turtling back her special tooth fairy surprise of a whole giant oatmeal cookie wrapped in a Thanksgiving napkin with a turkey in a pilgrim hat holding an ear of corn under one wing. She knew it would please her mama no end when she finally opened her eyes.

Yea, Though I Walk

August Early
Afternoon

Coming into the kitchen, Mr. Early almost bumped into the big-little girl standing smack in the doorway. Miss Cherille was asking her who she was. He remembered Miss Cherille from his tour, remembered her saying she ruled the roost.

"Cadence Greevey from Little Piney," came the answer. The girl was very polite. Mr. Early saw she carried an animal pelt with her the way a littler child might carry a blanket.

"Well, Cadence Greevey from Little Piney, come in out of that door. You're gumming up the works."

Miss Cherille waved Mr. Early in too. "I met you yesterday, I believe."

"Yes, ma'am. The day before."

Miss Cherille turned back to the girl saying she liked her dress.

"It's a dirndl," the girl told her with a little swish of the skirt. The rest of the folks in the room nodded their heads, Mr. Early along with them, though he had no idea what a "dirndl" was.

Miss Cherille got busy pouring Dixie cups of milk and plating any number of good-sized oatmeal cookies, all the while addressing him. "I've got my hands full with cooking, Mr. Early. Take a seat where you can. It's rush hour."

He tucked himself into the last available seat next to a very old man in a wheelchair. There was precious little to him. His skin was mottled yellow and red like a plum's with, under its thinness, dark veins. The man's fingers bent back nearly to his wrists. Under his bathrobe, his shoulders had all the substance of two smoothed-off doorknobs. He was watching Miss Cherille cook with a certain quickness of the eye until she gave him a look. "Mr. Katz, you're going to have to eat dinner in your room today. I got me a turkey to brine. I cannot have you under foot."

Mr. Katz spoke his words out one at a time like raindrops hitting the surface of a pond: "If you will permit me to point out, you let Miss Dawson eat with you."

He waved over at a woman who might be his twin in her thinness and paleness and bent-over body. She was gumming bits of oatmeal cookie, then carefully taking raisins from her mouth and laying them neatly on her plate.

"Why is Miss Dawson permitted to eat with you when I am not?"

At the sound of her name, the raisin lady lifted her gaze from the plate, but instead of looking at Mr. Katz, she locked onto Mr. Early. "Tobias! I haven't seen you in so long," her high voice sharp like a towhee bird, rising on the "you" as if greeting a long lost relative.

Which meant that everybody looked Mr. Early's way. Oh, how he wished he had his hat on. Anything he could pull down over his eyes.

"Behave yourself," Miss Cherille said and went right on with her conversation. "I don't play favorites, Mr. Katz. Now go to your room and eat some of that dinner I worked so hard on. Then maybe you can come back later."

Mr. Katz crossed his bathrobe over his chest. "Would three o'clock suit you?" He spoke like the prince in one of Sue-Sue's stories asking a princess what time to bring the pumpkin carriage around.

Miss Cherille might as well have been that princess, the way she smiled at him. "Three o'clock would be fine."

Mr. Katz wrapped his crooked fingers around each of the wheelchair wheels, nodding to Mr. Early. "Very pleased to make your acquaintance, sir. My hearing is not what it used to be. I did not catch your name."

Before Mr. Early could answer Miss Dawson was yelping, "Tobias, sweetheart! Give us a kiss!"

Miss Cherille cut her off, "He is not Tobias, Miss Dawson. Tobias has gone on. You know that. He's waiting for you just where he said he'd be, but he can't be here in this kitchen right now. You remember?"

"He's at the Dairy Queen."

"That's right."

"The Dairy Queen in the sky," whispered Mr. Katz to Mr. Early winking. "Call me Aram."

"August Early," Mr. Early said, hoping he would not have to shake either of those curled hands, but putting his own right around one when it was offered. He barely squeezed for fear of breaking it off.

"August," said Mr. Katz approvingly. "Do you know what that name means?"

"A month of the year."

Mr. Katz smiled. "Well, yes, but also nobility. Au-*gust*. " He said the name with emphasis at the end. "An au-*gust* person is a person of great dignity."

Mr. Early allowed as how he had not heard that.

Mr. Katz took his leave. Cadence-Greevey-from-Little-Piney stood up to go as well, holding out her empty milk cup. Since no one seemed to notice, Mr. Early took it from her. She scooted out the door, her pelt wrapped suspiciously around a napkin wadded in her hand.

Then Miss Burnice popped her head in from the hallway, waving at the cook. "They love that acorn squash."

"What's not to love? Nothing but brown sugar and a whole lot of butter."

Miss Burnice told Mr. Early that his wife had eaten a little something. "She'll sleep now." Mr. Early got up to go.

"Come on back later if you want supper and I'll fix you a plate," Miss Cherille called after him. "No use the both of you doing poorly."

Even though Mr. Early was extra quiet coming in, he woke Theo. She looked tidy in her bed. The bag of presents he'd brought was set at the far side, away from where her toes poked the blankets up.

"I brought you some things."

Fishing in the bag, his nerve almost failed him. Theo was bound not to like any of it. She would castigate him for spending money instead of putting it in the jar where they stored little bits as they had it, bills and change, for things the girls might need up the road.

He pulled his presents out in the order he found them, the plastic pitcher first. Theo stared as he turned it in front of her.

"It's green," he said. "Put me in mind of a squash vine. Or maybe cucumber. It'll be nice with the green salt and pepper you found over at the Rexall. I thought maybe you could put your water in it."

He pulled out the cup for her to look at. "To go with. It's a cup. Or a glass. I don't know which."

"A cup," she said. She held it.

"See, you tip it and them shells, they start to swimming. Right there in the glass."

"It's a baby's cup," said Theo.

"It's purty," said Mr. Early right away, thinking maybe it was not all right for him to have brought her a baby's cup. But she said, "It *is* purty."

He could have jumped like one of his dogs bouncing at the thought of a run in the woods. "See?" he reached and tipped her hands to tip the cup. "See how they's swimming?"

"I see it," said Theo.

"That's for your water to drink. And then I got you this."

He pulled out the pen.

"August Early, you done went crazy."

"It didn't cost but eight sixty-four for all of it. The pitcher was a red ticket and the rest was on sale." He demonstrated the pen, how the light clicked on inside. He pulled out the receipt. "See? Eight sixty-four." He wrote the numbers again so she could see the purple ink.

"Now, August, what am I going to do with a writing pen?"

"I thought you could make me a list, when you thought of it, or I could, of things you might want from home. So I won't forget nothing."

"Hmmm." That seemed to satisfy her. She took the pen and tried it on the receipt, making a squiggle that trailed off as her eyelids sagged.

Mr. Early knew he should ask her about the girls. Miss Susan Neville had pressed him to do so, but Theo looked peaceful now. The deep worry-wrinkle between her eyes had smoothed. Her mouth went easy. He tried slipping the pen from her hand, but that only made her grip it harder, so he left it there.

He tiptoed into the bathroom and filled up the new pitcher with water. He arranged it with the baby cup on her tray-stand.

Look, look, look! he was saying to her in his mind as he slid the silver-frame picture out of the bag. *Look, look, look!* She was fast asleep. He set the picture on the tray table, propping and turning it so that the first thing she'd see when she woke up would be the baby faces of Sue-Sue and Serena.

Then, in the way to which he had become accustomed, Mr. Early slid himself slowly backward into the chair by the bed.

For a while he was plagued with a vision of her in his mind, suitcase flung open, clothes slopped over her nightgown. He knew that he could never, ever again miss a day of coming to her, no matter if she waved him off, no matter if all he did was sit and sit and sit some more. She was an unusual woman, as Dr. Narduli had said, but he was to come to her.

Knowing that, pledging it like a prayer, Mr. Early settled back, waiting through the afternoon for supper hour to come.

To Everything Turn

Maggie Dull / Curtis-Michael Hipps
Suppertime

"Is this all right?" Curtis leaned over his menu.

"Are you kidding?" Maggie laughed. "I dream of the mu shu at Happiness." Happiness being the one and only Chinese joint in Big Piney, not to mention the only non-drive-through dinner option on the Piney side of Garnet.

"No, I mean, is it all right to leave your mother."

"Curtis? Jeez! Why'd I even tell you about her? You think I would leave her up on the mountain by her lonesome? Surely you don't think I'm that heartless."

Curtis sent a look over his menu that said, *I don't know, I've seen another side of you.*

It pleased her no end. There was something about this mountain boy. His lack of deference was a tonic.

"I hired a night nurse. Someone who knows what she's doing, though in this case, she is a he."

"A guy nurse?"

"Yeah. Got him from an agency."

"Man." Curtis shook his head. "I just can't see going for that. Dee Dee works with one: a big burly guy, Viet Nam vet named Bear, so that tells you something. But it's not for me."

"They make good money."

"Tell me about it. Still, I can't see me in the little white hat."

That got them both going. That and the first round of Budweisers. God forbid that Happiness should offer a Chinese beer, though Maggie sincerely doubted how authentically *Chinese* imported Chinese beers were. More likely generic Asian labels got slapped on some bottles of second-rate American brew. Besides, no one in the Pineys would be caught dead paying premium for some exotic quaff. Oh, they wanted mini corncobs and water chestnuts in their chow mein all right, but that didn't cost extra because the stuff came out of cans the size of her car. She'd seen the empties stacked in the parking lot out back. No, as far as beer went, folks in the Pineys wanted plenty of it. Cold. Reliably alcoholic. That was about all that mattered.

Curtis had tucked the two of them in the booth farthest from the door. Maggie reveled in the molded seats, nail-polish red trimmed in gold, fabricated somewhere in Guatemala and shipped straight out of Miami. She ought to know. She'd had to round up a roomful once for some Ameri-Asian food conglomerate, an industrial buffet whose winking theme was *Flour Drum Song*.

The capper at Happiness was the wall décor. Around the room in uneven groupings hung plastic bamboo frames with inside, not your classic lotus watercolor or indecipherable calligraphy, but technicolor photos of picturesque Blue Ridge scenes—dogwood blossoms close-up, the oft-snapped rushing brook tableau. Call it Mountain Oriental. It was so wrong. Maggie loved it.

She and Curtis leaned well back from each other. Chatter flowed and yet nothing much was said because neither wanted to say much. They pretended to catch up, getting-to-know-you in reverse.

Half a brew down and Maggie declared she wanted everything on the menu. *Egg rolls!* "Deep fried?" Curtis asked? *Hell, yes! The deeper the better.* She wanted sweet-and-sour. Then a big mound of mu shu, soggy and slightly gray no doubt, but hot, with plenty of no-discernable-trace-of-nourishment, bright-white rice glopped on the side.

When the waitress came, Curtis ordered for Maggie. "For the lady," he said, which was so un-Curtis it was funny.

Maggie took over for him. "Let me guess," then turning to the waitress, "He'll have wontons. The hot-and-sour soup. And a number twelve: beef and broccoli. With rice. Better double that rice. And a side of green beans." Winking at him, "How'd I do?"

"You missed one thing."

"Szechuan," she said.

"You got it."

Curtis hooted. Finally a woman who wasn't nibbling at a few cabbage strands. No way women fooled him. They didn't carry the curves they did, some of them even the heft, without powering some serious chow pretty regularly. But they liked to pretend they were living on air, as if a man found that attractive.

Curtis did not. He liked appetite. Besides, Maggie looked pretty damn good for a girl who apparently could eat like a horse.

They started on their second beers, swapping egg rolls for wontons, drenching every bite in all three of the neon-bright sauces, green, orange and high-gloss brown, adding drops of soy and squirts from a bottle of relabeled Mexican hot sauce. Curtis tried initiating some what-have-you-been-up-to chit-chat, but Maggie put the kibosh on all that. "Let's not. Or, I tell you what," licking her lips, mouth full of egg roll, "Let's do the speed version. Your life in ten words or less."

"Ten words? Dang, woman. You first."

"Okay." She was already saucing another forkful. "Wait. That doesn't count as one of my words. Okay: COLLEGE. CALIFORNIA. JOB. That's three. FIRED. That's a big one. MY OWN BUSINESS. That's worth three. DIVORCE. MONEY. NEW LIFE."

"That's eleven."

"New-dash-Life. Can we hyphenate that?"

"Always the cheater."

"All right, you get eleven."

Curtis caught the way she was leaning in at him, so he leaned back, putting his fork down, opening both arms on the molded seat. "Hell, I can do it in three: PAYLESS. MARRIED. KIDS."

"Four. Pay Less is two words. You've been working there all this time?"

"It ended up paying more."

Whoo-ee, how they laughed. Maggie had forgotten how funny dumb-funny could be. He could still get her going at the drop of a hat.

"Besides," he said, "Dee Dee does well. I bring home the bacon, but she brings home the ham." He raised his empty bottle, "Here's to happiness."

"Here's to happiness in Happiness." Maggie swung her bottle at the four corners of the restaurant. Then they crossed their empties like swords at the end of a fight, holding them high until the waitress brought them another round.

It was during the sweet-and-sour. Maggie was laughing so hard that the Crowes' simple, "Hey, y'all," had them both dropping their respective spoons, one with a clatter, the other with a splash. They looked up to see Pam and Walker along with Beau McCallum from the Rexall.

"Hey, back," Curtis said, wiping some soup off the memory-lane Doobie Brothers T-shirt he'd put on for the occasion. "You better watch it, sneaking up on a guy like that."

"Good to see you again, Margaret," said Pam, her tone way too honeyed, looking back and forth between her and Curtis.

"Please do call me Maggie, Miz Crowe."

"Please do call me Pam." More honey as she chided, "Why didn't you tell us about your mother?"

It didn't take Maggie but a tick of a minute to put it together. Mr. McCallum must have told them about the cancer. You don't run a pharmacy and not know the most appalling details of everyone's corporal business.

"Good to see you back home." That was all Beau said, waiting, no doubt, for her to raise the subject. She would not oblige. The last thing Maggie needed was a lot of hypocritical exclaiming over her mother.

Walker meanwhile was beaming, pouring on the affability. "How'd she like that redbird, Maggie?"

"Took right to it."

"Anything to cheer a body." Pam's eyes shifted back to Curtis, "And what are Dee Dee and the kids doing tonight?"

Was there a hint of something in her voice?

"Pining for me." Curtis winked Maggie's way. "Actually, it's pizza night at my house. Pizza and toenail painting for the girls. I make myself scarce."

Pam took hold of Curtis' shoulder, "Have you heard about Ms. Greevey's girl? The simple one?"

Walker looked like he'd swallowed something wrong. He took a step back, coughing.

Pam turned to Maggie. "That's who you were asking about yesterday, remember? The strange girl at the bus stop. It turns out, her mama's sick like yours. Cadence thought to take herself to the hospital on the bus, only she didn't know which hospital or where or how."

"She sat out there all day?" Maggie asked.

"No, she rode in and back several times. Can you believe that?" Pam was shaking her head. "It was Beau who found her."

Mr. McCallum told the whole story, going over the details like a tired man trudging in after a day clearing brush. Still, Pam wouldn't leave well-enough alone. "Cadence says her daddy—" she nodded toward Curtis, "— you remember Bobby O. Greevey?"

Lord, if there wasn't a good long pause. It looked like nobody *didn't* remember Bobby O., though everyone was too polite to say why.

" — he was supposed to be on his way down from up north to take care of Cadence, but he never showed. And this child all alone in the world! Here it is supper time and still no daddy."

"What happened?" Maggie asked.

"Nobody knows."

"To the girl I mean."

"The folks at Solace are keeping her tonight while we *talk*." Pam sent Walker a look, but he was fiddling with a leaf caught on his shoe.

The waitress arrived with a platter of mu shu. "You want table?" she asked the Crowes.

Walker pulled his wife back. "Y'all go on and eat before it gets cold." He got Pam headed toward a booth—thankfully on the far side of the restaurant—sandwiching her onto the rounded seat with a man on either side.

Curtis mouthed his first forkful. "Seems like everybody's sick."

"Can we hold off on the death talk?" Maggie waved her second empty bottle at the waitress.

It took Curtis noticing someone from the kitchen dry-mopping for them to realize that no one was left at any of the booths or tables. Beau McCallum and the Crowes were long gone. They missed, thank God, Maggie's knocking what was left of the extra rice, bowl and all, onto the floor. By then she and Curtis were well into round five.

Maggie had trouble getting herself into her jacket. Finally Curtis, who was not a gentleman-holding-the-lady's-coat type of guy, took her arm and crunched it into the sleeve the way a father might put a daughter into her snow coat. They were both aware they'd had one too many. Maybe four too many. They hit the parking lot before either knew what to do next.

Maggie stood—she hoped she wasn't swaying—by his beat-up Silverado which might, by the look of it, have been washed circa 1978. *Boys and their trucks,* Maggie thought, trying not to fall right over into his arms.

Curtis leaned against the side tail light. "You can't drive home," he said.

"That's for sure." She put her hand on his arm to steady herself. "Home is not where we're headed."

"No?" He was smiling.

Oooo, those eyes. Maggie loved how the upper lids sloped down like worry lines on a cartoon face.

"Where to?" he asked.

"Take me to the Dairy Queen!" She gave it to him. The look. The one she knew he liked. She saw him calculating.

"Get in," he said.

The Dairy Queen only opened summers. Fall-winter-spring, the little shack stayed shuttered until Memorial Day weekend when it got swept of leaves, patched for any water damage and dabbed with a little paint. That's when the picnic tables came out, benches and umbrellas, and it was ice cream time again. But on a moonless November night despite the weird warmth, when a body might actually welcome the chill of a Blizzard, the DQ sat dark and boarded, its parking lot deserted. Which might have been a problem except that Curtis knew how to circle around to the back lot where no one could see a parked Silverado from the road.

He shut off the engine and lights. Snapped off his belt. Turned in his seat.

He took her in. Everything was moving at half speed. Her eyelids slid down and up in slow motion. Her hand feeling around to undo her seatbelt seemed to be in no hurry.

What was that sound?

It was Maggie singing. To him. At him. About memories. In the corners of her mind.

"Mister Water Cooler Mem'ries…"

He hooted. "I believe the word is 'misty,'" he said. "And 'water-color…' not 'water cooler.'"

"That's how mother used to sing it," she said, throwing one leg over the stick shift.

The fact was, she couldn't sing. Never even qualified for the back row of the choir and the joke was that anybody could get into the Piney High Chorus. It didn't matter a damn to him. Not with her coming in close like that. Her swinging her leg over top of him, them laugh-griping about the damn stick shift in the way, him cupping a palmful of unbelievably soft thigh in each hand.

Curtis had thought about that kiss on and off for nigh onto fifteen years. Not telling anyone of course. Not a buddy over beer, not a brother off fishing. It wasn't anybody's business but his own. He wasn't into guilt trips. It came with the territory of his mind, part of his way-back thinking, something he knew for sure, as sure as he knew anything including how much he loved his wife, something he knew he could go to his grave with without troubling anybody. Least of all Dee Dee.

Fifteen years and Maggie was every bit as luscious as he remembered, more so even with her body both aged and toned. It made her somehow tender and firm at the same time.

She kept spilling out of his arms like mu shu dripping off the spoon. He scooped her for another taste, another, one more taste, while she laughed and hummed, laughed and sang, snippets of songs coming in between kisses, breathing songs close up on his cheek and mouth.

She was his big city woman, the fish that got away and here they were kissing at the DQ like no one had gone anywhere.

He told himself he just wanted to know whether she'd held up.

She had.

He told himself he wanted to know whether he still had the mojo.

Apparently he did.

He told himself he wanted to know if his thinking about her came even close to the real thing.

Boy, oh, boy.

They hadn't gotten any clothing clean off, but they'd gotten inside some, tingling flesh to tingling flesh, when Maggie started pulling at him, saying they should grab the tarp from the flatbed, that they should go down the back slope to the railroad tracks like the old days.

Curtis knew she wasn't all together there. Oh, her body was, one hundred percent present in his arms. But *she* wasn't. Insisting that they find a dark spot down behind the storage shed, completely forgetting that it was wintertime not summertime, that they were old folks now not kids, and that somebody might spot the truck parked there if they stayed too long.

Her desire poured like steam off the beef and broccoli, wrapping itself around him, chapping his lips, peeling the skin right off his face. The more she gave, the more he wanted. He could eat this buffet clean and still come up hungry.

He was thinking, *Why not.*

He was thinking, *I got the tarp in the back.*

He was thinking, *No one will ever know.* All the way through the blouse popping and the bra and his hand and her sounds.

But gradually something spoke to him through the beer haze. Not his mother. Not Dee Dee. It was him speaking. When Maggie started to open his door, a voice said, *Stop.* His own voice telling her to stop. Gently. Gently he began plucking her hands from him one finger at a time. Gently he held them so that they could not return to his buckle, his zipper, inside his zipper. One track of his mind was down in the wet leaves on top of the tarp, down in the pitch dark over her with the leaf smell and the feeling of her yielding. But there was another track running. A new one.

He smoothed the hair out of her eyes, coaxing her slowly-slowly back around the stick shift into the passenger seat with her crooning about honey and sugar and how she was his candy girl, and him thinking, *Dear God.* Peeling her fingers from him, trying not to set her off, when damn if she didn't flip right there, jerking away and wailing suddenly, "What in God's name is wrong?"

"Nothing, Mags. Nothing's wrong."

"What is wrong with me? Am I not a glamour puss?" He was zipping, managing the belt buckle somehow, pushing the key in the ignition, saying to her quick and strong and urgent, "Maggie Dull, you are all the glamour a man could ask for and twice the puss."

That did it. Her head went way back whooping—"Ha!"—shouting laughter into the roof of the cab, then down into her own lap as he did a 180 and pulled onto Main. He swiped the seatbelt across her with one hand as she bobbed her head up and down. Curtis had no business driving, he knew that. But if there was a scary-ass deep end into which the woman next to him might drop, Maggie was damn near close to going over the edge. He had to get her home. He figured there'd be no one out in Piney on a nothing November night. All he had to do was make it up a road he could drive in his sleep.

"Are you going to remember any of this tomorrow?"

More laughter, Maggie pulling her hair down into her face. "Oh, baby," she said, "'Til the end of time."

Curtis worked things out driving to the Dull house. He'd tell Dee Dee he'd had to drive her home. Which was true. He'd tell her she was in pretty bad shape. Which was true. Because her mother was pretty darned sick. Which was true enough.

Curtis was crystal clear about one thing: he hadn't done anything he regretted. And anything he *had* done was now locked deep in the vault he kept in the lowest, farthest, dimmest corner of his mind. The one he'd open for no one. Except maybe for Maggie someday.

He knew she wouldn't remember much. What little she did, she'd keep to herself. The fact was, Curtis knew this woman leaning against him now as she stepped one heel at a time down the rickety Dull steps from the drive. She ate what she liked. She kissed who she liked. And she held none of it to be anybody's business but her own.

Unsteady, Maggie had to root around in her purse for the house key. Curtis noticed a ladder by the door.

"This thing could fall over."

"Leave it," she said. "It's for the angels. That's what Mommy says."

He'd never heard her say "Mommy" before.

She got the door open. A big guy was standing by the sofa. A single braid, probably Cherokee. He looked normal enough in jeans and a plaid shirt. He held the TV remote in his hand.

"Hey there," said Curtis, all guy bluster.

Maggie did her best *I'm-okay* walk toward the bedroom.

Curtis tried to lighten things up. "I think you may have two of them on your hands tonight."

The guy didn't speak.

"Just wanted to be sure she got home okay. Her car is down in the Happiness parking lot in Little Piney. Maybe you could let her know in the morning. Or leave her a note."

Curtis could see he'd been sized up. He could also see the guy didn't care. He was too busy looking Maggie over, probably wondering if she was going to be sick too.

"I'm okay," said Maggie trundling herself down the hallway toward her bedroom.

She paused, all high drama, "Is mother okay?"

The guy-nurse waved her on. "Sleeping like a baby."

Curtis took the snapshot in his mind. Maggie holding onto the knob of the hall closet so as not to fall over, turning back and wiggling her pinky at him, slurring in a sing-song *la-dee-da,* "Goodnight sweet prince. *Fights* of angels…" Laughing. "Fights. Flights."

He was sure she wouldn't remember. But he would.

"It's been real," he said after her as she staggered through a doorway he knew led to her old bedroom, her old bed. He wondered if it was still covered with the same blanket, the wool one with the redbirds, a bunch of them stamped all over it, flying and singing and squeezing the life out of fat worms caught tight in their sharp little beaks.

I Pray The Lord

Cadence Greevey
Bedtime

Cadence began to be nervous after her supper in the Solace kitchen. First of all, the bear man— "Like a real bear, but nice"—came in to ask had she seen her mama's insurance card. Cadence wasn't sure what he meant. He did not seem mad, but he had those pictures on his skin, color pictures, drawn up around his neck, so she wasn't sure what to tell him. He said that insurance had to do with paying money and right there, thinking herself smart, she told him about the frozen assets.

He was out the door before she realized maybe she shouldn't mention that. Because maybe he'd figure out that frozen meant freezer. Then anybody could go to her house that very night, go right to the freezer and get every penny her mama had stored up in the plastic bags behind the picnic packs.

She hoped her daddy would already be there to stop a robber. Cadence liked that idea. Her daddy pulling up to the house just in time, scaring the robber so bad that he'd drop every dollar right there on the porch and take off down the mountain, tails between his legs.

But then she remembered what Uncle Walker had said. That her daddy had an accident in Krystal and he was in a hospital like her mama so no one knew when her daddy might be coming to see her.

Cadence thought maybe she should go home to wait for him. Things had not gone well with her riding the bus though and that wasn't even in the pitch black of night. There was no one to ask. Her mama never woke up now, not even to turn her head.

How about I start out? she thought. *Maybe walk as far as the front door to see how that would be.*

She headed up the hall to the fancy room with the colored glass window she liked so much. As dark as it was, she could still make out how it had many pieces. A candle burned in the corner. Cushions lay on the floor. Cadence thought they might be for sitting, so she tried one, crossing and un-crossing her legs, wondering how to get comfortable.

"Cadence Greevey?"

Cadence jumped up off the cushion.

"Cadence Greevey!"

A woman came through the door, a nurse in a real nurse outfit like on TV with a white dress and tie shoes.

"Are you Cadence Greevey?"

"Yes, ma'am." Cadence remembered the lady from her kitchen visit. A good bit rounder than Miss Lana and grayer skinned.

"I am Burnice," she said. "We have a lot going on this evening, sweetie, so if you decide to go someplace, how about you tell one of us first. All right?"

"Yes, Miss Burnice."

"No need to 'Miss' me. Burnice will do fine."

"Yes, ma'am."

Burnice was already leaving the doorway. Cadence knew she had to speak up.

"I got to go home."

Burnice turned halfway back. "At this hour?"

"I got to meet my daddy."

Burnice's eyes squinched up. "Won't he come pick you up?"

"I got bus money."

Burnice seemed to consider this. "Now, you and me, let's think this through. Do you think your daddy wants you climbing on a bus in the middle of the night?" She spoke in short phrases like piling up blocks to build a play-house.

"Probably not." Cadence hoped that was the right answer.

"Why don't you call him to come pick you up?"

"He's not here. He's in the hospital."

"I found her!" Burnice called over her shoulder to no one Cadence could see, all the while holding out her hand, "Come on, sweetie."

Cadence sat in a chair at the nurse desk while Burnice looked through papers and talked to the bear man saying, "We don't have enough on our plates, we're doing social work at all hours?" with the bear man saying back to her, "You made your bed!" on his way down the hall.

Burnice asked Cadence whether they might could call her daddy and Cadence said, "Yes," except she didn't have the number with her and anyway he wouldn't be there, they'd only get Paco.

"Mmmm-hmmm," said Burnice. "And what about your mama's people?"

Cadence mentioned Uncle Walker and Auntie Pam, but they weren't a real uncle or aunt, only pretend.

Burnice stopped flipping her papers. "Child. Do you *really* want to go home tonight?"

Cadence thought Burnice might be the smartest person she had ever come across after Miss Lana and Miss April Turner, the Weather Girl. She allowed as how she didn't want to go, how she was only worried for her daddy finding her and on and on until Burnice said, "Well then, why don't you stay put?"

Cadence felt her eyes get sting-hot. Burnice put her hand to Cadence's forehead just the way her mama would, first the back of it and then the palm. "Your mother's sleeping pretty good now. How 'bout we sit you down to watch some TV in the TV room?"

That was a treat. Cadence got to lie on a couch with her shoes off and her feet tucked under a blanket. Burnice gave her the remote that had more buttons than just the ones with numbers. She taught Cadence how to punch an arrow to go from one channel to the next. She told her not to touch the volume so it wouldn't disturb the others.

"Remember now: you take it in your head to go someplace, you ask me first. Promise?"

"I promise." But Cadence wanted to be sure she had things right. "Miss Burnice?"

"Yes."

"Can I go to see my mama?"

"Oh, yes. You can go in there anytime you like. You can go in there or stay in here." Burnice stood looking at a commercial that was playing. A grown man was sitting at a kitchen table, squared back in his chair like a raccoon fishing by a stream. He was playing with his silverware—something Cadence had been taught never to do—banging his fork and knife in time to the music and singing real loud, "'Cause I'm a re-e-e-eal Hungry Man!" Burnice laughed, wiping her eyes from the laughter. "Heaven help us," she said, shaking her head as she hurried out the door.

Cadence liked it in that TV room watching the shows flash by. With no one to tell her different, she could change the channel again and again, each time trying to guess right away what she was looking at by who was doing what. Samantha on *Bewitched.* All the friends on *Cheers.* Cadence liked *Cheers* because the bartender was handsome and always in love with the girls and the girls had pretty hairdos with bangs that never got in their eyes.

It occurred to Cadence watching *Cheers* where everybody knew your name, that maybe she could come live at Solace so everybody would know hers. She would sleep on the couch no problem. As long as folks told her what to do and where to stay out of like Mr. McCallum did at the Rexall, she'd make sure she was never underfoot. There were so many rooms to be in. And the TV room was a real family room, Cadence could tell, because the blanket she had around her had little figures stitched on it like any home-made thing.

Then she got a bad feeling because she was thinking something she knew she shouldn't: *What if mama don't come home?* Miss Lana had said the Lord had other plans for her. Cadence tried to picture her mama back at the Mountain Man when she was all better, standing behind the cash register, getting after her for her grades or spending too much on candy or some such thing.

There was a splatter noise at the window. Rain had come up suddenly the way rains could at night. Ropes of drops whipped the glass. Cadence heard high whining, a moan.

A ghost dog, she thought. Hershey crawling out of his grave, murder-mad at whoever put him there because maybe he wasn't quite dead when he was laid in the ground and that's why he was coming back. In third grade, on the playground, Spidey Weaver had said such a thing could happen. People that weren't dead got buried up to their necks, he said, and then over their heads with dirt snarfing down their nostrils until they were all plugged up and choking to death in the dark. Surely the same could happen to a dog. Hershey would have hated that.

"Ah, ah, ah." Cadence wrapped the blanket around her. She began walking around the room, heel-toe, heel-toe. Then up the hall to her mama's bedroom door, heel-toe, heel-toe.

Phew. Her mama was still there. Still with the ties on her two hands, her head tilted all the way back on the pillow, mouth wide.

"What are we doing, Missy?" Burnice, coming around the corner, made her jump.

"Hershey."

"Who's Hershey?" Burnice stopped with her in the doorway.

"He was my bestest, true dog."

"Mmmm-hmmm."

"He's a ghost dog now and he's coming for my mama." Cadence couldn't help using her outside voice, loud enough to where Burnice *shushed* her even as the bear man came from behind and past them on the run.

"Miz Early is making the change." He went around the bend in the hall with Burnice saying after him, "Give me five minutes."

He popped his hand back, fingers wide-stretched in the air. "Two is all you got." He was gone.

"What was that name again?" Burnice asked Cadence.

"Hershey."

"Do you see him in there?"

Cadence squinted her eyes for the wiggling of a tongue or the glint of teeth. "He's hiding," she whispered.

Burnice told Cadence not to move, not to make a peep, but just to fix her eyes into the dark places in her mama's room while she fetched what they needed. Cadence did so, watching floor shadows as they shifted from now a passing car, now the wind-stirrings of leaves.

The bear man came by again: "I'm calling Narduli."

"I'll be right there," said Burnice, back to Cadence before she could even gulp.

Burnice went first, stepping into the bedroom, shaking a plastic Bi-Lo bag as a summons. "Come here, child. With ghost dogs, you got to be doing, not muling." Cadence made herself scoot right up next to Burnice. She held onto her skirt.

"Here's what it is. They's been a wrong done. Somebody wronged your Hershey. And a ghost dog, without the human heart to know forgiveness, he may come back to exact a retribution from the living."

Cadence saw Ghost Hershey in her mind, all white with fangs, biting at her mother's arm even with the ties on, his teeth tight and his neck powerful, pulling the way he could pull as much as a buck or a bear carcass in life, hauling her own mama off the bed and into the shadows, down and away into hell. Cadence started to cry.

Burnice held up her one finger. "No, ma'am! None of that!" She dug around inside her bag. "All we need is a little extra protection around your mama in her weakness."

The first thing, she pulled out a tiny bottle, brown glass, like a doll might carry in her purse. A gold sticker star was stuck to one side identical to the one Miss Lana had given Cadence for keeping her mama's book of sickness so well.

"First, we got to confound a dog's sense of smell." Burnice untwisted the cap. "Go ahead."

Cadence put her nose down and good golly gracious what a sweet smell was there. Like as flowers, but strong.

"That's the rose essence," said Burnice. "Even on the cross, suffering and crying for His Father in heaven and giving up His soul for our salvation, Jesus smelled of the rose. Now, you ever seen a dog, even a living dog, go bury his nose in a flower?"

Cadence shook her head *No*.

"That's right. A dog will put his nose into anything, including garbage and old rotten leaves and most especially—you know this—right into the offal cast off by his buddies. But something sweet? Never. Come on, we got to hurry, child."

Burnice held the little bottle up high and went into each of the corners of the room, shaking down a single drop at a time. Then she put her finger to the bottle and traced two lines like a cross on her mama's pillow.

Cadence lifted her nose the way Hershey might lift his on a windy day, sniffing. The room smelled like bubble bath with the air itself as the water.

Burnice motioned for Cadence to hold the plastic bag. "Now we're going to post us some signs right quick."

She pulled out a Little Debbie box, empty of its cookies, but with Debbie herself on the top. Burnice faced the box into one of the back corners on the floor saying, "Little Debbie is a girl like you. Hershey knows to mind you, so Hershey will mind her and she's saying, "'Shoo! Get on outta here, ghost dog. Leave my mama alone!'"

Cadence wasn't crying anymore.

Finally, Burnice set out a card like the ones at the Rexall for birthdays and Easter. On the front was a heart with poking out of it a rainbow in rainbow colors. "I'm sure the folks who left this would want us to use it." She placed the card in another corner saying the rainbow would make Hershey think was it raining in there, that she didn't know of any dog that liked to get out in a downpour, so he'd stay away.

"Quick, close your eyes now and see how it feels in here." Cadence closed her eyes. She reached for Burnice's hand to hold it. "He's gone," she whispered.

"He *is* gone," Burnice said. "Now you can sleep in here with your mama even like a baby and won't nothing come after either of you. Does that sound good?"

Cadence nodded *Yes.*

"Are you sleepy?"

Cadence nodded *Yes* again.

"You want to sleep with your mama or with the TV?"

Cadence pointed away from her mama's room.

"That's fine."

Cadence would not let go of Burnice's hand as they walked, heel-toe, heel-toe. "Can I come and live with you here?" she asked.

"No, sweetie. This place is for sick people. Even I don't live here, though it sometimes feels like I do." Burnice got her back on the TV couch, "But I tell you what. You study real hard in school and maybe you can work here when you're all grown up."

Cadence's eyes stung again. "I don't do good in school. Can it only be people that do good in school who work here?"

Burnice pushed the blanket up around her. "No, ma'am! Look what good you did tonight." She patted her arm. "You keep doing the best you can. The Lord will show you your path as He showed me mine. And mine right now—" she was prying her hand out of Cadence's lock-hold "—is to see to Miz Early." She was leaving.

"Can I come visit?"

"You can visit any time. That's what this place is about."

Burnice was gone.

Cadence curled herself up, wiping her eyes with the top of one of her puffy sleeves. A plan was coming to her mind. She would grow roses for the rose smell. They didn't grow roses at home because her mama said they were expensive down at Macon's Luscious Lawns and they didn't grow easy in the cold mountain air. But once, after school, she and her mother had made a trip in the car to Garnet to see a museum house that was as big as a palace, and what Cadence remembered was the roses everywhere in a garden that had, instead of rows, circle paths of white stones, so you could walk around rose trees as high as your head, each one a different color.

She was sure now: she would learn how to grow them. She already knew how to put corn seeds in, pushing a finger halfway down into the soil and then spacing the seeds a finger apart. She knew how to water the beans and tomatoes every day. Why not grow roses for Solace? She would be Miss Burnice's helper and Miss Burnice would love her like a daughter and maybe take her to *her* house sometime for a holiday picnic or a barbecue with her people there in the backyard, maybe on a river bank with a big tree and Miss Burnice pushing Cadence out over the water on a tire tied to a high branch for a swing.

He Maketh Me To Lie Down

August Early
The Dead of Night

"She's making the change." That's how the man who called himself Bear told it to Mr. Early. Woke him out of sleep and said to come quick.

She's making the change. Mr. Early said it to himself all the way down the mountain, around every left-right switchback of the headlights, speeding on a road nobody else was on or likely to be on for the hour it was and the no-moon and the chill and the night rain.

She's making the change.

Rain black-silvering the road like the heaving side of a caught-up fish. Rain making the tires slip at the tightest part of each curve.

Coming—*Bang!*—out of the overhang of pines onto the flat running along the river, here came the moon now, a splotch of dirty grey light, night clouds blowing in front with the weak moon behind, the spine of the Blue Ridge beyond like the back of an angry porcupine, something you never wanted to see up ahead of you on the trail.

She's making the change.

He could hear his mama's voice, *The hospital's the place where you come to die.*

Run, he thought. *Run the other way.*

The hospital's the place.

She's making the change.

He sat dead still at a red light the way the law told him to, even though there was no sense in it, since there was nobody coming from any direction except himself. It would have disturbed no one to drive through, but August Early waited as the curling line of stink from the tailpipe wound by his window, white in the chill.

Please don't change, he thought, willing away the green light, pleading with the red to stay with him, to keep him there forever.

Please don't change.

The light went green. He had to go.

He had to go.

He felt bad about the brightness of the headlights sweeping across the windows before he could quick shut them off. What if the sound of the truck woke somebody? He could hear Theo calling to the dogs to *Lay off that racket!* when they got to pack-baying, egging each other on once one of them heard a stone turn over or a branch scrape.

He sat in the darkness of the cab, dash gone lightless. No radio. Only the sound of the rain on the windshield. Black rain.

She's making the change.

Theo.

He leaned on the door handle hard. Threw himself out into the wet, a few cold drops touching his chest where his parka was open, the rest spattering off his hat, his shoulders.

The umbrellas in the hallway were wet. Lots of them.

It was not like during the day. No light came from the kitchen. Somewhere down the hall he could hear a TV. Maybe in the family room. He remembered it from Miss Hazel's tour of the place. Nothing else stirred. No sounds came from the room with his wife, just a pale spill of light.

A giant of a man stood next to the bed. "Bear," he said, by way of giving his name. He came around to shake Mr. Early's hand.

Theo was in a different sleep. Or maybe not sleep. Her eyes were shut tight. Not easy tight, bad-dream tight. Squinched shut, her mouth squinched too.

Bear reached under the blanket.

"She was spiking a fever an hour ago. That's not uncommon, Mr. Early. We have a few cool packs on her to help keep her comfortable."

Mr. Early could not get his eyes to see what they were seeing. She was breathing, her chest coming up like somebody blowing up a balloon. Coming way up. And then, *whomp,* collapsing down hard like someone had pushed on her. Then nothing. A long nothing. Then the blowing up again. No mask on her now nor nothing at all beyond the line of something going to her wrist, but there she was breathing like somebody was breathing for her.

"She's making the change," Bear said.

There must have been something on Mr. Early's face because the next thing he knew the man called Bear had walked him backward into the re-cliner chair and got down to kneel right next to him, even a little in front of him, a big man, so much bigger than Mr. Early's own daddy had been, as big as he'd always imagined the story men to be, Daniel Boone, Paul Bunyan, Davy Crockett.

"You okay, man?" Bear patted his knee short and quick, his hand paw-like, plump.

Mr. Early nodded *Yes.* His eyes were with Theo, watching the breathing.

"This is what happens," Bear said. "She's all right."

"No she ain't."

Mr. Early's hands went round and round the rim of his hat, turning it between his knees, the rain running off to his feet.

Up went her chest. Up, up, up. And then, *whomp,* down. Her eyelids rolled this way, then that. Mr. Early could see her one hand, the one closest to him, was crabbed up.

"She's not feeling anything."

Mr. Early stood so that Bear had to rock back.

"She is."

Bear stood with him. Much taller than his daddy.

"No, Mr. Early—"

"Listen here," Mr. Early said with a voice he'd heard only a couple of times before. Once when Serena was walking up ahead of him along Cane Creek and not seeing the timber rattler on the rock to her left. Once with Rocky running so hard after a squirrel he was just about underneath the Hamilton Sanitation truck rounding into the driveway.

"She told me. She plain-told me and I am telling you. She does not want to know. She does not—" Mr. Early swung his hat over her. "She ain't all right."

"We're doing what we can…"

"Hunh-unh. No." Mr. Early put his hat down on the recliner, pulling off his parka, walking nowhere as he spoke. "She ain't right." Walking around Bear. "She does not want to know." Walking to the end of her bed, to the rounds of her feet there under the blanket.

"We've got her on really strong pain medication. That's what the drip is." Bear pointed to the line going into Theo's wrist. "We're doing what we can."

"Do more."

Mr. Early felt he could kill the man right there with his bare hands. He'd heard tell of it in Bible stories, over and over again on TV, but he'd never known the feeling facing another human being. And now here was this big man, tattoos on his neck, this man who had surely done things Mr. Early had not done and could not do, short as he was and prone to a fluttery heart. At least that was what the doctor had said years ago, telling Mr. Early he could not serve his country, that no war would take him. He'd been left behind as boys his age went off, some of them never coming back. But Mr. Early was no shrinking violet. He'd taken lives, plenty of them in the woods. He'd shot any kind of thing for fur or eating. He knew his way around a rifle, just not to point one at a man. And yet here he was at Theo's feet looking square on at the big fellow, feeling it, by God, that he could kill him right then and there. Shoot him dead. He knew he could by the roar of it up through his body into his ears.

"Do more," he said, like snapping on a lead line to bring a headstrong horse to attention, bringing it around, *snap,* to have it jump forward, even not wanting to, onto the big scales.

He saw Bear come to attention.

"It's something we have to call the doctor about."

"Call."

Bear left him.

Mr. Early could see it clear from where he was standing, the crabbing of Theo's hand on the bed.

When it gets bad, she'd said.

This was bad.

Mr. Early picked up his parka from the floor. He hung it in the closet without knowing he was doing it, pulling the wet fabric away so as not to damp her bathrobe. He put his hat on the closet shelf.

And sat.

Sat next to her. As close as a chair could get to a bed.

He would give Bear twenty minutes. And then he'd be going to get him.

It took less than ten. Bear went right around to the stand where the line was coming into Theo's wrist. "We got Dr. Narduli. We'll up her dose. Now, this is something you can do, Mr. Early. I'm going to wheel this around to you."

Holding the line up, Bear brought the pole with the small bag around to Mr. Early's side. He showed him the button he could push if he thought she wanted more medicine.

"You can't give her too much," he said. "If you push too much, it will just wait until it's time to give her more. So you can push on it all you like. And when it's time, she'll get the kind of medicine that means she won't feel any pain."

"She'll sleep easy?"

"She should. Let's give it a try. Here."

Bear put the switch with the button right into Mr. Early's hand.

Mr. Early pushed it. Immediately.

"See? The light goes on. That means she got a dose. So you can push this whenever you like. Let's wait and see how she does."

Mr. Early could not say, "Thank you," or anything. He was watching Theo's face.

"I'll pull the door to so you have some privacy, but we're here if you need us. Would you like some music?"

"No, sir."

Mr. Early did not watch him go. He watched Theo. The room was dead quiet except for her strange breathing.

How long should he wait? Ten minutes, he thought. Leaving the house, he had not put his watch on, but there was a clock by the bed.

After the second time punching the button, Theo's hand loosened a little. The skin around her eyes eased.

It went on. Sometimes when he pressed, the light would blink, other times it would not. Her mouth opened. She lay flat still with each time him thinking *Breathe, Breathe* until her chest wrenched upward and dropped again.

Breathe, Theo.

He took her slack hand now. A beautiful hand. After everything, still smooth.

He looked for the breath. There.

"Theo." He was speaking now. Looking around to see was he alone. He was. The door was closed. He could hear nothing in the hallway.

He squeezed her hand. It felt like loose sticks in a sack of water. A cold sack.

"Theo." He let go of the button to lift her hair away from her ear. It lay in lines of wet gray curl down the pillow and onto the bed. He stroked it slowly. He could feel a hardness under the sheets. They must to have lined it in plastic.

"Theo." He got down close to her ear, so that he would be speaking only to her, so that even if someone were standing outside the door, only she could hear.

"I made up my mind," he said. "I'm gonna keep those babies. I know you want them to go to Miss Susan. I know you want her to raise them on account of she's a woman and women are the ones to do the raising."

God knows, Theo had said it to him many a time.

"I know that. But in this one thing, Theo, I'm going to do the way I see fit. They's my grandbabies too. They come from my stock as well as yours. I love them like nobody can, Theo, so I'm gonna take them and I'm gonna raise them right. Miss Susan, she can be of help. But I'm gonna raise them sure as I'm sitting here. They're gonna be fine. Don't you worry."

He lifted himself up to look into her eyes which were just eyelids now, grey and not moving, staring at them as if he could see through to where she was maybe watching him back.

"I ain't never once let you down, Theodora Early. I been a good man, like you said. And I'll be the best of daddies to those girls. I will get them growed up, by God, and happy and healthy and never gone to those things that took their own mama. Never. They'll be the finest girls you ever did see."

Mr. Early tipped his head to lay it beside hers, watching from the side, way up close, seeing the one eyelid and her ear cleared now of hair, and him next to her, breathing with her except more often.

There was no way to tell if she heard him.

He could feel his own mama looking down from heaven now, busting with pride over her one son and his stepping up, as the preacher would say, to do what a man is called to do. To take care of his own.

"Excuse me."

Mr. Early sat up quick, letting go of his wife's hand as if it had bitten him.

The lady spoke in a very quiet voice, coming around and putting her hands, like Bear had done, under the blankets. It was Miss Burnice in her nurse dress.

"I don't think we need these anymore." She pulled two plastic packs out from Theo's feet. "She's not hot, she's cold," pulling a second blanket up. "She'll go hot and cold now. That's natural. We'll try to keep her comfortable."

Mr. Early watched the nurse take Theo's wrist and hold it for a time, looking at her watch. "Is there anything I can do for you?"

Lord, he'd forgotten. He grabbed up the button and pressed it. The light went on.

"No, ma'am."

Miss Burnice left him alone, neglecting to pull the door to the way Bear had done, so that it was half open to the hallway. Mr. Early thought about closing it, but he didn't want to let go of the button. He didn't want to move.

The blinds in Theo's room had been drawn. There was no way to see what might to be moving in the world outside. Surely everyone was long asleep. Little children long since dreaming. Tired wives crawling out of beds from husbands already snoring for hours now. Wives kept up by the snoring maybe. Or by worries. Worries over children. Walking floors with their wooly bathrobes cinched up around the waist and slippers crusted with dirt from walking out in the garden to put hose water in dog bowls. Pacing as their husbands snored, unaware of wakeful women.

What was he doing?

How long had he been lying there, his head next to hers?

He looked.

She seemed all right.

He pressed the button.

The light went on.

She did not want to know.

He did not want her to know.

From time to time, he touched her hand. Not enough to stir her, he told himself. Just to check. Always, it was cold.

He hoped her feet were not cold as well. Theo could not abide cold feet. She wore winter socks even in the flush of summer. Up on the ridge, mornings came with a chill. By nine, there'd be sun enough to make tomatoes split and roses blow open. Still, in the dawn hours, even in summer, Theo kept her socks on and complained of cold.

Mr. Early got up to tuck the covers tighter around each foot, tamping down to keep the air out and what heat she made close by.

He came back to his chair. He wanted his head down next to hers again, but his aching neck would not allow it. All he could do was lean back the other way in the recliner, the button still in his hand.

How could he be sleepy? He could not afford sleepiness anymore. Not if he was going to take care of those girls. It used to be Rocky or Shirley would cough even one short bark in the darkness of a night, and Mr. Early would come straight out of sleep to listen and wait for more, for the dogs telling him *Something's coming!* a possum or a raccoon. He'd listen in particular for the string of no-let-up barking that would say *Human Being!* to him. That would say, *Human Being on the property! Human Being coming down the driveway!*

That was the kind of man he'd have to be again. Ready like the young for anything.

He heard his mother's voice now, stern: *Come away, son, so He can do His work.* She might as well have been standing right next to the chair. *Make room, boy. Make room for Jesus.*

Mr. Early leaned forward, his neck grabbing so bad he made a sound.

Hush up, August. Don't you stir this woman.

He spoke back at her in his mind. *This woman? This woman is my wife!* He wanted his mother out of there.

She belongs to Jesus.

He'd heard her say it once before. On a bad day. On the afternoon, late, when Chuck Henry and Perry Loop, two boys from the other side of Little Piney, had bushwhacked their way up to the second trestle and over to one of the abandoned pitshafts at the old emerald mine and looked down with the sun topping the ridge so that light came onto the rainwater at its bottom to show a little girl floating there. At least that's what they said. Mr. Early had wanted to go see, but his mama wouldn't let him and by the time he'd scrambled his way up to check on it, the little girl was gone. "Pulled out to be buried," the boys said. Oh, but he could see her there anyway. Looking down into the black water, he could see her there still.

"She belongs to Jesus," his mama said when he came back home. He knew better. "No, mama. She belongs to that dark hole all alone."

Theo? He sees a little girl in the water. She has on Theo's nightgown, the white one with the yellow flowers.

Theo? Amazing how the sound echoes. Surely it will wake her, lying so far down in the cold, cold water.

Theo?

He is a boy again. A strapping boy. The biggest of mountain boys with big boots on. He has a rope and a knife. He has his dogs. And he's looking down into the shaft as the dogs play back and forth, excited by his excitement and maddened to see where he is looking.

He's a Rescue Boy. Strapping. Sizing up a tree strong enough to tie himself, waist to trunk, so that he can go over the edge and lower himself to just above the water to pluck her out, little as she is, hoisting her over his shoulder with one arm, getting her balanced so that he can use his two hands, levering back on his feet to rope-walk them both up the middle of the crumbly timber and soil of the pitshaft wall, bits of things tumbling past them into the water from the sheering of the rope above, *splash splash,* but climbing steady and true with never a worry that the girl might slip off and down again. Because he is a Rescue Boy. Looking up, tilting his head enough to see, without losing her, the quilting of leaves high overhead crowning not only the shaft but the whole of the earth, a shimmering of sun-green before a blue sky. Blue. No clouds. Rescue Boy takes one last deep breath as he pulls with his top hand, shifts one foot above the other, swings the two of them up over the lip and into the open air, into the light.

It might to have been a second. Or hours. Or days. With no sense of drifting off, his coming to made no sense.

His head was clean over his left shoulder when he started to see. The pitshaft was still in his sight with the sight, too, of the room he knew himself to be in, the water and the little girl and Theo's hand all mixed up together.

Mr. Early drew his head up to look.

There was no sound.

He looked.

He looked and looked.

He waited.

No sound.

Her chest did not move.

Nothing.

Her face was pure slacked now. Eyes open.

It was what they'd said. Chuck and Perry speaking of the little girl. They said she was gray. *Not white,* they said. Not like a ghost. Gray. Like fish skin.

Graying even as he looked. The color under her skin graying.

He stood up.

She was gone.

He thought he might be sick.

He made a sound, an awful sound. A coughing. Because something was coming up from him. Tears made him take his head way back to keep them in his eyes, tipping his head up to where his mama should have been high above him in the ceiling. Or Jesus. Or the angels. But there was nobody.

He could not make the heaving stop. He was ashamed to be a grown man doing that way.

He sat.

He had to get ahold of himself.

He could not look at her face. Her hand outside the cover was gray, the arm mottling into spots. He could see it.

Hadn't her hand been under the cover when he fell asleep? Had she reached for him?

Oh! There was the sound again. He had to gather his shirt up around his face to smother it, pushing his collar up around his eyes and mouth to get it to stop.

But he couldn't. Not before there was a knock at the door and Bear coming in. *Why can't it be the lady nurse? Miss Burnice?* But no, it was Bear coming in. And coming right over. Mr. Early had his head in his shirt he was so ashamed. Coming right over and getting down there with him, putting his big bear paw hand on his shoulder and saying, "Hey, man," which was just about the best thing anybody had ever said or could ever say then or at any time.

"Hey, man," he said, rocking him back and forth with his paw on his shoulder as a way of saying, *I'm here.*

Mr. Early could not speak for the wracking. But he had to. He had to. Looking up into that bare ceiling with the no-Jesus and the no-mama and crying out in anguish, "I fell asleep!"

He couldn't help it. "I fell asleep!"

"It's okay, man."

Bear was gripping his shoulder hard, but Mr. Early shook his head *No,* rocking back and forth in the chair.

Bear did not let go. "Listen. Listen now."

Here came more coughing from deep inside him.

"Hey." Bear swung around to both knees and got the other paw on him, pushing on both of Mr. Early's shoulders to hold him down, to keep him in the chair.

"I seen this a million times. You gotta trust me."

His voice was deep. Deeper than any preacher's.

"Listen. Listen to me. As long as you were with her, she could not go."

The words came in through a jibber of sobbing and coughing and not being able to breathe. *What was he saying?*

"She could not go as long as you were here. You understand me?"

How often had Mr. Early heard his mother say that—"You understand me?"—as a warning to mind her.

He looked into Bear's face, the long, fat moustache around his upper lip, the weight of skin below his chin.

"She needed you to go so she could go."

God. Heaven. Angels. Mr. Early felt his stomach come back below his throat. The tears stayed on his cheeks, but they stopped, instantly turned off from his eyes.

Bear smiled at him.

"She needed you to fall asleep."

Mr. Early found his voice. "I can't see Jesus."

Bear let go of his shoulders, sitting back on his heels, "That's because He's busy carrying her home."

Both of them looked toward the ceiling.

Mr. Early took in her face now, seeing not the gray and the awful open eyes and not anything but seeing her.

He found his voice. "Sometimes she'd go on the back porch instead of coming out front to say goodbye."

"That's right," said Bear. Standing to give Mr. Early some space.

"She hated a goodbye."

Bear waited. Mr. Early looked at him now.

"She lost her baby, you know. Got her clean growed up and then we lost her to the drugs."

"Your daughter?"

"Yes, sir."

Bear nodded at his feet. "Don't I know all about that. I come out of 'Nam."

Now Mr. Early was nodding at Theo. "After that, she wasn't good for goodbyes or nothing but doing for her grandbabies and keeping quiet about the rest."

"That's it," said Bear, nodding some more. "You let her go the way she needed, Mr. Early. You did what a good man does."

There was nothing in Mr. Early. He could feel it. And it was a relief, the nothing. The nothing of it all, looking down at the horror picture of what once was his bride in its frozen scream face thinking, *She never liked a good-bye.*

"Is there anyone we should call to come be with you?"

"No sir. There's the girls, but she did not want them seeing her like this. That was her wish."

"What's this?" asked Bear. He was fingering something on the blanket.

Mr. Early knew it right away. The animal pelt, most likely rabbit, a beautiful gray-brown color, its soft, ragged edges curled. It lay neatly on the other side of the bed just at Theo's left hand so that part of it lay under her fingers.

"Is this yours?" Bear asked.

"No sir."

"You sure?"

"I believe it belongs to the little girl. The big girl. The one from Little Piney."

"Humph," said Bear. He took his time. His tone changed. "If you'd care to step outside for a moment, Burnice and I, we could close your wife's eyes and straighten her a little. In case you wanted to sit with her some more. Would that be all right?"

Bear had his elbow, passing him to Burnice who was suddenly there to take him down the hall. "How 'bout you sit in the parlor for a minute, Mr. Early," she was saying, "and we'll come get you."

Burnice steered him into one of two armchairs at the front window. The blinds were open.

"What time is it?" Mr. Early asked.

"Just past seven."

Mr. Early could see the sun's first light barely coming below the mountains, dawn approaching as the rain cleared. A car, headlights on, splashed through a puddle and chugged up the street toward the stoplight.

Mr. Early looked down. The pelt was in his hand. The fur was soft. What was it doing there?

"You can keep him."

Mr. Early turned. The big-little girl was standing in the parlor door, wearing her dirndl dress. It was wrinkled.

"He's Rabbit," she said.

Mr. Early held it out to her.

"You can keep him." She smiled a bright smile. "Merry Thanksgiving."

Thanksgiving? Was that what it was?

The girl turned away, walking from the door heel-to-toe the way he'd seen the twins do when they were bored.

He would have to tell them. He did not know how. Or what. Everything was drifting away inside of him. Theo was right. They should never see such a thing. Her face, eyes staring. This was a horror pure and simple. And a mercy. To go just as she had gone.

All gone. What his mother used to say when he cleaned his plate as a boy. *All gone.*

He held the pelt up to his cheek.

Rabbit.

He closed his eyes to talk to God.

This ain't no fair trade, he said into the darkness of his thoughts, sending the words up to heaven where he hoped the Big Man, Jesus' Father, the Father of Fathers, was listening. *A skin of something dead for a wife?* he said to Him. *This ain't no fair trade.*

He did not care if it made God angry.

He did not care.

After a time, he opened his eyes. There was light enough to see a pine tree across the way. And a buzzard. Black shouldered against the dawn-dark sky with its head too small for its body. It had landed on a limb just under the crown, a limb that stuck out so that Mr. Buzzard could surely see all the way to Tennessee from there. He looked like he was standing, a man in a black suit way up high, unearthly still, so still as to define stillness, watching.

Below, a sapling, beech, bobbed like crazy. Its branches criss-crossed in the wind, a last few leaves shearing off.

Wind down here, Mr. Early thought, *but not a trace up there with the buz-zard.* How was that possible? How could it be a big wind down here on earth, but way up in the sky nothing?

THURSDAY

November 23, 1989

Thanksgiving

Surely Goodness And Mercy

Maggie Dull
Early Morning

Maggie heard her mother in the family room: "Use the swan boats!"

Swan boats? What swan boats? Maggie tried sipping her already sweating glass of instant iced tea. Stomach and head lurched. She closed her eyes. A plateful of mu shu morphed into Curtis' face floating way too close. Nope. Better to keep the eyes open apparently.

In all her years including any number of basement binges in junior high, Maggie had been able to drink everyone under the table, even the boys. Invariably they ended up passed out while she could always get herself back to wherever she belonged. Drunk, yes. Sick, never. It was some miracle of her constitution. Until now.

Gone the way of all youth, she thought. Maggie powered three aspirin dry, closing her eyes. Here was Curtis' face again. His lips. *Dear God,* his fingers on her—

"Use the swan boats!"

Maggie held onto the kitchen counter with both hands, leaning her head down to see if that would help, thinking, *If I were a swan boat, where would I be?*

Right away she was picturing a Tunnel of Love. She and Curtis sailing through the mouth of it in a plastic bird dinghy. Sailing inside an industrial-sized tube that would smell of mold and chlorination whose waters, if ever seen by the light of day, would surely be strewn with litter tossed by hormone-crazed teens in the throes of the forbidden. What would she and Curtis do in there? Neck for the few minutes it would take their swan to go from one end to the other? Like last night? Or *not* like last night? Her memory was spotty. Not for what she'd *wanted*, mind you. That she remembered exactly. Exactly what she'd put on and spiffed up and gone to dinner for. But how far had they gone in their Tunnel of Love?

Her mother called again: "You have to beat the bees."

All right. Bees. Swans. Maggie swung herself up and out to the family room where she'd battened the old girl in an easy chair next the sliding glass door, a chevroned pink and green (*Pink and green, for God's sake!*) blanket their Cousin Peggy had crocheted up around her legs. Her mother insisted on wearing yellow. She was yellow head to foot. Even the turban around her singed pate was wound with a sunburst scarf. *Scheherazade meets I Love Lucy,* thought Maggie.

"Get the swan boats!"

"Where would they be, Mommy?" Maggie was going with the Mommy thing now. Whether her mother understood it or not was another story, but at least she was playing along.

"In the high boy."

With exaggerated indulgence, Maggie opened drawer after drawer, each one squeaking with the weight of the linens inside to show her mother, *See, no swan boats.*

But of course they were there. In the bottom-most drawer, sitting on top of a Christmas tablecloth. Two ceramic gravy boats shaped like white cobs, their tails arching unnaturally to form handles so that, Maggie noted, picking them up, one had to place one's fingers way too close to a part of the swan one would never want to get near. Their necks rounded into open bills, blunt and black-tipped, to form pouring spouts.

Maggie squatted on the ottoman in front of her mother, one swan in each hand.

"I don't think we're going to have gravy, Mommy."

"No, no," her mother said, all Marie Antoinette suddenly. "For the flowers."

"Put flowers in them?"

"High on the log."

Flowers in a gravy boat? Well, why not?

"You have to beat the bees," her mother said, this time agitated.

"I don't know what you mean."

Her mother pointed out through the window to the garden. "When the sun hits, the bees come."

My God. Her mother wanted flowers in a swan. Flowers cut before the hot sun brought out the bees. Never mind that it was November. To her mother it was still summer, offering an object lesson for every self-appointed guru on the other coast: seasons were but a state of mind.

Out Maggie went into the morning, headache trailing her like—well, like bees. Angry bees swarming from behind, a cloud of pain.

She scrounged around the porch to find, sure enough, her mother's rusted garden scissors and some canvas gloves. She slid one on.

Whomp, the glove disappeared. Here was Curtis' hand covering hers. She could feel the marvelous fleshy padding of his thumb, his elbow, his lovely big neck, his lower jaw as she kissed him.

Whomp, she was back on the porch wielding scissors. She leaned over, praying to any God who might be listening, *Don't let me hurl,* until the feeling passed. Then she filled her swans with the garden hose and set off in search of something, anything flower-like with which to make a table display. There were no bees in sight.

It turned out there was plenty to choose from. Gobs of rosemary—she'd have paid a premium for that in Palo Alto—and mint which wouldn't last long in the water, but long enough. Low mounds of oregano had taken over where her mother used to plant lettuces. That would work. But she needed some fuller leaves to hold things up. A branch or two of laurel did the trick. Best of all, she rounded the house to find a line of bush roses still covered in orange-red clusters. Sheaves of them, an old strain. Dogwood-like in the spareness of the petals. Maggie knew they weren't cutting roses, but damn if they wouldn't provide a splash of color, even browned at the tips, for the few scant hours they'd be needed.

She did her arranging on the porch, head pounding, pushing things into each swan until they were perfect, symmetrical but not identical.

"What do you think?" Backing in, hands full, Maggie wasn't aware that her mother had nodded over in her morning snooze. *Hallelujah.* At least now she could get on with things in peace. The whole meal would have to be improvised. Maggie set her swans mid-counter and went spelunking in the kitchen.

It was news to no one that Dolores Dull was one tragic figure at the cookstove. She could make the basics, an entrée meat, a vegetable, starch and dessert, but somehow everything she touched turned flavorless. How had she given life to Maggie, a girl who could whip a trifle out of some fruit cup and a Twinkie?

There was some skim milk in the fridge along with half a box of Special K. Some white bread. Mayo. A stick of butter. Pickles. A jar of Smuckers scraped down to the last spoonfuls.

Damn, Mother.

Maggie tried the freezer. It was filled with home-bagged fare, none of which Maggie could identity confidently enough to reach for.

Next the pantry. And here she had some luck. There was an unopened box of Uncle Ben's Converted Rice. Ben, mind you, had never converted Maggie. She considered it one step down from cardboard with less taste. But her mother had always loved a plateful of it, dry and unadorned beyond butter and pepper. Fake pepper. The minute black specks sold in paper picnic shakers.

Next to Uncle Ben stood two cans of Petite peas, silver wrapping encircling identically silver cans. Her mother loved these particular peas because they were tiny, unfazed apparently by the fact that they poured out an incredible shade of gray-green, a color that said *Bacteria! Botulism! Sudden death!* But they were tiny. That was all her mother cared about.

Maggie checked the date. Small peas, small miracles. They'd been bought within the year.

Peas and rice. They were halfway to Thanksgiving. What else? What about the boiled peanuts? Perhaps she could pop down to the Bi-Lo, grab a can and get back before her mother knew. In her mind, Maggie was already down the road in the Tracer, jumping potholes, cornering hairpins, sailing into Big Piney hangover-free and then—*Whoa!*—on past the Bi-Lo, out onto the highway, heading west, going—where?

She could see the local news anchor, prim-suited, grim-faced: "Margaret Dull, also known as Maggie Dulé, left her mother's home in Little Piney on Thanksgiving morning. She was last seen..."

Maybe she could leave it all behind. Meaning *all.* Meaning move to the middle of the country, to Nobody, Indiana or Nowhere, Oklahoma, a place where she would never have to see old boyfriends or drooling shells of mothers ever again. She could change her name. Again. She could start over. Again.

"Her car was found on Route 70. Her mother was found dead..."

Starved to death, Maggie thought. *Hoping for a Thanksgiving dinner that never got served.*

Maggie put her disappearing act on hold, filed it under When Things Get Bad Enough. *Which might be any minute now,* she told herself, *but isn't quite yet.* She could not leave her mother for boiled peanuts or boiled anything. Maggie would have to make do.

She re-checked the fridge. No peanuts. Fine. But there was peanut butter in the door shelf. And peanut butter was the color of cooked turkey...

Maggie had it. She'd make little turkeys. Thanksgiving canapés, signifiers of the bird of honor in shape and color, one-bite jokes to reference the occasion. Her mother loved tiny. She'd get it in spades.

Maggie made two sketches, one of the live bird, tail fanned, the other of the cooked bird, drumsticks to one side. She pulled out a slice of Wonder Bread from the fridge to try one of each. Deft work with a serrated knife that probably came free with a jar of concord grape jelly left quite a mess. No way anyone would guess *Turkey!* looking at either one. On the other hand, these were shapes never seen on a plate before. They spoke to originality. Maggie would get points for trying.

Her kitchen sense kicked in. Canapé carving had to come after peanut-butter spreading. And the bread had to be toasted first to stand up to both. Maggie dosed the peanut butter with a spoonful of mayonnaise to thin it. The thought of the taste made her nauseous, but she knew it might suit her mother.

She crisped up her turkey prototypes, swiped them with the peanut-mayo combo and laid them on a bread-and-butter plate, complete with a mini-sprig of rosemary and a dollop of strawberry jam standing in for cranberry sauce.

"Can I stay with you?"

Maggie just about jumped out of her skin. Her mother was standing shaky in the kitchen door, holding onto the frame, her turban slipping down toward her right eyebrow.

Maggie ran to get a chair, seating her in the doorway so that she could keep an eye on her. "I think you're asking me if I would stay with you."

"No!" There was that stubborn, angry look. "Can I *stay?*"

Maggie got it. The woman did not mean cohabiting. Not in this house. Not in any house. She meant *staying.* As in not dying.

Maggie had braved burning planes. She had asked the doctor, "How long?" She had fired medical personnel for magical thinking. But she could see, in this moment, how it had all been lip service, lip sync. She'd mouthed certainties while denying the one truth: that her mother would not stay. That her mother's already narrowed world, the dreadful island upon which she lived, the one that folks had deserted in droves—friends, husband, children—that now even *she* would not live there. Now it would be Maggie alone on that island.

Incredible. For years, maybe all the years of her life, Maggie had felt alone. Never noticing she'd had a little (not so little) shadow that went in and out with her: her mother, lurking among the vineyards and spas like some California Yeti; her mother, strange, terrible, invisible, but company nonetheless. And perhaps the reverse was true as well. Perhaps she, Maggie, had been splitting her time, *doppelganging* in the mountains, in the blue light, haunting her mother's garden, ghosting her mother's bedroom. Each each other's shade. Each each other's comfort.

Maggie would have welcomed a couple of angels coming down the chimney right about then, just to kibitz, to get their take on not only the true, but also the right thing to say.

"I want you to stay, Mommy."

"With you?"

"With us. With all of us." How to tell her. Or whether. Maggie took a breath. "I want you to stay. But I may not be able to stay with you." Easing that in. Watching for her response.

God bless the bliss of addle-ation. It was as if Maggie had not spoken. Her mother focused past her into the kitchen. "Look what you've done!"

"Yes, it's a surprise."

"You're making a party?"

"I am."

"A birthday?"

"No, it's Thanksgiving, remember?"

"Boiled peanuts!"

"I couldn't find them, Mommy. I'm so sorry. But how about some pecan pie?"

Maggie told her mother to stay put while she emptied several jars onto the counter. There were traces of flour in one. Some sugar. And a baglet of walnuts, not full, open for God knows how many years, but tied up pretty good. No trace of mold at least. Maggie figured if she sprinkled them with the sugar, a little cinnamon from the spice rack and did a light roast she might have something.

"Look at you," her mother said. "Where'd you learn to do that?"

"From you, Mommy." Maggie spoke before she knew she was thinking it. But then she was thinking it. "You showed me how to make something from nothing."

"I made you, didn't I?" Her mother cackled, amusing herself.

No glamour puss, thought Maggie. And then she was standing at the kitchen sink, head bent way over to spare her mother, but the sound was bad enough, her stomach heaving up whatever it could until it quieted and she could pass some cold water over her lips and forehead. She rested there for a minute.

It felt good with her head on her elbow. From that perspective, her mother's legs appeared to hang sideways from her chair, defying gravity.

"High on the log, Mommy."

Maggie got herself upright and began scouring the sink. The blood in her brain throbbed, then settled.

While her mother dozed and watched, dozed and watched, Maggie improvised a dough, scraping flour together, spiking it with Special K. She kneaded in butter until the texture looked right, made tiny cups to bake for just minutes and then filled them with the sweet walnuts. It would be a dry confection, to be sure, but all they needed was a taste.

By the time Maggie's pie-lets were oven-bound, her mother was fast asleep, listing in the chair wedged in the kitchen doorway, her turban coiled to the floor, her face drained of anger, drained of anything at all, hanging inches from a pair of swan boats.

He Leadeth Me Beside

Walker Crowe / Bobby O. Greevey / Cadence Greevey
Morning

"Take Cadence to the parade. It's what the child wants."

Certainly it was what the child wanted. Walker could see that. Cadence wouldn't stand still for jumping up and down slap next to the sick bed, her dress in a muddle from a whole night of sleeping in it while her mother languished in her last moments on this earth.

It was the rest of what Pam said that struck Walker as dead wrong: "Take her out of here. She doesn't understand."

Walker thought there was no better indication than insisting on a parade that the child understood perfectly well what was going on. Furthermore, her begging for floats and marching bands at a time like this could only presage years to come with a deeply confused, motherless child-adult who would surely turn the Crowe household topsy-turvy while his wife maintained that all the child needed was a parade.

But he didn't argue. Pam was in her glory. Tending to the needy was what she lived for. And he—for better *and* for worse, he reminded himself—had pledged to live for her.

They'd gotten the phone call early enough to wake to.

"She's making the change."

That's what Walker heard. He said the words to Pam the way Beau McCallum said them to him. She grabbed the phone away to tell Beau that, No, no, he should stay home with his family for Thanksgiving and let her see to things. "All we got coming is my cousin Ida and her kin," she said, "and they can go to the in-laws. We'll take care of it."

She'd barely hung up the phone before she was throwing on yesterday's pants saying that they would have to go in straight away. Thank God, she said, no turkey had gotten near an oven yet. She called Ida to communicate the emergency. She was waiting with the car engine running before Walker could even find his glasses.

"They tied her to the bed," Cadence announced as Pam rushed to her side, but there was no evidence of tying nor any need thereof. Poor Verleana lay still except for the sweat drenching and a slight moaning. Walker thought her face looked bad. Punched up and bruisy.

He stayed by the door listening as Cadence veered in her chatter from tooth fairies to *Cheers* to Thanksgiving parades. Under normal circumstances, he'd have jumped at the slightest hint of an escape route. He had no stomach for standing by to watch the dying. But the notion of a shotgun marriage with him bound to this strange girl, his own wife brandishing a double-barrel in their direction, did not thrill him. Which was what dragging a simpleton around town through holiday crowds was going to feel like.

It took Pam saying, "Do it for me. It's what the child needs."

The child. Grown up and tall, yes. Too big for her clothing. But that's what Cadence was: she was a child.

Walker held out his hand. "I'll take you."

Cadence did not move. She was riveted on Pam scooping an empty Little Debbie box off the floor.

"That's for ghost dogs," Cadence told her.

Walker got the *What did I tell you?* look from Pam as she tossed the box in the wastebasket. "Cadence, honey, there'll be no ghost talk nor any such thing now that we're here with you. Your mama is in good hands. You go on with your Uncle Walker."

They all jumped.

A phone was ringing.

A phone by the bed.

It had never rung before, so no one knew it was there. Now it was ringing loud and scary. Pam picked it up right away. She spoke for a time. Then she said, "Cadence, it's for you. It's your father."

Cadence grabbed the receiver. "Daddy?"

She listened for a moment.

"Don't cry, Daddy."

Pam came over to Walker, taking hold of him at the waist, gripping tight hard. He put his arm over her shoulder.

Cadence became quite animated. "I saw her feet go up, Daddy." Instinctively Pam reached for Cadence saying "Let your father talk, sweetheart," but Walker pulled her back as Cadence said loudly, "I saw both her two feet go straight up in the air!"

For a moment Bobby could not trust himself to speak. Cadence's voice sounded more grown up now. What did she mean she saw feet? He didn't want her hearing his tears. Paco offered him a paper towel from the kitchen roller. Bobby pulled himself together.

"Cadence? Can you listen to Daddy for a minute?"

There was a silence. Then her new grown-up voice, "Daddy, are you in the hospital?"

"No. I was. But then I had to come home to get better."

"To Cincinnati?"

"Yes."

He could hear her breathing, waiting.

"I'm okay now. Are you there with your mommy?"

"Yes, sir."

"She's not doing too well, is she?"

"No, sir."

"You say you saw your mommy's feet go up?"

"No, sir. Not her."

"Oh."

"Mommy's okay now. We got her so the ghost dogs can't get her. You remember Hershey?"

"The dog?"

"Miss Burnice says he's a ghost dog without a human heart to know forgiveness, but Mama's going to heaven, don't you think, Daddy? And she'll be safe in heaven."

"Cadence, I need you to focus. Can you listen for a minute?"

"Yes, sir."

Cadence felt happy with him talking to her, as happy as she'd felt in a good long while.

He said he would be there in a week and they'd have a talk. He said, meantime, that Uncle Walker and Auntie Pam would look after her.

"Is that all right with you?"

"I'm going to live here at Solace."

"You can't live there, Cadence. You have to go home with the Crowes and we'll figure out where you're going to live when I get down there next week, okay?"

"Yes, sir."

She waited. She did not speak.

"You can come live with Daddy if you want to."

Cadence did not know what to say. She knew to be polite, but she was thinking about sitting at the pool in Cincinnati not knowing anybody and nobody talking to her and the long hours in the house with just the piano lid-shut and everything brand-clean but quiet with no dogs or children to play with.

"But you don't have to. We can talk about it."

"Yes sir." She was looking over at Auntie Pam who had her hanky out and was wiping her eyes.

"I gotta go, Daddy."

"All right. I'm going to see you real soon. We love you, Cadence."

"I'm going to the parade."

"Paco sends his love."

"I gotta go."

"Give me back to Miz Crowe, sweetie. Bye-bye."

Walker thought his wife was going to dissolve right there with nothing but his holding to keep her on her feet until Cadence reached the phone to her. Then he could feel her require herself to rise to the occasion. She and

Cadence traded places, Cadence coming to tuck in next to him as if they'd been father and child their whole lives.

What a trusting soul, Walker thought, feeling the girl lean in. He liked the way she'd spoken to her father, or rather, not spoken. The way she'd been attentive and said "Yes, sir."

Pam waved the two of them away. Clearly she wanted time on the phone alone.

"I'm hungry," Walker said to the child. "What do you say we go looking for something to eat?" He remembered this from his own three children when they were much younger. How when you made things a treasure hunt, children went along. He thought they might swing over to the Griddle House on 4th which was open even on holidays, order up a big plate of pancakes and then maybe mosey to the square just as the parade was starting so as to cut down on any standing-around-doing-nothing time. He figured he couldn't go wrong feeding the girl. She looked to be an eater the way she fit in her dress.

Which had to be changed, apparently. Pam put her hand over the mouth-piece of the phone as they were going out the door, nodding and listening and at the same time hissing to Walker, "She's not going anywhere like that," waving toward the bag she'd packed with fresh pressed clothes.

Walker sent Cadence into the public bathroom off the parlor to dress herself. She came out with a little water still on her face and her hair patted down to look presentable. They headed toward the front door when Cadence stopped dead. "Aren't we going to eat?"

"We are indeed."

"It's this way," and she was gone down the hall before Walker knew she was going.

Lord help him, he'd have to keep an eye on her.

"Cadence?"

He didn't know if he could keep this up, chasing the girl zigging and zagging ahead like a calf separated from its mother while he did his best to trot along behind, hoping to catch her before she got into trouble. This was not the reward he'd hoped for in his twilight years, a far cry from his quiet porch, exertion reduced to the rocking of the rocking chair when it pleased him and the occasional lifting of a bottled beer for a swig. A far cry.

There she was.

"Cadence!"

And then she wasn't, darting around a corner, out of sight.

Our Maker Doth Provide

Maggie Dull
Dinnertime

Things had gone just fine for the minutes that Maggie's mother had been awake. She marveled at her plate full of small treats like a dollhouse tea. The spoonful of rice. The peas. She took to her peanut-mayo canapé, nibbling at it, nodding when Maggie told her it was in the shape of a turkey. As far gone as she was, Maggie could swear she grasped the ingenuity of it all.

"You're my mother of invention," Maggie said to her, feeling how *non sequitur* was now *sequitured,* how things didn't need to follow on any longer, but could be said out of the blue and understood without understanding.

Her mother gummed every bite. Maggie saw she tasted nothing, pretending up a storm, exclaiming over first one thing, then the next. *Pretending for my sake,* Maggie thought. *Using her waning energy to keep the party going. Like daughter, like mother.*

Maggie watched her, transfixed by the swan boats, peering closely at the oregano, the laurel, the roses, turning them slowly on the Lazy Susan as if they were swimming in a miniature parade. By all measures the woman seemed content, though she never got to her pie-let. She fell asleep at the table, her chin on her shoulder.

It looked uncomfortable, but Maggie didn't want to wake her. She didn't want to do anything at all except sit at the table now, placing herself, finally, where she was. For days she'd been drifting somewhere far away, neither in Palo Alto nor Little Piney, but hovering like some weather satellite, drifting round and round like the swans, wondering what it might be like down there on earth where people lived. Wondering. Wandering.

Now, however, Maggie felt herself irising in from above, frame by frame coming down into the mountains on the east coast, not the west, into a weirdly warm Thursday in November with the leaves turning late and the bees gone, into a house with a garden whose bush roses were still red, to sit at a dining table looking at stray tinsel on the drapery rods, trace glitter in the carpet, noting pill trays and water glasses and tissues and towels, attending a little doll party of alien foods that only she and her mother could understand.

She was here now.

Things smelled of warmed gray peas.

Her mother snorted.

Maggie turned the Lazy Susan. The swans swam round and round. Where was ESP when you needed it? Gone, gone. Round and round. *Perhaps*, Maggie thought, *I have outgrown not only a taste for foreknowledge, but the need.*

She wondered how would she manage now.

The business.

Her life.

Oh, for God's sake! She could hear her mother's voice rising from memory, the old mom, the tough one, saying, *You call that a life?*

Her mother was right of course. That was why it had been so easy to hop on a plane, to de-camp even with this year's party season in full frenzy. There was lots of busyness in Palo Alto for Maggie, she knew that, but not much life. So leaving was a snap. Besides, Maggie was a world-class leaver. She'd been leaving people, places her whole life. One coast for another. One town to the next. Planes and motels. Hiding. From whom? With whom? It really didn't matter. Or hadn't until now.

Maggie felt how her life—lives—the lives of a serial leaver—how they had shifted from them to this, from then to right here.

Born again. Maggie smiled and put her head down in the exact position of her mother's so that she could watch her sleep in the shape of sleep.

How would she manage? Maggie had no idea. It was not a matter of faith. Just the opposite. *Nothing left to lose.* She decided she might as well be present for this losing, this loss, this going, this gone.

Let Not Your Heart

Walker Crowe
Dinnertime

Walker followed Cadence down an ivied hall into a full-blown kitchen filled with the wall-to-wall bustle of folks cooking and tending. He excused the both of them, tugging at Cadence, "They got to do for those that are sick, honey. Why don't we get our breakfast down the street." But she was having none of it, explaining that it was fine to eat at Solace as long as they stayed on *this* side of the table.

"Find yourself a seat." A tiny woman with very short hair was in the middle of untrussing a good-sized turkey, stuffing pouring from its nether-end, the skin butter-browned. It smelled out of this world.

"Miss Cherille," she introduced herself. Clipping string and slicing meat, she said it was no bother, that she had biscuits. She bobbed her head toward the table where, sure enough, there were biscuits piled high on a plate. She said to sit themselves down and did he want any coffee.

"You see?" said Cadence. She took the one stool and commenced to babbling, telling Miss Cherille all about the parade they were going to. "Isn't that something," Miss Cherille said as she fetched coffee and a glass of milk and minded her to take just one biscuit at a time. Walker stood behind.

"Happy Thanksgiving." The voice came from another woman, solidly built, wearing a purple dress as if for church with a single strand of pearls.

Cadence waved, bobbing up and down, her mouth half-glued with biscuit, "Merry Thanksgiving, Miss Burnice."

Walker told her to finish chewing. "Merry's for Christmas," he said. "Happy's for Thanksgiving."

Cadence repeated it, "Merry's for Christmas. Happy's for Thanksgiving."

Miss Cherille slid a cardboard box across the table with newly carved slices of turkey plastic-wrapped on top. "Here it is, Burnie."

"Well, this looks like heaven." Burnice reached for the box, then turned and held out her hand to Walker who took it.

"Burnice Kling," she said. "I looked after your Cadence last night." He thanked her for her trouble.

"Oh, it was no trouble." She bent down to Cadence, "I see you got you a good breakfast." Cadence nodded with her mouth full. "Better leave some room for turkey."

She turned back to Walker, "Are you her daddy?"

Cadence piped up, "We're going to the parade."

Walker said they were family friends and that he and his wife were going to take care of Cadence until arrangements could be made with her daddy.

"She has a good heart," Burnice told him.

Walker nodded. "I am gathering that very thing."

"Well, I best be going. Happy Thanksgiving," Burnice called to everyone.

"Happy is for Thanksgiving!" Cadence called after.

Walker finished his biscuit. He watched Cadence start in on her second.

Two men came through the kitchen door. The first Walker recognized, the one called Bear. Lord, what a block of a fellow he was at a distance, the dress shirt he had on at odds with those tattoos and the fu manchu. Next to him, holding his hat in his hands, was a short man, wiry. At the sight of them, Miss Cherille set down her rolling pin, wiping her hands good on the towel stuck in her apron band. Her voice went motherly, "Mr. Early, won't you stay here with us for some Thanksgiving?"

Walker realized with a terrible thud that this Mr. Early had been crying. It was not something a man wanted to see of another man. His eyes were red. The skin around them, top and bottom, was raw. He kept turning his hat in his hands, not meeting anyone's eyes, certainly not those of strangers.

Bear spoke up, "He says he's got to get home to his family."

"You got you children?" Miss Cherille asked.

The man named Early looked up and tried to speak, nodded, then looked up again and said, "Grandbabies."

Walker saw that Cadence had paused in mid-chew, staring intently.

"God bless you," Miss Cherille said. "Of course you want to get back to them. I am so sorry for your loss, Mr. Early." She took a moment. "Tell you what, why don't I pack you up enough to take home so y'all'll at least have something for Thanksgiving dinner. You know they might could do better what with some turkey and dressing."

She was packing things as she spoke, pulling potatoes and green beans out of the oven, wrapping turkey, foiling stuffing.

When she had it done, packed tight down in a box, she walked around to him, clasping his hands as he took hold of things. "Now Mr. Early, we expect to see you here next week. Isn't that right, Bear? You and your family. Bring the babies and the grandbabies. Everybody. You come down to the grief counseling we do here every Tuesday night. It will do you a world of good. You promise?"

The man named Early nodded his head *Yes*.

Turning to Bear, he spoke very slowly, very quietly, as if his words might fall apart for speaking them. "I wonder, would you tell the doctor, we thank him for all he done."

"Dr. Narduli?" Bear asked.

The man named Early nodded again.

Walker hadn't seen Cadence get up. He would have stopped her, but she was already past and over to the poor fellow, talking like they knew each other, saying, "Her feet lifted up!"

Walker went after her. "Hush!" he said, but Cadence kept talking, fixed to Mr. Early's face.

"Last night. I come in with Rabbit. You was asleep in the chair, you remember? So I put Rabbit on her like this—" Cadence smoothed her tummy with her hand. The sight of it made Mr. Early tip his head to the side.

"That's enough," said Walker, not unkind or sharp, because this was no time to be sharp with a child in such a situation, but trying to get her to stop.

She paid him no mind. "You was asleep so I put Rabbit on her and that's when her two feet, they raised up in the bed like this—" Cadence lifted one of her legs straight up. "And then she went, 'Hunh!'" Here Cadence took a big deep breath and pushed it out. "And then they come down." She lowered her leg so that her shoe slapped the floor, which made Mr. Early jump. He stared at her, neither one of them speaking.

Oh, here we go, Walker thought, *This is what it's like to raise the simple-minded,* even as he was saying, "Cadence, I believe we've bothered this gentleman enough," when didn't the child pipe up like she was announcing their trip to the parade to say, "My mama's going to Jesus."

Miss Cherille spoke up immediately, "That's right, baby."

But the short man, Mr. Early, was keyed on Cadence in a different way, like a shipwrecked sailor discovering an island mate. He spoke directly to her. "Is your mama going right now?"

"They tied her up, but she's not tied no more."

"Well, then she'll need this." He pulled from the inside pocket of his parka a fur pelt.

"Rabbit!" Cadence clapped her hands around it.

"Don't you think she might could use it?"

"Yes, sir, I surely do," said Cadence just as polite as any child could ever be.

Mr. Early nodded to Walker with his red eyes. "She was good enough to loan it to my wife last night." He looked back to Cadence. "You go on now and take that to your mama."

Cadence took off straight for her mother's room with Walker calling for her to wait, trying to clean up their biscuit mess, while Bear held the box of food so Mr. Early could get his hat on, Mr. Early thanking him once and twice and once again and heading with his box toward the front door, Miss Cherille watching him go, watching until she took up her rolling pin and asked Bear, "You pulling a double shift?" and him saying, "Yes," saying, "Dee Dee needed time with her family," as Walker finally got things neat enough to excuse himself to go run after the girl with a rabbit pelt in her hand.

Come Ye Thankful People

Maggie Dull
Late for Dinner

Maggie's neck cricked when she sat up. Someone was knocking at the door. Alone on the mountainside with all normal people at home carving turkey, who would come calling? An escaped convict? Someone's Alzheimer relative roaming the hills? Maggie wondered about the deer rifle they used to keep in the closet. Was it still there?

She peered out of the drapes through the sliding glass door.

Dear God in heaven.

Curtis-Michael.

And family.

A woman.

The wife. Surely it had to be.

And three children there, all dressed up as if coming from church.

The woman had her hat on.

Helmeted, Maggie thought. Like a spaceman standing in the forward door of a 737.

In front of the children? she was thinking as she opened the door. *This woman is going to fight for her man in front of the children?* as she managed to say, "Happy Thanksgiving" with the woman saying "Happy Thanksgiving" at the same time. Maggie saw she was carrying a foil-covered casserole. The children each carried one too. Even the little boy had a small version. Maggie could see cranberry through plastic wrap.

Her eyes bounced the once. Curtis smiled tight-lipped. Maggie opened the door wider, asking them in.

The family came through with Curtis trailing and the woman turning the second she was inside to face Maggie, face her straight on, saying "I am Dee

Dee Hipps. Curtis-Michael told me you were here by yourself."

Maggie's eyes bounced to him again. Still the tight smile. Registering that the wife called him Curtis-Michael, used the whole name.

"We didn't think it was right for you to be alone on a holiday."

The children, having come in gingerly the way new visitors did, focused right away on the table and the sight of her mother coming out of her snoring with the noise. Maggie could feel how they were frozen seeing her, shocked perhaps at her mother's straggle.

But Dee Dee's eyes never moved. "We thought you might could use some turkey and fixings. We always make more than enough, don't we?" She was reaching her arm toward the children without shifting her gaze. "Brian, Abigail, Carleton come say hello to Miz—Dooley is it? Doley?"

"It's Dull," said Maggie. "Same as it always was."

"Oh, I'd heard something different." A flicker there.

This time Maggie did not shift her eyes to Curtis hanging back near the door. "Please call me Maggie."

The children came over balancing their various dishes and offering their various hands. The eldest boy was nine maybe. In a coat and tie, not a suit, but dressed old-style as people of her mother's age dressed for church. He had his daddy's eyes.

The skirt on the daughter, younger than the boy, was short—surely there had been some arguments about that—but she was done up nonetheless. She even had a little lipstick, pink, over the hint of braces Maggie could see when she smiled.

The baby, Carleton, wore a summer suit with short pants, hem and socks meeting at the knee.

Dee-Dee herself had on low heels and a summer dress, a good knock-off from T.J. Maxx or Ross, a flower print in blues to below the knee. Blues that popped under her blond curls.

"Let them eat steak!" That was her mother piping up now, pointing at the pie-let crumbling before her.

Still Dee Dee's eyes never moved. "Curtis-Michael, would you take this on into the kitchen for me, please?" She handed her casserole over waving in the direction of the stove that could be seen through the doorway. She waited until he'd shepherded the kids ahead of him. Then and only then did she turn her attention to Maggie's mother, going to her with a kindness, a keen attentiveness, saying backwards as she went, "I don't know if Curtis-Michael told you, but I'm a supervising nurse at Solace."

Would wonders never cease?

It was just the two of them talking now. Two and a half, if Maggie counted her mother. Curtis and the children were in the kitchen. Maggie could hear the opening and closing of the refrigerator, drawers sliding out and shutting again.

"No, I did not know that," Maggie said. "Curtis didn't mention it. He said you were a nurse..."

"A bird in the land!" Maggie's mother was excited by the company.

"That's hand, Mommy."

Dee-Dee pulled a chair in close and took her mother's hand, pressing it, soothing. "Ms. Dull, I am Dee-Dee Hipps. I work with Miss Burnice at Solace. You remember?"

Curtis and the children came back into the kitchen doorway. The baby, Carleton, got whimpery. Curtis hoisted him into his arms.

Dee Dee surveyed the peas and rice and canapés. "Look what you have done. You have made a feast here," she said and looked up.

Therein, there-across, something passed between the two women. An acknowledgment as from one soldier to another, two blood adversaries meeting in the middle, in a no-man's land, sliding sabers back into sheaths, touching hands to caps, nodding to one another in deference to each other's resourcefulness before bowing and returning to the fray.

"I am so glad that Curtis-Michael told me about your being here," Dee Dee said very quietly. "He almost didn't. To spare me the trouble." She was standing now, her eyes unnaturally bright, looking to her husband, all the while holding onto Maggie's mother, taking her hand with her as she stood, speaking to Maggie, but never letting her gaze go away from the man, her man, the father of her children. "We were so touched that you wanted to be here for your mother. For your family. Nothing matters more than family. Am I right?"

Maggie looked where Dee Dee was looking. There was her answer. In Curtis's face.

"'Not as the world giveth,'" Dee Dee said.

"'Give I unto you,'" he answered.

They started, all of them. A woman stood haloed in the front doorway knocking on the jam. She bore yet another casserole, a whole box of casseroles by the look of it.

"Burnice!" Maggie's mother cried as Dee Dee said the same. Burnice Kling did not move, looking for all the world like a cornered thief, like someone caught sneaking out instead of coming in. She wore a real dress not a nurse's, royal purple, with sandals, a pink bow of leather on top of each toe. She was staring at Dee Dee who stared right back.

The children called out "Hey" and "Happy Thanksgiving," rushing over while everyone talked at once, Maggie saying to come in with Burnice explaining to Dee Dee, "I thought I should bring some food by," and Dee Dee explaining to Burnice at the very same time, "We thought we should bring some food by."

Burnice handed the box to Maggie. "From the Solace kitchen," she said.

All of the commotion got Maggie's mother going. She began circling both hands in front of her like a magician over a hat.

"The Lord moves in wisteria's ways."

"That's mysterious, Mommy."

Maggie's mother extended a single crabbed finger toward her, hushing the hubbub to ask the assembled. "Have you met my friend?"

She pointed to Maggie.

She blinked.

Then something changed.

"I know you!" Her voice pitched upwards. "I know you! You're my Maggie."

"That's right," said Burnice. "She's your baby."

Maggie could not move.

Her mother smiled, waving at the swan boats. "Please porridge yacht!" She winked at Maggie. A big wink.

"Please porridge mold!" Maggie winked right back. A bigger wink. Silly. Which made Carleton laugh. Which made everyone laugh, even Maggie's mother, wheezy and unsure of the joke, but bright with the cheer of it.

Their laughter rose. Then died in fits and sighs.

No one knew what to say next.

Curtis was looking down at his shoes, pale, with the children grouped around him, watchful, uncertain.

Dee Dee took Maggie's box of food and handed it to him, remarking that it was a kindness of Burnice to think of such a thing for a client, artfully avoiding any mention of irregularities with her work in this particular house, in the Dull house. Burnice, meanwhile, was backing herself toward the front door. "I did not mean to intrude."

Maggie followed her onto the porch. "I am so glad you came by, Ms. Kling. I was too strong speaking to you the other day. I regret that. It's been a while since I've been home. I forgot how people do."

"Not as the world liveth!" her mother chirped behind her, waving a napkin.

"There's no need," Burnice said. "I'm fine. Dee-Dee can tell you. I didn't mean to interrupt anything." She all but ran for the steps up to the driveway, calling back, "You take good care."

"Wait wait! I've got your table cloth. It's your mother's, isn't it?" Maggie's words stopped Burnice. "And the baby rattle. I believe that's yours too."

Burnice waited as Maggie fetched her things from the back bedroom, neatly folded and stacked, walking them up the stairs to her. "I couldn't get all the glitter off."

"That's fine. It will make special occasions all the more special." Burnice clutched the fabric to her. She looked like she couldn't get away fast enough, glancing toward Dee Dee and then scooting up the driveway toward her car.

"Ms. Kling!" Maggie called. "Would you be willing to help us again?"

Burnice stood in her car door. "That's not up to me. It's up to Dee Dee. She's in charge. Happy Thanksgiving."

Maggie wanted to do a better job with her apology, but Burnice was already maneuvering her car between the Tracer and—*Ah, God!* Maggie's heart lurched—the Silverado. The Silverado that had come up that very same mountain twice, hauling first her, and now his family to her door. She could see the tarp on the flatbed. Things that had sunk below alcoholic mists began to resurface. She saw a stick shift. She tasted Szechuan. She heard the good solid steel of a zipper catching and giving, teeth parting, inching down.

Burnice's car rolled by, headed toward town.

Maggie looked back at the house. Dee Dee was standing in the front door with her children watching, as if she lived there and it was Maggie who needed either to be welcomed or turned away.

Dee-Dee nosed the children ahead, saying up to her, "Your mama looks like she needs her rest." Brian-Abigail-Carleton passed Maggie on the steps—Carleton doing the best he could, holding tight to his sister's hand. They hovered from above as the two women met mid-stair. Curtis lingered on the porch.

"How long are you planning to stay?"

"I don't know."

Neither spoke. Then:

"I can't leave her." Not a complaint. A declaration.

Dee Dee nodded.

"I will stay at least until she no longer needs me."

"At least?"

"At least."

Here, finally, Dee Dee let slip the slightest hint of impatience—just a trace, Maggie heard it—as she signaled her children to go on and get in the truck. It looked as if she wanted Curtis gone as well. Instead he came in right beside her, taking her by the shoulders with one arm, his face dropped of anything and everything except the truth of all the years Maggie had missed, his life encoded there, his life with her.

Dee Dee's voice went nurse-professional. "We won't leave the two of you alone, Ms. Dull. We'll have Hazel Gurley come by."

"I'd rather see Ms. Kling again. Really. I'd prefer it. So would my mother."

If Dee Dee was surprised she didn't show it. She allowed as how she would leave that up to Burnice and Maggie agreed.

Maggie spoke in such a way that she made the choosing of her words very clear. "Thank you for coming."

She looked at Dee Dee.

She looked at Curtis.

She looked at Dee Dee again. "We are neighbors. And I plan to be a good neighbor. You can count on that."

The thought of Curtis's hand came to her—*oh that hand,* feeling the weight of it under her blouse and—

"Is somebody there?" Her mother was calling.

Maggie let it all go. She looked at him as a neighbor now and he did the same, both of them putting away childish things, firmly putting them away, watching each other do so.

Their parting was nothing. Swift. Ordinary.

Goodbye.

Goodbye.

Goodbye.

Neighbors taking their leave. A couple climbing up to a dirty truck with three children waiting inside. A middle-aged woman left behind, standing in her doorway, watching them go.

The Silverado roared off the gravel and barreled down the mountain, scattering crows.

Maggie took a deep breath. The air was warm, still.

She eased the door shut and turned to find her mother struggling to stand herself up from the flotsam of the table, swans and pie-lets, an uneaten canapé, a couple of stray serving spoons the children had left behind.

"Are you real?" her mother asked.

A flip response flashed through Maggie's mind, a snappy comeback. Instead she said, "I am."

All Are Safely Gathered

August Early
Late for Dinner

The dogs came swarming. Hollering up a storm. Straight to the driver's side this time, being smart dogs, at least Shirley, the bright one, with the others following. Bumping up to where it was hard for him to get the door open without clobbering one in its swing.

They knew better than to jump, but on this morning, perhaps because of his going out sudden in the night, Mr. T and Shirley both got to popping their front paws up to his chest and yelping as if to say, *He's mine! No, he's mine!*

Mr. Early left her things on the side seat, then thought better of it. He could see himself forgetting and opening that door and Sue-Sue or Serena looking in to see her bathrobe or her pink suitcase or the silver framed image of themselves looking out at themselves. He pushed it all to the floor, grabbed a tarp from the back and covered it.

"Get on outta here!" he snapped at Shirley who'd jumped into the driver's seat as if she'd ever been invited to ride cab-side when there was plenty of room for dogs on the flatbed. It was no wonder. She could smell turkey and gravy coming out from under the foil.

"Git!" The dogs jumped back, heaping onto Shirley as she made her exit, checking to see if maybe she'd gotten a scrap or two and could they get some.

Mr. Early grabbed the box of food. He kicked the truck door closed good and tight. His boots crunched on the gravel heading toward Miss Susan, *crunch, crunch, crunch*. It was a good sound. Making a faint trail, he knew, in the rough rock, a path of his footsteps that could be followed by a passel of dogs, say, or a ghost, newly departed, the spirit of a grandmother, fussy and bossy to the end, on beyond the end, tailing him to be sure he did right by her, by them. The thought of it made him smile.

I'm going on ahead of you, he thought backward to his wife. *You just see if you can keep up.*

Setting down the box. Taking off his hat. Toe-heeling the mud off his boots in the open doorway. The girls running to him, "Daddy!" Him squatting to scoop them up, one in each arm—he still could—scooping them off the floor, their skirts scotching over their bottoms, his arms pressing in to catch them from falling, hugging them to him, hugging with two girls pressed to either side of his neck squealing, "Daddy!"

He looked up to see Miss Susan Neville in the background. Saw her catch it all in his face and turn for the kitchen. One of the dogs whined through the screen door.

He squeezed his eyes tight-tight to concentrate on the feel of the girls. The softness of their hair on his cheeks. The weight of them.

I got 'em, he was saying. To her, not to them. To the ghost standing with the dogs on the other side of the door. *I got 'em,* he was saying to her. *You can go now.*

All Creatures Great

Cadence Greevey
Afternoon

Cadence thought she had seen nothing prettier on this earth than the pair of—what did Uncle Walker call them?—Mamas?—"No, Yah-Mahs," he said—"Spelled with L's," he said—a pair of them making their way down Garnet Avenue on leashes, each one like a dog except they were much bigger with long necks and their heads way higher than the heads of the two girls holding those leashes. Lucky girls! Each as tall as Cadence but all grown up, Cadence could tell. Like the girls in her class who had a look to them that Cadence didn't see when she looked in the mirror at herself. The Yah-Mahs were covered with fur the color of Rabbit only curly. Cadence wished she could pat them. They carried pretty blankets on their backs like saddles, though you could see they would never work for saddles because how would you stay on?

Cadence thought maybe she could make a blanket like that for Rabbit, a little one of many colors to set on top. She jumped up and down saying "Mama, Yah-Mah" with Uncle Walker calling after her, "That's enough," coming to get her by the hand, because people around them were trying to see and one man asked, "Can't you get your girl to sit down?"

They found a place along the curb where Cadence could sit in among the baby strollers which she was willing to do after Uncle Walker explained that she could see the parade better from there and wasn't that just the best place to be?

Cadence thought the Yah-Mahs were the prettiest things in the parade until she saw the capes, the short ones, on top of the jackets every one of the marching band got to wear as they walked. Dark blue and red with gold stripes. Same as their gloves. Same as their hats. Cadence stood up when she heard the music, dancing as they high-stepped by until Uncle Walker told her she had to sit back down so that folks behind could get a look at them too.

It wasn't like on TV. In a TV parade there was one thing and then another and then another, but it was all far away and small on the set. Here, sitting on the curb, it took time for each thing to come which made the parade seem longer. And Uncle Walker was right—everything looked so big! The tassel boots of the marching bands. The clown shoes Mr. MacLaine had put on to wheel his big-wheel wheelbarrow, all cleaned of its mud, with inside it a music box playing music that made everybody clap as he came by.

It was good to be down low, too, when the Christ Mount bus passed with twirly paper and flowers all over it like for a birthday party and flags on top. In each window of the bus was a person from the church tossing out candies to everybody watching, and where do you think those candies fell but right there where Cadence was sitting so that she could scoop up handsful, passing them back to Uncle Walker to get more.

He said it nicely, but she was embarrassed when he told her she might could share some of those candies with the littler children. His words made her remember from her mama's teaching that she was taking too many and she hadn't done right. "Suffer the little children." She knew that from Sunday school. Cadence took some of her candy back from him and gave it to the stroller babies—well, to their parents—and to the older ones who were just the age she often wished could be a brother or a sister to her, because they were more fun to play with than the children in her class.

Cadence did her best when Uncle Walker tried to get her talking to him in between the bands and the trucks, even though she was concentrating on what was coming next. He kept asking how she was feeling. Which each time he did, she said Fine-fine-fine, but wanting him to stop asking, because truthfully she was fine-fine-fine, but his asking made her wonder if there was something wrong and if so what it was.

He kept asking about her daddy. She said right away her daddy wasn't mad at her, which she believed to be true. She said even Mr. McCallum wasn't mad after she didn't tell nobody and rode the bus. She said what her daddy told her, which was that he was coming and then they would talk. Which was all the talking she wanted to do about it.

But Uncle Walker's asking made her worry, was someone mad. She thought her mama wasn't because she never woke up now. And Auntie Pammy wasn't because she'd brought Cadence her second favorite dress that morning, the one with the seashells, the one she was wearing that very minute. "In honor of Thanksgiving," Auntie Pammy said. Which was just what her mama let her do each year, even though all they did was watch the parade on TV. Cadence begged to go to Garnet to see the real one for real, but it never happened. They'd only gone the once when she was little and her daddy was with them. Still, most years she got to dress up like as if they were going to see it in the real true way, even though all they did was sit in front of the television set. Her mama got dressed up too before she got sick.

Cadence jumped and twirled, showing off her seashell skirt and her sweater, bright blue. Nobody said, *Sit!* because there was nothing coming along right at that moment. In fact two other little girls, much littler than Cadence, got up to jump and twirl with her, until the grown-ups started to applaud and Uncle Walker called to them to sit back down, that the big trucks were coming.

The first was the fire truck. *Ding-ding-ding!* with the men in their helmets waving and the white dog with spots. Everybody allowed as how it was the prettiest truck in the whole world. Cadence did too to be agreeable. But secretly her favorite was what came last. The Hamilton Sanitation truck. Oh, it was so big! The brightest of shiny white-white and all belly, roly-poly round, with a bright green cab and the men inside in green caps throwing out green peppermints for the children to go and get.

This time, Cadence stopped herself from taking too many. *Let the little ones have some.* She could hear her mama's voice saying that, reminding her she was a big girl now.

So she let the babies get the candy while she waved like mad to the Hamilton Sanitation men, waving so hard they caught sight of her and waved back, like they all knew each other. Waving and waving until the men went by, turning their attention to where they were driving even though they were going real slow and there was nobody in the road.

Hamilton Sanitation always came last in the parade except for the Pilgrim and the Indian carrying the HAPPY THANKSGIVING banner that had not changed since Cadence was a baby.

The banner went by. Then five Hamilton Sanitation workers in their green hats and jackets, three men and two women, pushed push brooms down the street to clean up what was there, fishing out any wrapped candies that had been missed and handing them to children who had not gone home yet with their hands still out.

They walked by, pushing their brooms on down the road behind the Pilgrim and the Indian.

Then nothing. Nothing else came.

People began leaving the curb.

Cadence couldn't help it. She tried not to, because she thought Uncle Walker wouldn't like it, but she started to cry. The parade was over. She had looked forward to it all morning. She had thought it would be longer and it seemed long, but then it was over in a minute and gone and past and there was nothing to look forward to anymore. She saw parents scooting the other children away from where she sat, one mama saying to her little boy, "Don't stare."

Uncle Walker stood over her for a while. Then he sat down. Just sat. He patted in between her shoulders. He shuffled in his pockets for a cloth hanky where she could bury her eyes and try-try-try to get her crying to stop.

Cadence knew he was doing his best, but he didn't know what to say. How could he? He wasn't her daddy. He patted her like a person thumping on a dog, thinking it feels good to the dog and the dog wagging its tail to show its appreciation, but probably thinking, like she was, *That thumping's not helping one bit.*

After a while, it was dead quiet. Just the two of them. Cadence kept her face in the hanky, but she wasn't crying anymore.

Uncle Walker reached over. "Who's there?" he said, pulling the hanky down a little bit like hide-and-seek. That made her smile. He pulled it down a little more until he could see her eyes looking out at him in just a peek.

He said, "I wonder what the very prettiest thing is of a Thanksgiving," and Cadence said right away, "Yah-Mahs!" and Uncle Walker said, "No-o-o-o," and Cadence said, "Mr. Hamilton's truck!" and Uncle Walker said, "No-o-o-o." He had the hanky pulled down over her fingers now, so that he could see her nose, which was stinging.

Then it came to her. "Turkey!"

"Turkey!" he said back.

"And dressing and cranberries and mashed potatoes and gravy!" They said it together. Cadence scrambled up with him now, setting her hand in his, pulling, "With Miss Cherille, yes?"

"Yes, indeed."

"At Solace?"

"Yes, ma'am."

She stopped him with her two hands. "Uncle Walker, I am going to live there." She said it in her big girl voice. "Miss Burnice told me I can go to Solace after school and tend the roses to make the rose scent for them as need it, because ghost dogs, they hate the smell of anything sweet. Did you know that, Uncle Walker?"

He looked quite surprised, shaking his head *No* at her question, but listening with a serious face that she liked.

"I've thought all about it. I can't work for Mr. McCallum no more because I got to get a job at Macon's Luscious Lawns because they have the roses there and that way I can learn. See, I got a plan. Like mama with the pails and the washcloths."

Again, he had the serious face with a look like they were meeting for the first time, or like she had said something truly unusual as of a spaceship falling out of the sky right into their backyard, which her mama would have told her never to say, because it would not be true.

"I know the rules at Solace," she told him. "'You make your bed.' That's what the bear man said. And, 'You got to be doing, not muling.' That's what Miss Burnice said and I followed every word and didn't we chase those ghost dogs right to kingdom come!"

Cadence rattled on as they went, twirling her seashell skirt. They headed away from Garnet Square, her pulling him some and him pulling her when she went in the wrong direction. Along the way, she picked up the occasional stray candy, even a perfect yellow leaf—"Ginkgo," he told her—to take back with them to whoever was at the table on the side where it was okay to go, to wait for the prettiest of all Thanksgiving pretties to be set before them, to say grace, "God bless this food to our use and us to Thy service" with a big "Amen" which Cadence would surely say extra loud, and then to dig in.

Thanks

To Leslie Keenan for being the dream editor every novelist hopes to find. To Deborah Grabien, Marlene Adelstein, Ruth Wilson and many others for their keen editorial insights. To Alice Acheson for years of above-and-beyond guidance. To Patricia Volonakis Davis for the gift of her support. To Kelly Preston, Jane Hunter and Heather Fitz for their help birthing and promoting this book. To Tanya Quinlan for her beautiful cover and book design. To early readers Dave Stanton, Jeff Langley, Bob Kertzner and Julie Miles for their encouragement. To the cherished readers who crafted this book's thoughtful endorsements. To Rebecca Cooney for years of wisdom at her kitchen table. To Lynne Morrow for years of wisdom at Northlight. To Edwin Gardner for insisting, long ago, that written words beg to be read out loud. To Maia Danziger for opening a door to what's coming and to Eric Weiner for opening a door to Maia. To a beloved passel of McTigues and Kniselys and Stantons for having my back. And to Tom for the everything that is our life together.

About the Author

Amanda McTigue hails from a long line of talkers. Her daddy's people were immigrant Irish Catholics who wound up stateside in the Appalachian coal-mining country of West Virginia. Her mother's people were Presbyterian preachers from the Blue Ridge mountains of North Carolina. An author, teacher, and stage director, Amanda's children's books and companion CDs are on bookstore shelves. Her written works for the theater have been seen on stages ranging from community playhouses to the likes of Juilliard, Carnegie Hall and the Minnesota Opera. *Going to Solace* is her first novel. You can keep up with her doings at www.amandamctigue.com.

CPSIA information can be obtained at www.ICGtesting.com
Printed in the USA
LVOW081548080513

332883LV00009B/1120/P